Tips and Tricks for the iPad® for Seniors

Studio Visual Steps

Tips and Tricks for the iPad® for Seniors

Get more out of your iPad

www.visualsteps.com

This book has been written using the Visual Steps™ method.
Cover design by Studio Willemien Haagsma bNO

© 2013 Visual Steps
Author: Studio Visual Steps

First printing: October 2013
ISBN 978 90 5905 099 0

Resources used: A number of definitions and explanations of computer terminology are taken over from the *iPad User Guide*.

Do you have questions or suggestions?
Email: info@visualsteps.com

Would you like more information?
www.visualsteps.com

Website for this book:
www.visualsteps.com/tipsipad

Subscribe to the free Visual Steps Newsletter:
www.visualsteps.com/newsletter

Table of Contents

Foreword

The iPad has many great features. Once you have mastered the basic operations of this handy device, there are many more possibilities to discover.

This book allows you to explore some of the lesser known features on the iPad that will make it easier to use. You will learn how to use the touch screen in new ways and how to adjust the sound, notification and privacy settings to suit your own preferences.

Most apps offer additional settings that you can apply. Here are just a few examples: choose whether or not to accept cookies in *Safari* and synchronize your calendar with your email account. You can also decide which messages are shown in the *Notification Center* and learn how to set up *Home Sharing* in *iTunes.* You can even enhance your listening experience by setting certain options in the *Music* app.

Besides the tips for the standard apps on your iPad, we also give you a few tips for apps that you can purchase or download for free in the *App Store*. The *App Store* contains millions of apps, so you are sure to find other apps to suit your particular interests.

Now dive into this book and discover what more the iPad can do for you!

Alex Wit
Studio Visual Steps

PS We welcome your comments and suggestions.
Our email address is: info@visualsteps.com

Visual Steps Newsletter

All Visual Steps books follow the same methodology: clear and concise step-by-step instructions with screen shots to demonstrate each task.
A complete list of all our books can be found on our website **www.visualsteps.com**
You can also sign up to receive our **free Visual Steps Newsletter**.

In this Newsletter you will receive periodic information by email regarding:
- the latest titles and previously released books;
- special offers, supplemental chapters, tips and free informative booklets.
Also, our Newsletter subscribers may download any of the documents listed on the web pages **www.visualsteps.com/info_downloads**

When you subscribe to our Newsletter you can be assured that we will never use your email address for any purpose other than sending you the information as previously described. We will not share this address with any third-party. Each Newsletter also contains a one-click link to unsubscribe.

Introduction to Visual Steps™

The Visual Steps handbooks and manuals are the best instructional materials available for learning how to work with mobile devices, computers and software applications. Nowhere else will you find better support to help you get started with a *Windows* computer, *Mac*, iPad or other tablet, iPhone, the Internet or various software programs.

Properties of the Visual Steps books:
- **Comprehensible contents**
  Addresses the needs of the beginner or intermediate computer user for a manual written in simple, straight-forward English.
- **Clear structure**
  Precise, easy to follow instructions. The material is broken down into small enough segments to allow for easy absorption.
- **Screen shots of every step**
  Quickly compare what you see on your screen with the screen shots in the book. Pointers and tips guide you when new windows are opened so you always know what to do next.
- **Get started right away**
  All you have to do is have your tablet or computer and your book at hand. Sit some where's comfortable, begin reading and perform the operations as indicated on your own device.
- **Layout**
  The text is printed in a large size font and is clearly legible.

In short, I believe these manuals will be excellent guides for you.

Dr. H. van der Meij
Faculty of Applied Education, Department of Instructional Technology, University of Twente, the Netherlands

What You Will Need

To be able to work through this book, you will need a number of things:

An iPad 2, the new iPad (third generation or fourth generation), iPad Air, iPad mini or iPad Mini 2 with Wi-Fi or 3G/4G.

Probably, this book can also be used for a later edition of the iPad. For more information, see the webpage **www.visualsteps.com/tipsipad**

A computer, laptop or a notebook computer with the *iTunes* program already installed.

If you do not own a computer or a notebook, certain sections of this book will not be applicable. But it is not absolutely necessary to use a computer when you are working with an iPad.

How to Use This Book

This book has been written using the Visual Steps™ method. The method is simple: you put the book next to your iPad and perform each task step by step, directly on your own iPad. With the clear instructions and the multitude of screen shots, you will always know exactly what to do. By working through all the tasks in each chapter, you will gain a full understanding of your iPad and its many lesser known features. You can also of course, skip a chapter and go to one that suits your needs.

In this Visual Steps™ book, you will see various icons. This is what they mean:

Techniques
These icons indicate an action to be carried out:

   The index finger indicates you need to do something on the iPad's screen, for instance, tap something, or type a text.

⌨   The keyboard icon means you should type something on the keyboard of your iPad or your computer.

🖱   The mouse icon means you should do something on your computer with the mouse.

The hand icon means you should do something else, for example rotate the iPad or turn it off. The hand can also indicate a series of operations which you learned at an earlier stage.

Apart from these operations, in some parts of this book extra assistance is provided to help you gain more understanding of your iPad.

Help

These icons indicate that extra help is available:

 The arrow icon warns you about something.

 The bandage icon will help you if something has gone wrong.

1 Have you forgotten how to do something? The number next to the footsteps tells you where to look it up at the end of the book in the appendix *How Do I Do That Again?*

In separate boxes you will find general information or tips concerning the iPad.

Extra information

Information boxes are denoted by these icons:

 The book icon gives you extra background information that you can read at your convenience. This extra information is not necessary for working through the book.

 The light bulb icon indicates an extra tip for using the iPad.

Website

On the website that accompanies this book, **www.visualsteps.com/tipsipad**, you will find more information about this book. This website will also keep you informed of changes you need to know as a user of the book. Visit this website regularly and check if there are any recent updates or additions to this book, or possible errata.

Test Your Knowledge

After you have worked through this book, you can test your knowledge online, at the **www.ccforseniors.com** website.

By answering a number of multiple choice questions you will be able to test your knowledge of the iPad. After you have finished the test, your *Computer Certificate* will be sent to the email address you have entered.
Participating in the test is **free of charge**. The computer certificate website is a free Visual Steps service.

For Teachers

The Visual Steps books have been written as self-study guides for individual use. They are also well suited for use in a group or a classroom setting. For this purpose, some of our books come with a free teacher's manual. You can download the available teacher's manuals and additional materials from the website:
www.visualsteps.com/instructor
After you have registered at this website, you can use this service for free.

The Screen Shots

The screen shots in this book indicate which button, file or hyperlink you need to click on your computer or iPad screen. In the instruction text (in **bold** letters) you will see a small image of the item you need to click. The black line will point you to the right place on your screen.
The small screen shots that are printed in this book are not meant to be completely legible all the time. This is not necessary, as you will see these images on your own iPad screen in real size and fully legible.

Here you see an example of such an instruction text and a screen shot of the item you need to click. The black line indicates where to find this item on your own screen:

In some cases, the screen shot only displays part of the screen. Below you see an example of this:

At the bottom of the screen:

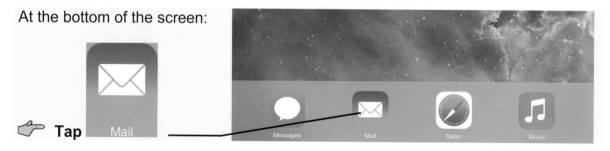

We would like to emphasize that we **do not intend you** to read the information in all of the screen shots in this book. Always use the screen shots in combination with the display on your iPad screen.

1. General Options and Settings

It is recommended that you regularly update your iPad and all of its installed apps. These updates often contain small changes, for instance, to the options available for the iPad or the app. The updates may also include new security options, which will better protect your iPad.
It is also a good idea to create regular backups of the data on your iPad. You can safely store your data in *iTunes* or *iCloud* and save the products you have purchased or downloaded.

You can fine-tune the settings on the iPad to suit your needs. This will make the iPad easier to use. You make changes to the settings in the *Settings* app.
For example, this is the place where you can set up the sounds that are played when certain events occur, and where you can set the current date and time. There are also settings to protect your privacy and secure the iPad with a code lock.

You will be typing text on your iPad on a regular basis. For example, in an email message, in your calendar, or in a text editor app. This is easy enough if you use the onscreen keyboard, but there are several tricks which can make it even easier to type a text. Such as the automatic insertion of a period and a blank space at the end of a sentence.

If you have specific problems while using your iPad, such as loss of hearing or sight, you can use the accessibility settings to make it easier to work with the iPad.

In this chapter you will find tips on the following subjects, among other things:

- checking for updates for your iPad and for the apps;
- viewing information about your iPad;
- sound settings and enabling the rotation lock;
- changing the location and privacy settings;
- automatically setting up a lock and a passcode lock;
- autocorrection and suggestions for words;
- disabling the typing sounds while you type;
- multitasking gestures and accessibility settings in case you have problems with your hearing, sight, or motor skills;
- creating a backup;
- various settings for the iPad and *iCloud*;
- resetting the iPad to the original factory settings;
- printing with your iPad, and using the iPad to communicate with your computer.

Tip

Dictionary
At the end of your book you will find several appendices. One of them, the *Appendix B. Dictionary* contains an overview and explanation of the terminology used in this book.

1.1 Checking for iPad Updates

Apple regularly releases new versions of the iPad software. These new releases may contain new functionality, or include fixes for certain problems. You will often see an automatic message appearing on your screen concerning such new releases, but is also important that you check for new iPad software yourself.

☞ **Open the *Settings* app** 📖¹

👉 **Tap** ⚙ **General**

👉 **Tap**
Software Update

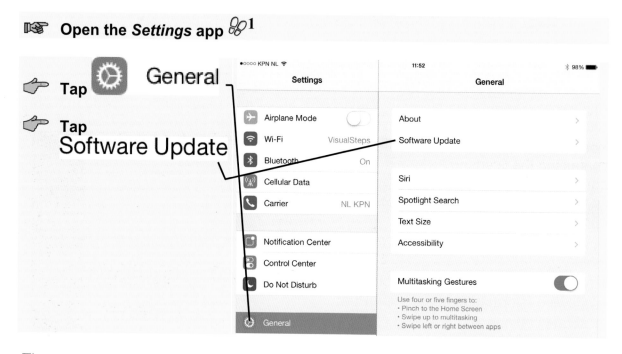

The system will check whether there is new software available for the iPad:

In this example, the most recent version of the software is already installed on the iPad:

To go back to the *Settings* screen:

☞ **Tap** ❮ General

If a newer version has been found, you will need to install the update:

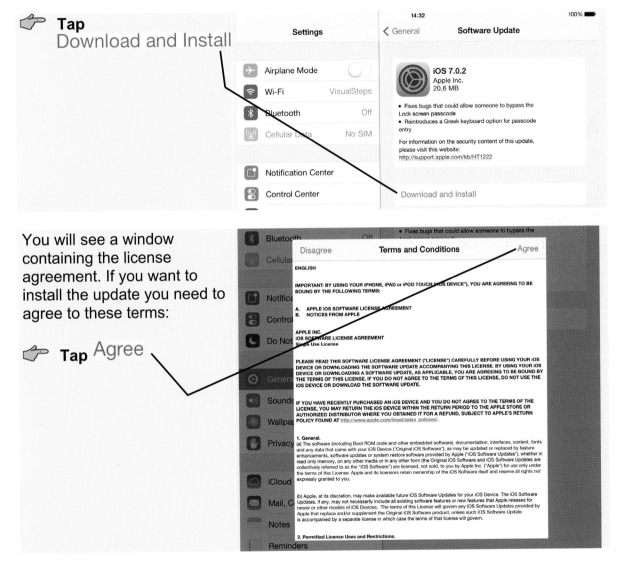

☞ **Tap**
Download and Install

You will see a window containing the license agreement. If you want to install the update you need to agree to these terms:

☞ **Tap** Agree

You may see a warning message:

 If necessary, tap the desired option

The update will be
downloaded and prepared:

Next, your screen will turn dark and the installation procedure will begin. This may take a while. After the update has been installed you will automatically return to the Start screen.

If you see different screens while you are installing the software update:

☞ **Follow the instructions on the screen**

1.2 Checking for Updates for Your Apps

Every so often, the apps installed on your iPad will also need to be updated. These updates are free, and may be essential for solving any problems. An update may also add new functions or options, such as a new level for a games app. You can install these updates through the *App Store*:

☞ **Open the *App Store*** ✂¹

You can tell right away that an update is available when a badge ② appears on the *Updates* button at the bottom of your screen:

☞ **Tap** Updates

In this example, a second update has been found after the *Updates* page has been opened. Both updates are free. Here is how to install these updates:

👉 **Tap** Update All

If you only want to download an update for a specific app, just tap the UPDATE button.

The apps will be updated. You will see a progress circle 🔘.

1.3 Viewing Information About Your iPad

Although you may not need it very often, it can be useful to know where to go to find additional information about your iPad. For example, if you have a lot of photos or music stored on the iPad, it is good to know how much available memory you have left. You can also write down the iPad's serial number, in case your iPad is stolen.

This is how to access the information concerning your iPad:

👉 **Open the *Settings* app** 👣¹

👉 **Tap** ⚙️ General

👉 **Tap** About

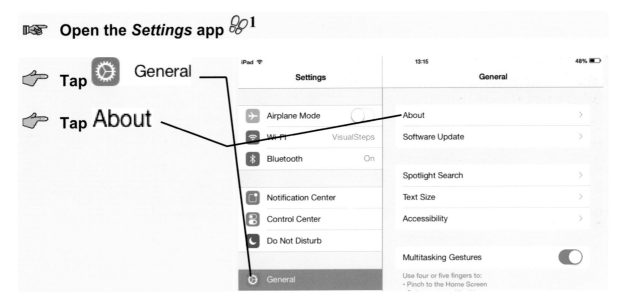

You will see all sorts of information about the iPad:

Owner of the iPad:

Total memory capacity:

Available capacity:

Version of the *iOS* operating system:

Serial number of this iPad:

Wi-Fi and Bluetooth address:

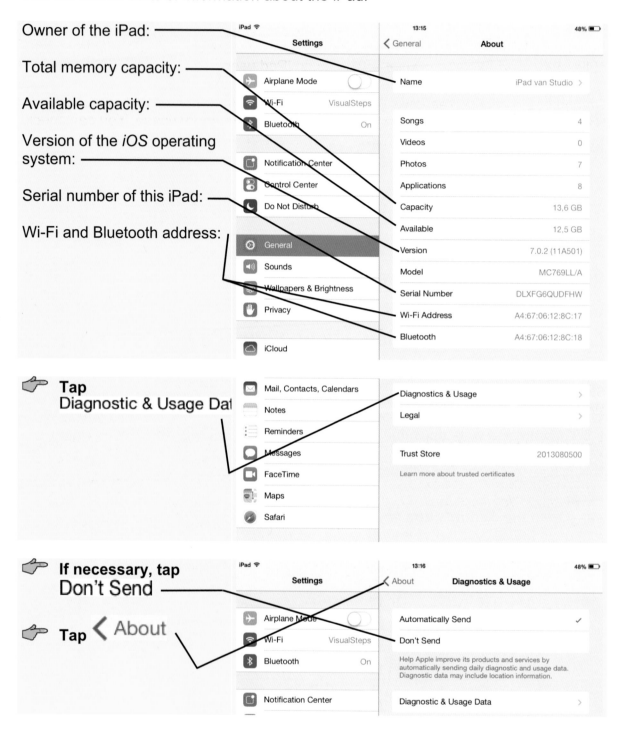

☞ **Tap**
Diagnostic & Usage Data

☞ **If necessary, tap**
Don't Send

☞ **Tap ❮ About**

💡 Tip

Legal information

By tapping Legal you can find additional information about your rights and obligations, and about your guarantees as an iPad user.

On one of the other screens you can find even more information about your iPad. Here you can find specific information concerning the memory usage. You can check whether you still have enough memory space available, and how you can free up some extra space:

👉 **If necessary, tap**

General

👉 **Tap** Usage

Storage available and used storage:

Space used for specific apps: You can read more about this topic in *section 4.23 Viewing the Memory Usage of the Apps.*

Space in *iCloud*:

👉 **Tap** < General

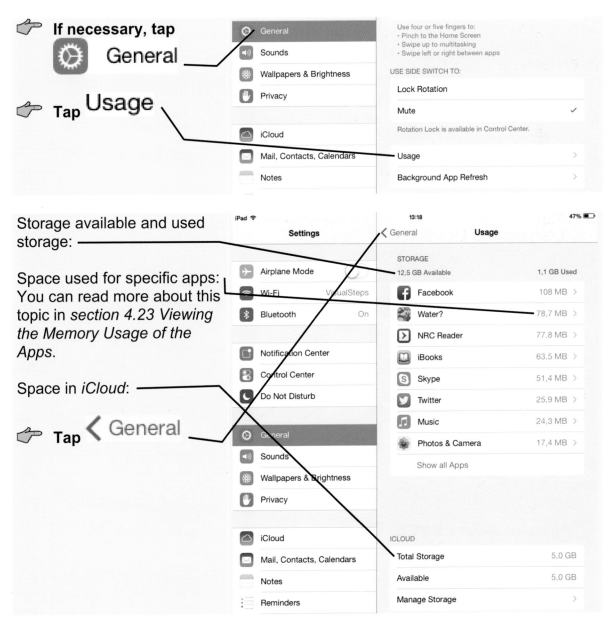

1.4 Battery Usage

If you use your iPad without connecting it to a power outlet, it is important to monitor your battery usage. Here is how to do that:

☞ **Open the** *Settings* **app** 🐾**1**

By default, you will see the battery percentage on the status bar:

To see more detailed information:

☞ **Tap** ⚙ **General**

☞ **Tap Usage**

The time the iPad is in use since it was last fully charged:

The time that has elapsed in standby mode:

Display battery percentage on status bar:

If you do not want to display the battery percentage on the status bar all the time:

☞ **Drag the slider ⬭ by Battery Percentage to the left**

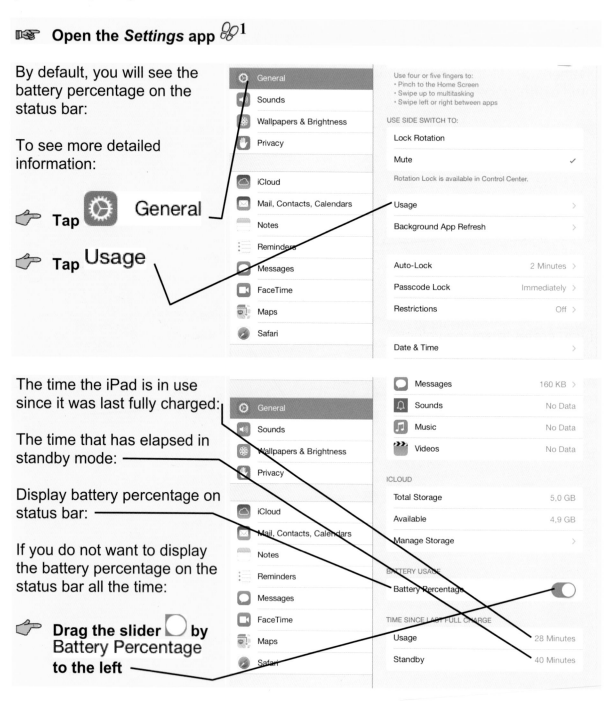

1.5 Sound Settings

Many actions and events on the iPad are associated with certain sounds. For instance, when you receive an email or lock the iPad, you will hear a sound signal. You can set up your own combinations of events and sounds, and select the volume level as well.

If you do not want to hear sounds for certain events, or for all of the events, you can turn the sound options off:

☞ **Open the *Settings* app** 🐾**1**

☞ **Tap** 🔊 **Sounds**

To set the sound level for the sound signals:

☞ **Drag the slider** ⚪ **by**

If you prefer to set the volume with the volume controls on the side of the iPad:

☞ **Drag the slider** ⚪ **by**
Change with Buttons
to the right

The current sound signals are displayed next to the events:

You can set a different sound for each individual event:

☞ **Tap an event, for**
example, New Mail

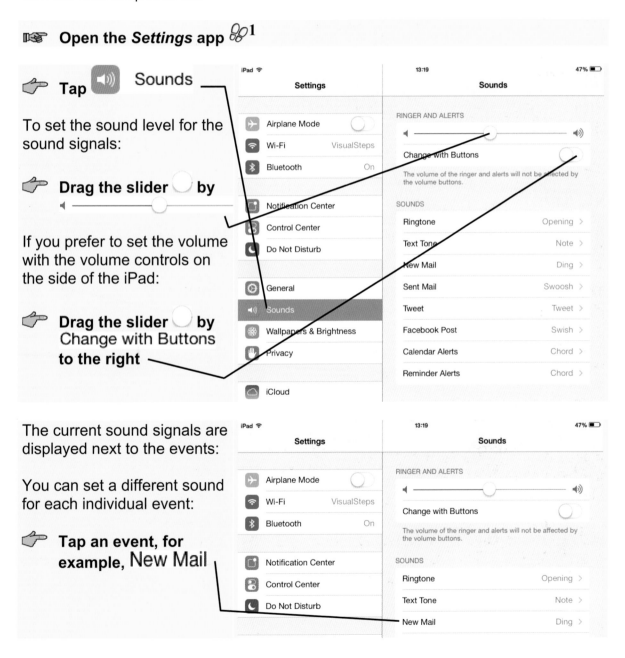

You can select a sound from the list:

☞ **Tap a sound, for example,** Popcorn

You will hear a sample of the audio file.

If you prefer not to hear any sounds, tap None.

Confirm these settings:

☞ **Tap** < Sounds

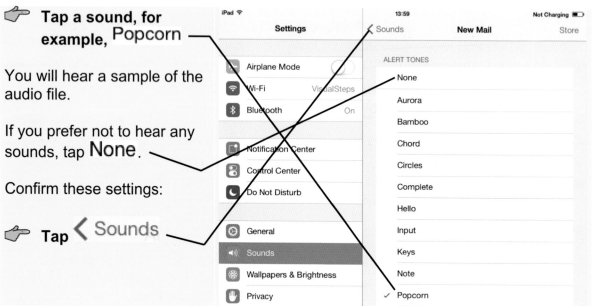

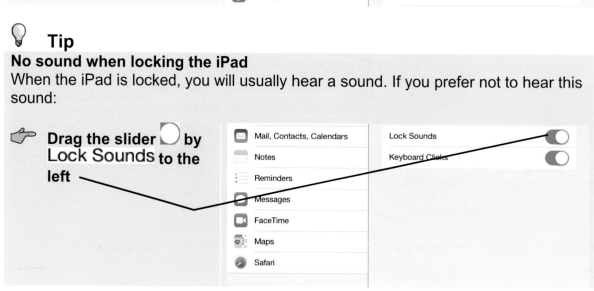

💡 **Tip**

No sound when locking the iPad
When the iPad is locked, you will usually hear a sound. If you prefer not to hear this sound:

☞ **Drag the slider ⬭ by** Lock Sounds **to the left**

1.6 Turning On the Rotation Lock

☞ **Open the *Settings* app** ✇¹

The side switch on the iPad can be used in two different ways:
- *Rotation lock*: lock the screen in portrait or landscape mode.
- *Mute*: mute the volume of notifications and sound signals.

By default, the *Mute* function is selected. You can easily change the function of the side switch to *Rotation lock* if you prefer: You do that like this:

☞ **If necessary, push the side switch upwards**

☞ **If necessary, tap**
⚙ **General**

☞ **Tap Auto-Lock**

		Use four or five fingers to: • Pinch to the Home Screen • Swipe up to multitasking • Swipe left or right between apps
⚙	General	USE SIDE SWITCH TO:
🔊	Sounds	Lock Rotation
❋	Wallpapers & Brightness	Mute ✓
✋	Privacy	Rotation Lock is available in Control Center.
☁	iCloud	
✉	Mail, Contacts, Calendars	Usage >
	Notes	Background App Refresh >
	Reminders	
💬	Messages	Auto-Lock 2 Minutes >
🎥	FaceTime	Passcode Lock Immediately >
	Maps	Restrictions Off >
🧭	Safari	Date & Time >

Now you can use the side switch to lock the screen in the current position.

1.7 Selecting Location and Privacy Settings

You may not reflect on this while you are using your iPad, but certain apps on the iPad may pass along sensitive personal information through the Internet. For instance, information on how you use your iPad, or the current location of the iPad. This last option is called Location Services. By the way, you will not just protect your privacy by turning off these options, you will be extending your iPad's battery life as well.

You can decide for yourself what type of data can be used by these apps. For example, you can turn off Location Services:

☞ **Open the *Settings* app** 🐾¹

👉 **Tap** ✋ Privacy

Depending on the option you selected when you set up your iPad, the Location Services have been turned on or off:

👉 **Tap**

⬆ Location Services

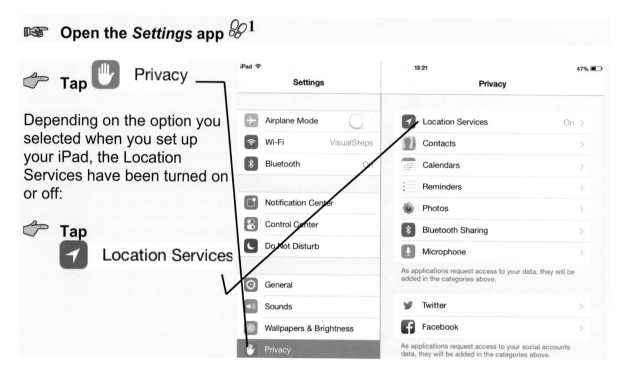

The settings for the Location Services are displayed:

You will also see a description:

If you want to turn off the Location Services for all apps:

👉 **Drag the slider** ⬭ **by** Location Services **to the left**

You may see various apps for which Location Services have previously been turned on or off. If you want to turn off Location Services for a specific app:

👉 **Drag the slider** ⬭ **by the app to the left**

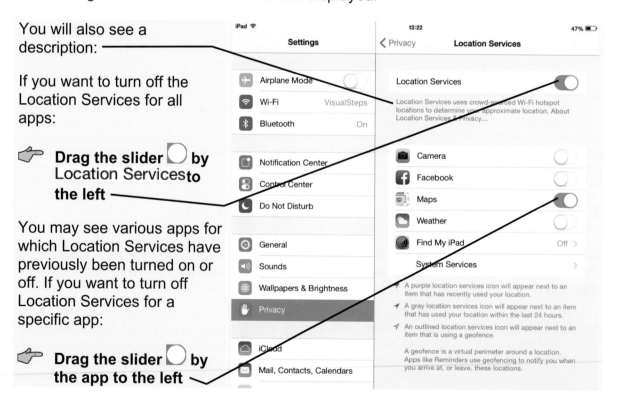

Please note:

An app that uses Location Services will automatically ask you whether this option needs to be turned on again. Then you can choose the option you want to use. If you have turned off all Location Services, some apps may not function properly.

You can display an icon on the status bar if a certain app uses Location Services:

☞ **Tap** System Services

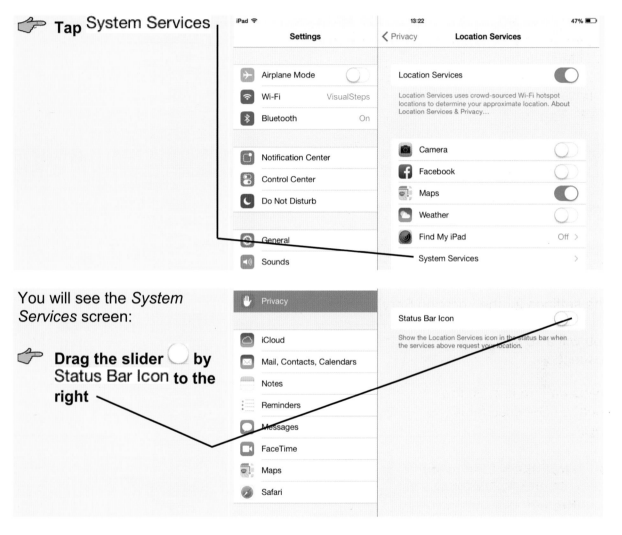

You will see the *System Services* screen:

☞ **Drag the slider ○ by Status Bar Icon to the right**

On the *System Services* screen you can see where the system has recently used Location Services. This may occur for example, when you set up the correct time zone for your area. For each function you can select a default setting and allow the system to use (or not use) Location Services.

To turn off Location Services
for a specific function:

☞ **Drag the slider** ◯ **by
the function to the left**

☞ **Tap**
   ❮ Location Services

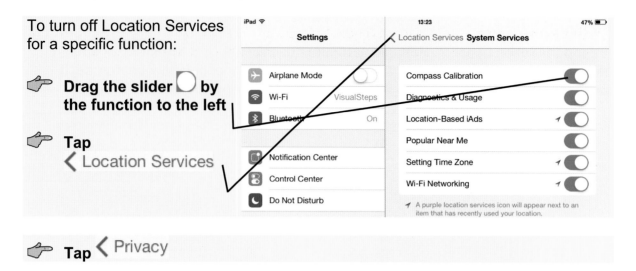

☞ **Tap** ❮ Privacy

On the *Privacy* screen you can see which apps have tried to gain access to certain
apps and functions on your iPad. In this way you can monitor the apps that try to gain
access to your data, and disable or remove these apps, if you wish. You can find out
which apps wanted to view your photos, for example:

☞ **Tap** 🌸 Photos

In this example the *Facebook*
app has asked to access your
photos, and has been allowed
to view these photos:

If you want, you can drag the
slider ◯ by the app and
block the access rights for
this app:

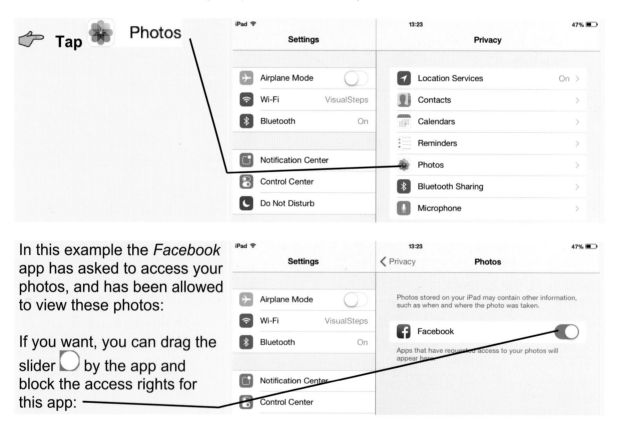

On the *Privacy* screen you can also select an option to send on information from your iPad for advertising and diagnostic purposes (or you can choose not to do this):

👉 **Tap** ‹ Privacy

👉 **Tap** Advertising

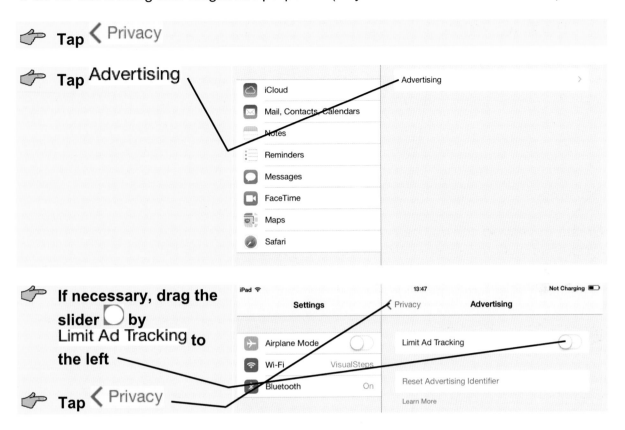

👉 **If necessary, drag the slider ⬭ by** Limit Ad Tracking **to the left**

👉 **Tap** ‹ Privacy

1.8 Setting Up the Automatic Lock

By now, you have probably come across the automatic lock feature while using your iPad. If you do not use your iPad for a certain period of time, the automatic lock will put the iPad into sleep mode and lock the device. The screen will turn dark and the activities on the iPad will slow down. This saves battery life.

By default, the automatic lock is set for two minutes. But many people feel this period of time is too short. What if you are lingering on a page while reading a book, or using the iPad while making notes, following a recipe as you cook or displaying sheet music? These are moments when you do not want your iPad to turn off so quickly.

Fortunately, you can change the amount of time to elapse before the automatic lock is activated:

👉 **Open the** *Settings* **app** 🦶¹

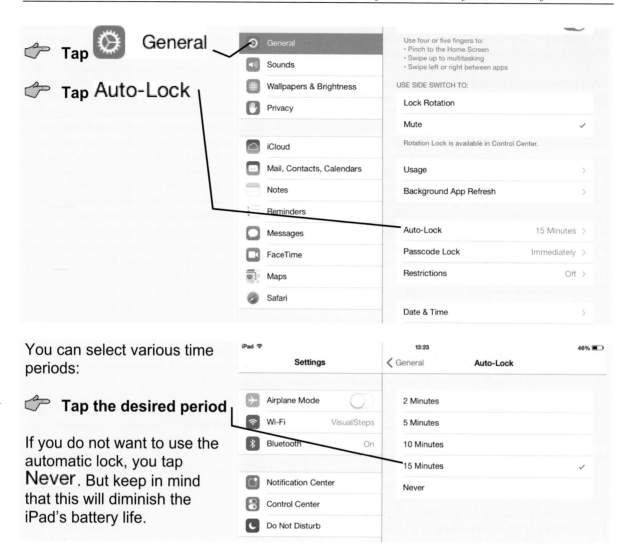

☞ Tap ⚙️ General

☞ Tap Auto-Lock

You can select various time periods:

 Tap the desired period

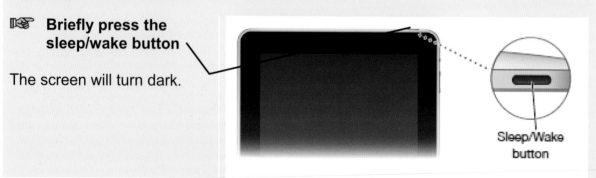

If you do not want to use the automatic lock, you tap Never. But keep in mind that this will diminish the iPad's battery life.

💡 **Tip**

Manually put the iPad into sleep mode
Remember you can put the iPad into sleep mode yourself, for instance, when you need to go out for a while.

☞ **Briefly press the sleep/wake button**

The screen will turn dark.

1.9 Setting Up the Passcode Lock

You can secure your iPad with a passcode lock. This code must be entered before the iPad will unlock (or whenever you want to wake up your iPad from sleep mode). This way, you can prevent unauthorized access to your iPad.

This is how you set up the passcode lock:

☞ **Open the *Settings* app** 🐾¹

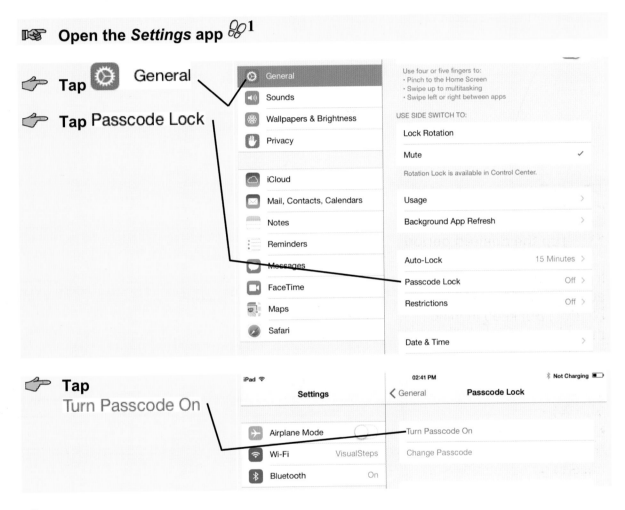

☞ **Tap** ⚙ General

☞ **Tap Passcode Lock**

☞ **Tap Turn Passcode On**

 Tip

Extensive code
An extensive code consists of letters and numbers. If you create such a code, it is more difficult to break, but might be harder for you to remember than the 4-digit passcode. Both types of codes are set up in the same way.

You can make up your own passcode:

 Type a 4-digit passcode

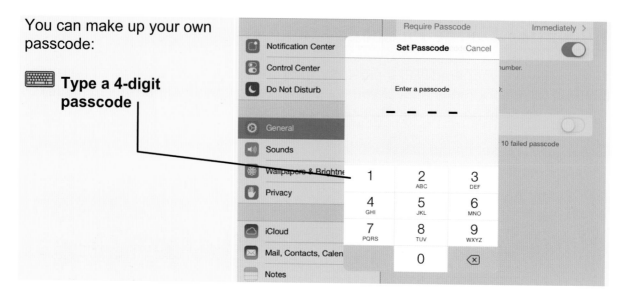

In the next window:

 Re-type your passcode

Please note:

Write down your passcode and save this code in a safe place. If you forget the code you will no longer be able to unlock your iPad.

When you lock the iPad and put it into sleep mode, you must enter the code in order to unlock it again (wake it up). But you can also set how long the iPad can be in sleep mode before requiring you to enter the passcode. If this set amount of time has not elapsed, you will not need to enter the code to wake it up.

Tap Require Passcode

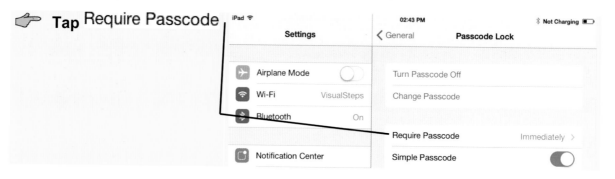

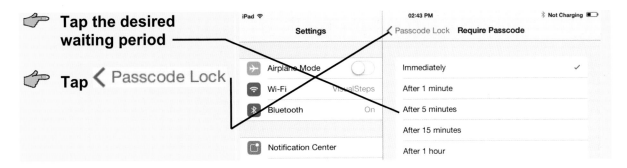

👉 **Tap the desired waiting period**

👉 **Tap** ‹ Passcode Lock

💡 **Tip**

Delete data after ten attempts to unlock the device

When setting up the passcode lock you can choose to have all the data on the iPad deleted after ten attempts to access the iPad have failed. This is an extra security measure for your iPad, in case it contains personal information you do not want to share with others. If you are going to use this option it is recommended that you create regular backups of your data, so you can use the backup in case the data on the iPad is deleted.

👉 **Drag the slider** ⬭ **by** Erase Data **to the right**

If you no longer want to use the passcode lock on your iPad, you can turn it off:

In the *Passcode Lock* screen:

👉 **Tap**
Turn Passcode Off

⌨ **Type your passcode**

Now the passcode lock has been disabled.

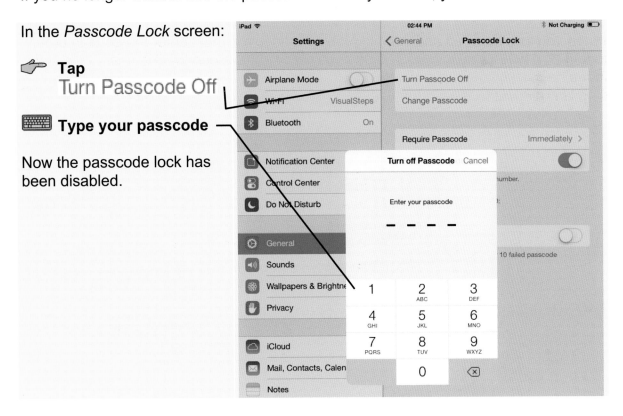

1.10 Setting up Restrictions for Use

If your iPad is also used by your children or grandchildren, you may want to set up certain restrictions for them. For instance, you can decide which apps they are allowed to use, and what type of films they can view:

☞ **Open the *Settings* app** ✍¹

☞ **Tap** ⚙ **General**

☞ **Tap Restrictions**

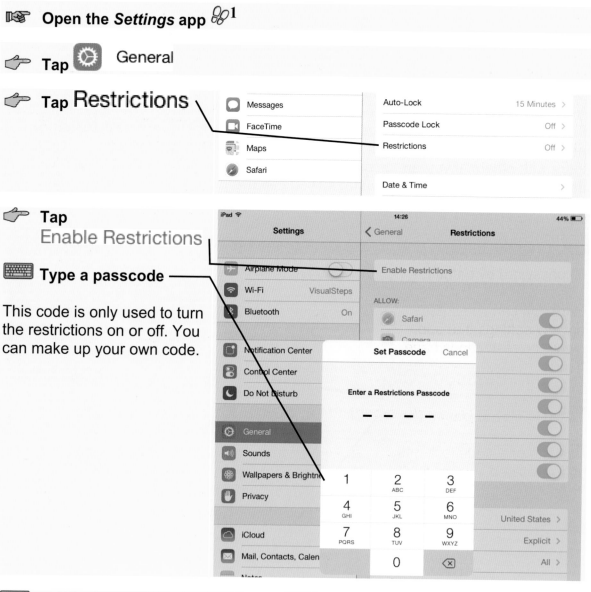

☞ **Tap Enable Restrictions**

⌨ **Type a passcode**

This code is only used to turn the restrictions on or off. You can make up your own code.

⌨ **Re-type the passcode**

At the top you see the apps that may be used. If you want to disable one of these apps:

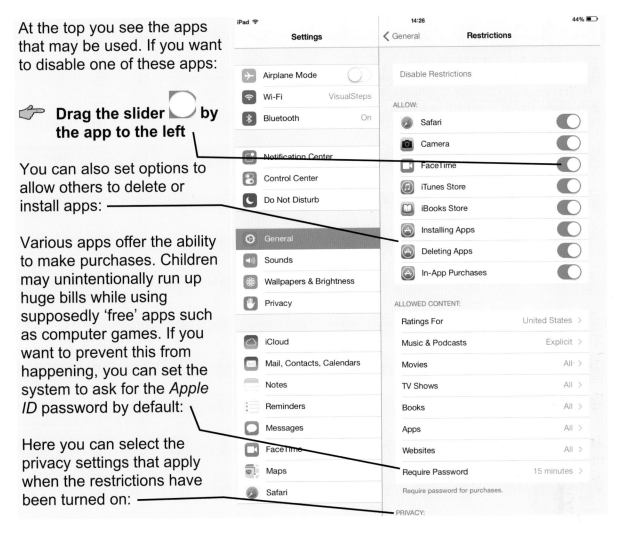

☞ **Drag the slider** ⬭ **by the app to the left**

You can also set options to allow others to delete or install apps:

Various apps offer the ability to make purchases. Children may unintentionally run up huge bills while using supposedly 'free' apps such as computer games. If you want to prevent this from happening, you can set the system to ask for the *Apple ID* password by default:

Here you can select the privacy settings that apply when the restrictions have been turned on:

You can also set age limits regarding the use of music and films:

By ALLOWED CONTENT: you can enter the age limits for your country:

☞ **Tap** Ratings For

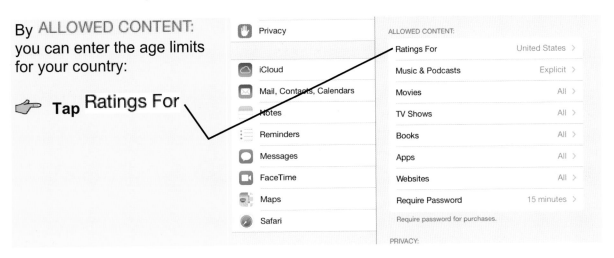

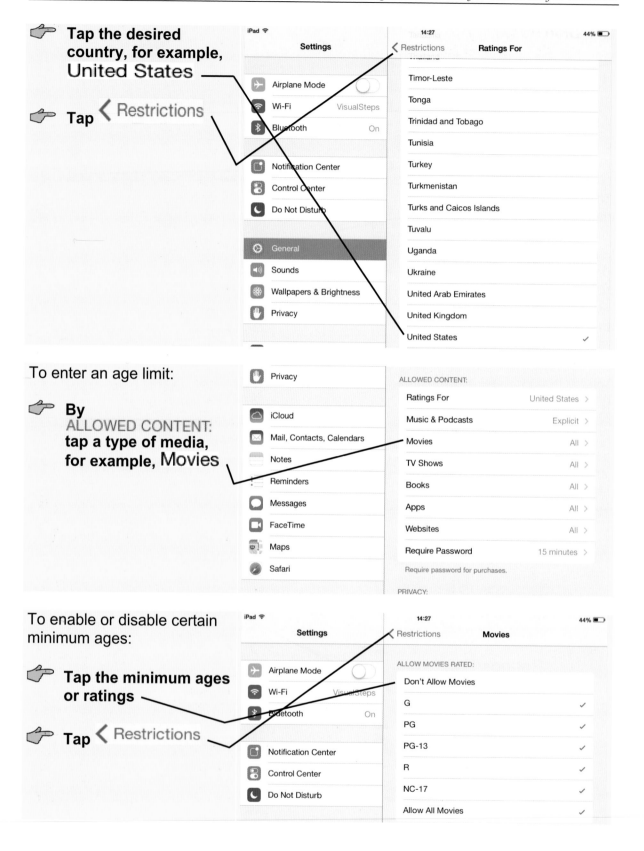

Tap the desired country, for example, United States

Tap ‹ Restrictions

To enter an age limit:

By ALLOWED CONTENT: tap a type of media, for example, Movies

To enable or disable certain minimum ages:

Tap the minimum ages or ratings

Tap ‹ Restrictions

☞ **Drag upwards across the right side of the screen**

Furthermore, you can allow or restrict changes to be made to email accounts, contacts, and calendars:

Restrict access to volume control:

It is often possible to play games with others, and add friends. You can allow this option to be enabled or disabled as well:

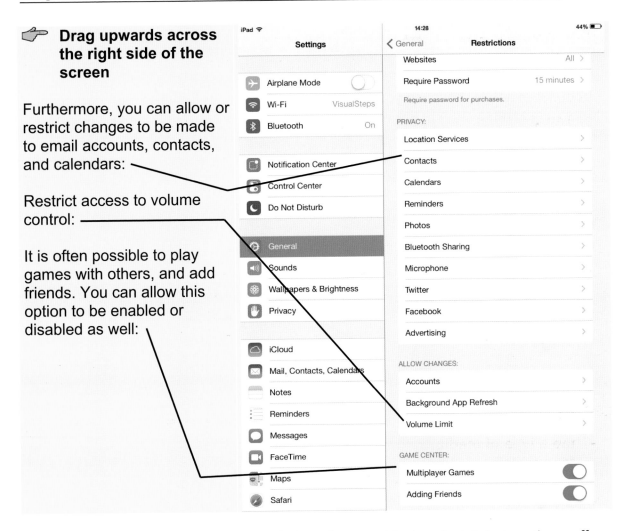

If you no longer want to use the restrictions for your iPad and wish to turn them off:

☞ **Drag downwards across the right side of the screen**

☞ **Tap**
Disable Restrictions

⌨ **Type the restrictions passcode**

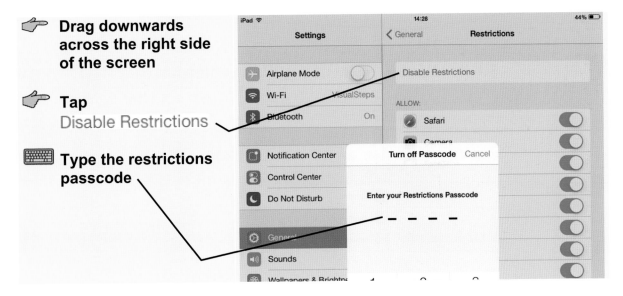

1.11 Setting the Date and Time

The date and time on your iPad are set automatically. If the date and time are not correct, for example, because you have turned off Location Services, you can adjust them. You can also change the way the date and time are displayed. For instance, you can select a 12-hour clock instead of a 24-hour clock:

☞ **Open the *Settings* app** 👣**1**

☞ **Tap** ⚙ **General**

☞ **Drag upwards across the right side of the screen**

☞ **Tap Date & Time**

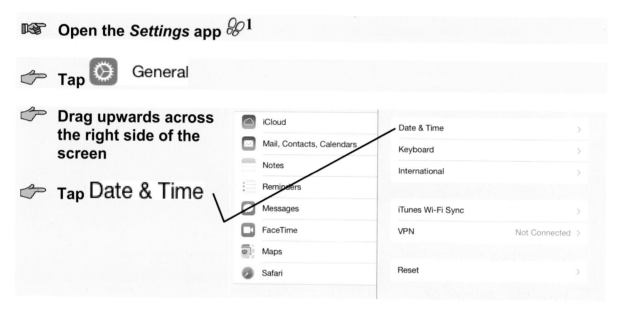

To use the 12-hour clock:

☞ **Drag the slider by 24-Hour Time to the left**

Now the time is displayed in AM and PM:

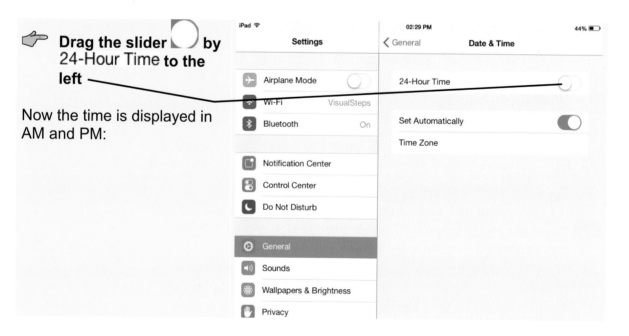

The time and the time zone are automatically set through the iPad and the Internet. If you do not want this, you can also set them manually. This may be useful if you have disabled Location Services and are travelling to a different time zone:

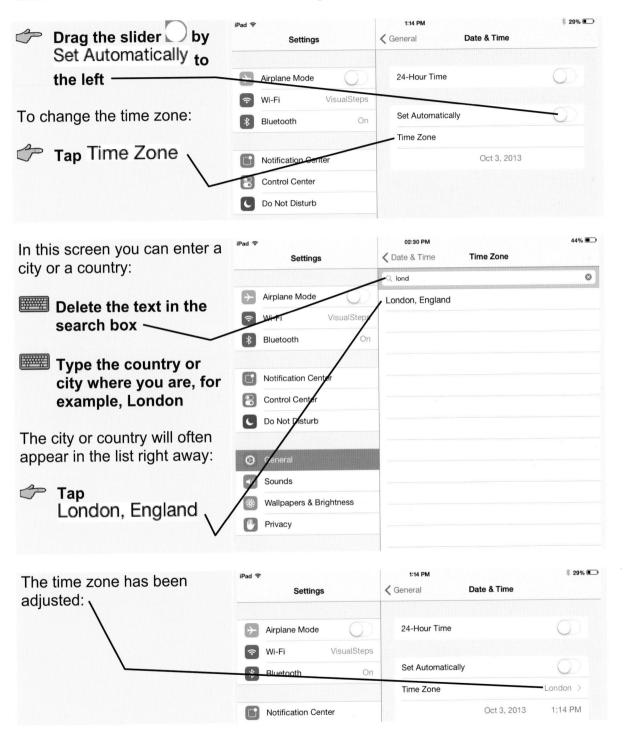

☞ **Drag the slider** ⬭ **by** Set Automatically **to the left** ————

To change the time zone:

☞ **Tap** Time Zone

In this screen you can enter a city or a country:

⌨ **Delete the text in the search box**

⌨ **Type the country or city where you are, for example, London**

The city or country will often appear in the list right away:

☞ **Tap** London, England

The time zone has been adjusted:

You can also change the date and time:

☞ **Tap the date**

First, you set the time:

☞ **Swipe your finger over the wheel, until you see the correct time**

In the same way you can change the date, if necessary:

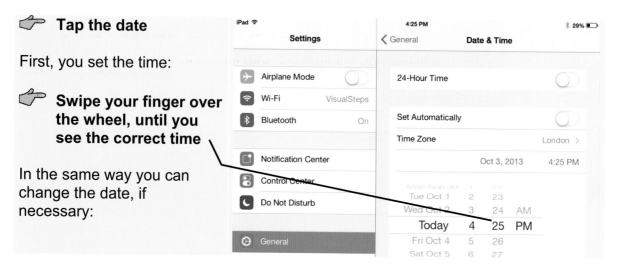

To automatically set the date and time back to the correct time zone:

☞ **Drag the slider ◯ by Set Automatically to the right**

To put back the 24-hour clock:

☞ **Drag the slider ◯ by 24-Hour Time to the right**

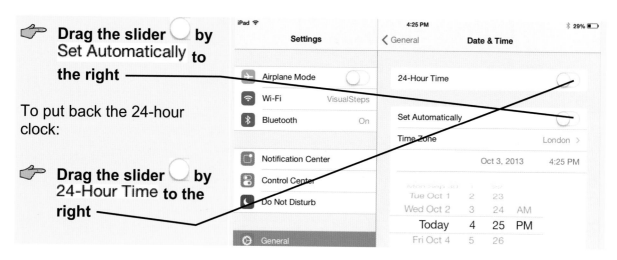

 Tip

Regional settings
By using the regional settings you can also change the way the date, time, and phone numbers are displayed for a specific country. Some countries use a day-month notation, while other countries write the month first, followed by the day. This is how you change these settings:

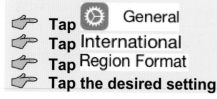

☞ **Tap** ⚙ General
☞ **Tap** International
☞ **Tap** Region Format
☞ **Tap the desired setting**

1.12 Setting the Language

You can change the language used by your iPad. The names of the apps and all other texts on your iPad will then be displayed in that language. You can use this option if you are working abroad, or if your native language is different from the English language:

☞ **Open the** *Settings* **app** 🐾¹

👉 **Tap** ⚙ General

👉 **Tap** International

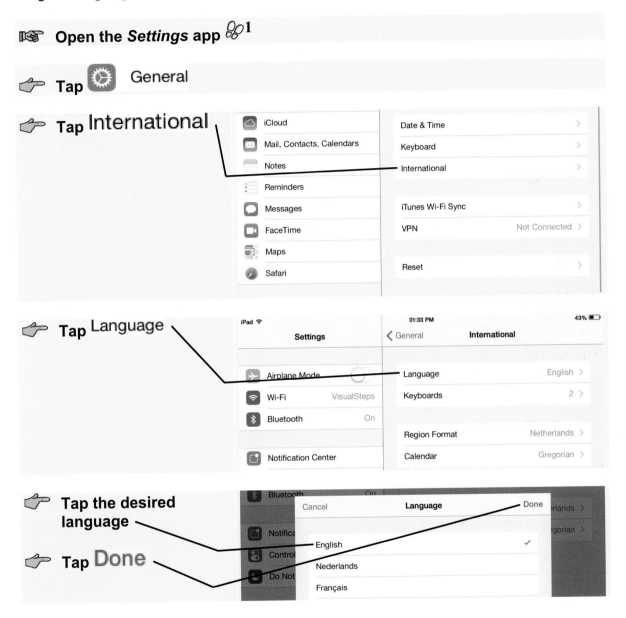

👉 **Tap** Language

👉 **Tap the desired language**

👉 **Tap** Done

The language setting will be changed. This may take a while.

1.13 Quickly Type Spaces

There are various apps on your iPad where you need to type text, for example, when composing an email message. There are many things you can do to make typing easier. In the next few sections we will acquaint you with various keyboard shortcuts.

Usually, you end each sentence with a period, followed by a space. You can do this a lot quicker by using a keyboard shortcut:

☞ **Open the *Notes* app, or any other app that lets you type text** 𝒢𝒢**1**

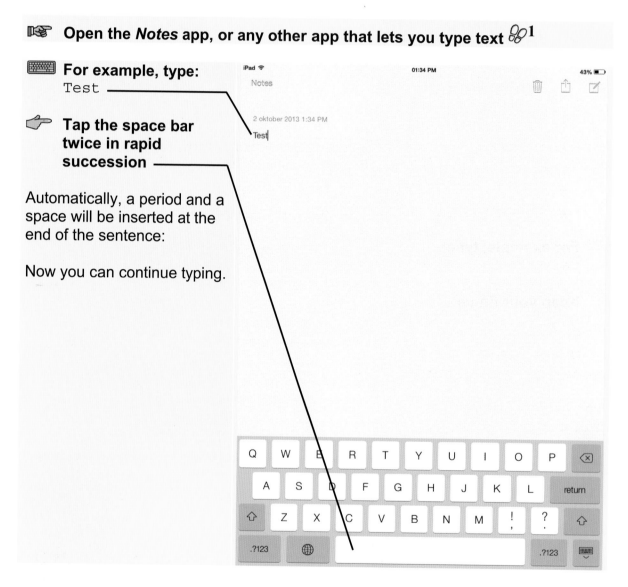

⌨ **For example, type:**
Test

☞ **Tap the space bar twice in rapid succession**

Automatically, a period and a space will be inserted at the end of the sentence:

Now you can continue typing.

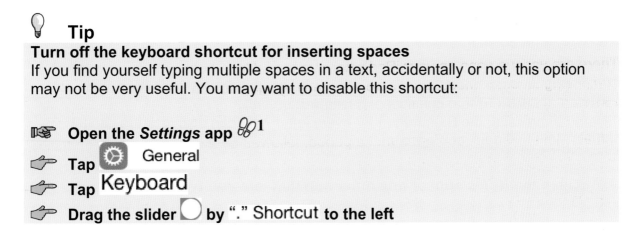

Tip

Turn off the keyboard shortcut for inserting spaces

If you find yourself typing multiple spaces in a text, accidentally or not, this option may not be very useful. You may want to disable this shortcut:

☞ **Open the *Settings* app** 👣1

☞ **Tap** ⚙ General

☞ **Tap** Keyboard

☞ **Drag the slider** ⬭ **by** "." Shortcut **to the left**

1.14 Using Accents

On the onscreen keyboard you will not see any diacritical marks (symbols added to letters), such as ë, é, or ï. This is how you type one of these letters:

☞ **Open the *Notes* app, or any other app that lets you type text** 👣1

⌨ **For example, type:**
Caf ————————— Caf|

☞ **Keep your finger**

pressed on the E key

A small window appears with different diacritical marks for the letter e, such as é and ë:

☞ **Slide your finger from**

the E to the é

☞ **Release the key**

The e with the diacritical mark will appear in the text.

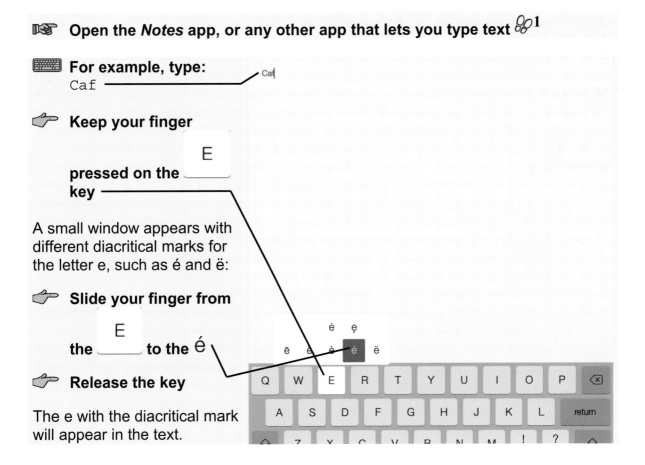

1.15 Using Caps Lock

Usually you will just type one capital letter at a time, at the beginning of a sentence. But sometimes you need to type more than one capital, for instance, when you are entering a password that consists of capital letters only.

Instead of pressing the Shift button for every letter, you can also lock the capital letters with the Caps Lock setting:

☞ **Open the *Notes* app, or any other app that lets you type text** 🦶¹

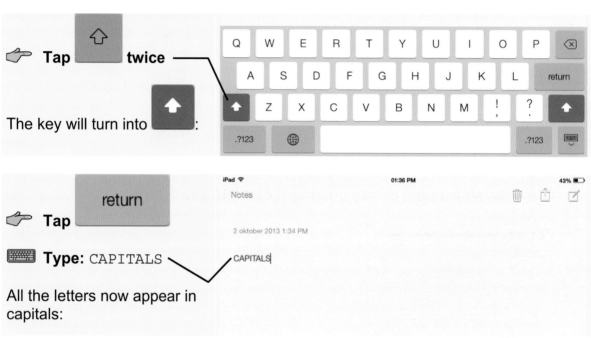

☞ **Tap** ⬆ **twice**

The key will turn into ⬆ :

☞ **Tap** return

⌨ **Type:** CAPITALS

All the letters now appear in capitals:

To go back to the normal function of this key:

☞ **Tap** ⬆

➥ **Please note:**

Only use capital letters in emails and other messages when necessary. On the Internet, typing an entire sentence in capital letters is perceived as shouting.

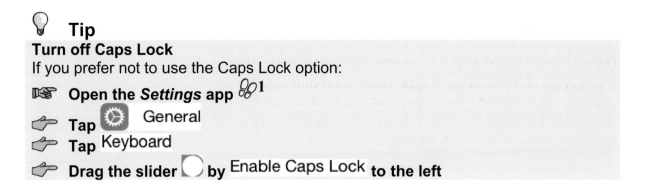

Tip

Turn off Caps Lock

If you prefer not to use the Caps Lock option:

☞ **Open the *Settings* app** ✂1

☞ **Tap** ⚙ General

☞ **Tap** Keyboard

☞ **Drag the slider** ◯ **by** Enable Caps Lock **to the left**

1.16 Auto-correction and Word Suggestions

In certain apps you can display suggestions for words while you are typing. This feature is called *auto-correction* and will help you to spell words correctly.

There are two ways in which you can display these suggestions. The first method is to get suggestions while you are typing:

☞ **Open the *Notes* app, or any other app that lets you type text** ✂1

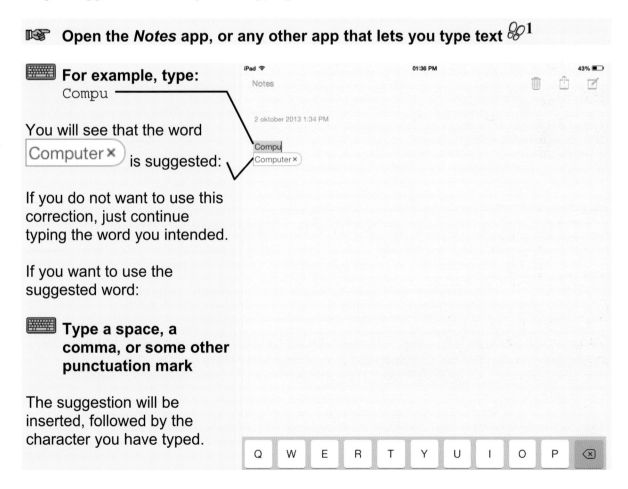

⌨ **For example, type:**
Compu

You will see that the word
Computer ✕ is suggested:

If you do not want to use this correction, just continue typing the word you intended.

If you want to use the suggested word:

⌨ **Type a space, a comma, or some other punctuation mark**

The suggestion will be inserted, followed by the character you have typed.

You can also get a suggestion by selecting a word you have already typed:

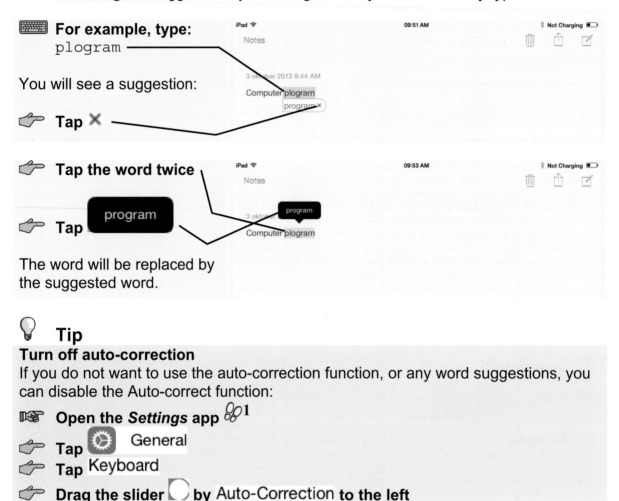

For example, type:

plogram

You will see a suggestion:

☞ Tap ✕

☞ Tap the word twice

☞ Tap

The word will be replaced by the suggested word.

💡 **Tip**

Turn off auto-correction
If you do not want to use the auto-correction function, or any word suggestions, you can disable the Auto-correct function:

☞ **Open the *Settings* app** 👣¹

☞ **Tap** ⚙ General

☞ **Tap** Keyboard

☞ **Drag the slider** ⬭ **by** Auto-Correction **to the left**

1.17 How to Undock or Split the Onscreen Keyboard

The standard position of the onscreen keyboard is at the bottom of the screen. But it might sometimes be easier to put the keyboard in the middle of the screen. On the iPad, this is called *undocking*.

This function is especially useful when you hold the iPad in a vertical position. This way, the keyboard will be closer to the text, which will give you a better overview. This is how you undock the onscreen keyboard:

☞ **Open the *Notes* app, or any other app that lets you type text** 👣¹

☞ **Put your finger on**

☞ **Swipe to** Undock

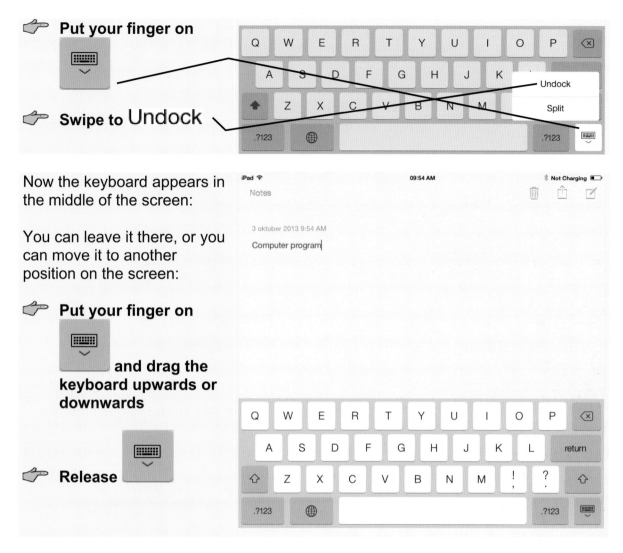

Now the keyboard appears in the middle of the screen:

You can leave it there, or you can move it to another position on the screen:

☞ **Put your finger on**

and drag the keyboard upwards or downwards

☞ **Release**

➥ Please note:
This function works best when you hold the iPad in the horizontal position. Afterwards you can turn the iPad to a vertical position and continue typing the text.

You can also put the keyboard back into its fixed position:

☞ **Put your finger on**

☞ **Tap** Dock

Another option is to split the onscreen keyboard. The keyboard will then be displayed in two halves, on both sides of the screen. This can be useful when you need more space on your screen, in order to type text:

☞ **Put your finger on**

☞ **Tap** Split

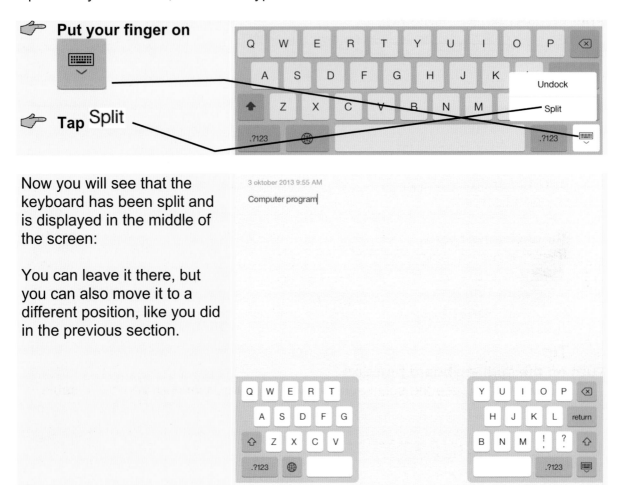

Now you will see that the keyboard has been split and is displayed in the middle of the screen:

You can leave it there, but you can also move it to a different position, like you did in the previous section.

3 oktober 2013 9:55 AM

Computer program

To merge the keyboard again:

☞ **Put your finger on**

☞ **Tap** Merge

Or, if you want to put the keyboard back to its original position at the bottom of the screen:

☞ **Put your finger on**

☞ **Tap** Dock and Merge

💡 **Tip**

Split the keyboard by dragging
You can also split the keyboard with a dragging gesture:

☞ **Put your thumbs in the middle of the keyboard**

☞ **Press lightly with your thumbs and drag outwards. You will see the two halves.**

You can join the keyboard together again by dragging both halves towards each other.

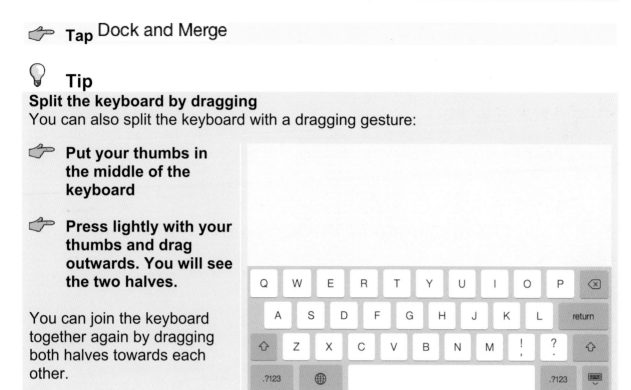

💡 **Tip**

Turn off the split keyboard function
If you do not want to use the split keyboard while you are working, you can disable this function:

☞ **Open the *Settings* app** **[1]**
☞ **Tap** ⚙ General
☞ **Tap** Keyboard

☞ **Drag the slider** ⬭ **by** Split Keyboard **to the left**

💡 **Tip**

Larger keys
If you disable the rotation lock and turn the iPad sideways (landscape orientation), the keys on the onscreen keyboard will become larger.
This can be very useful if you have problems tapping the right keys.

Tip

Wireless keyboard
Although the iPad onscreen keyboard can be used for most typing purposes, it may sometimes be awkward to use. For example, if you need to type large amounts of text, it may be easier to use an actual keyboard. A wireless keyboard can solve these problems. The keys you tap are wirelessly transferred to the iPad through Bluetooth. In *section 1.21 Setting Up Bluetooth* you can read more about connecting such a keyboard.

1.18 Turn Off the Sound of the Keyboard While You Type

Some people are annoyed by the sound the iPad makes while they tap the keys. You can disable these clicking sounds quite easily:

☞ **Open the *Settings* app** 🐾¹

☞ **Tap** 🔊 Sounds

☞ **Drag the slider ⬭ by Keyboard Clicks to the left**

Now you will no longer hear those clicking sounds as you type.

1.19 Setting up Multitasking Gestures

You have already used various gestures for one or two fingers to control the iPad. But the iPad will also respond to gestures made with four or five fingers at once. These gestures are called multitasking gestures. First, you need to check whether the multitasking gestures have been enabled on your iPad:

☞ **Open the *Settings* app** 🐾¹

☞ **Tap** ⚙ General

👉 **If necessary, drag the slider ⬭ by Multitasking Gestures to the right**

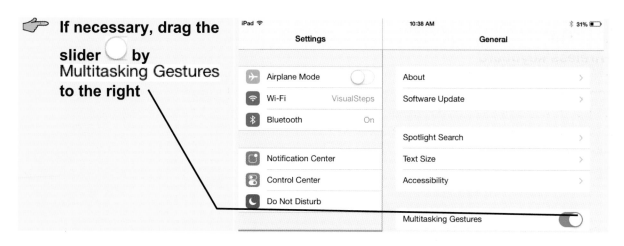

There are three different multitasking gestures:

👉 **Swipe upwards across the screen, with four or five fingers at once**

The multitasking bar is displayed. On this bar you can find the most recently used apps. You can quickly open an app by tapping it. To close an app, tap the app with one finger and flick it upwards: ⎯⎯⎯⎯

This is how you close the multitasking bar again:

👉 **Swipe downwards across the screen, with four or five fingers at once**

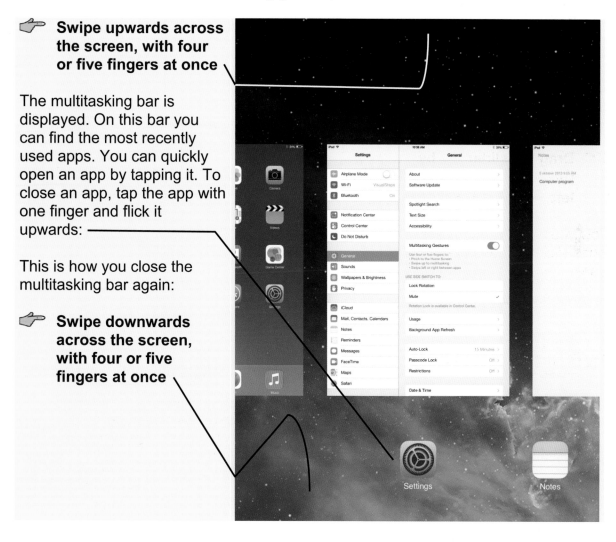

You can also use multitasking to quickly switch between the apps you have opened:

This is how you display the next open app from within the screen of another open app:

 **Swipe across the screen from left to right, with four or five fingers at once**

This is how you display the previous open app:

 **Swipe across the screen from right to left, with four or five fingers at once**

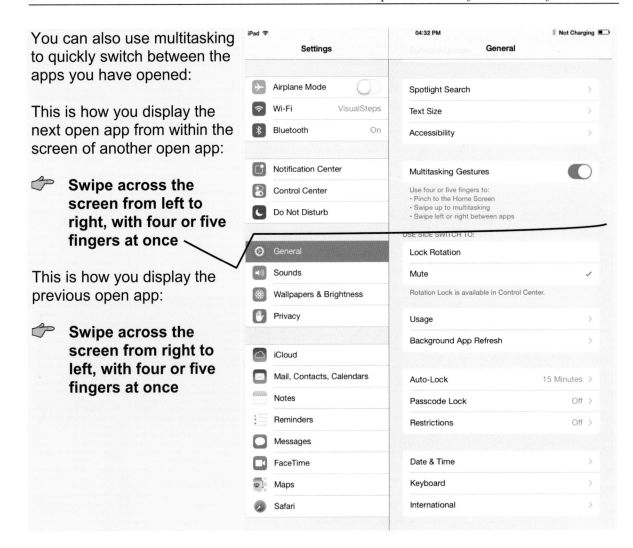

You can also use a multitasking gesture to go back to the Start screen at once, without using the Home button:

In the screen of an app:

 **Use your thumb and three or four fingers top make a pinching gesture on the screen**

You will see the home screen.

1.20 Accessibility Settings for People with Impaired Vision, Auditory Disabilities, or Impaired Motor Skills

Do you have problems using the iPad? Is the text difficult to read? Take a look at some of the accessibility features available on the iPad:

☞ **Open the *Settings* app** ✂️¹

☞ **Tap** ⚙️ General

☞ **Tap** Accessibility

You will see various accessibility options, divided into several categories:

Settings for impaired vision:

Settings for auditory problems:

Guided access to an app:

Settings for problems with physical and motor skills:

At the bottom of the screen you find quick access to a function by triple clicking the

Home button ⬛ :

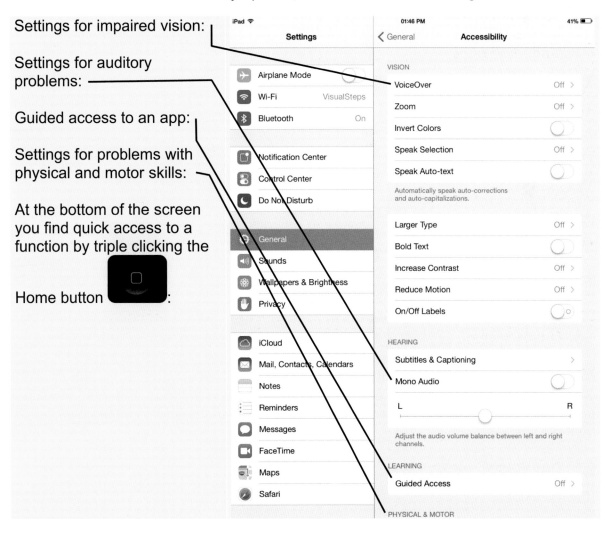

You can use one of these accessibility functions or multiple functions at once, to make working with the iPad easier. In the remainder of this section we will discuss some of these options. If you wish, you can take a look at the other functions by yourself.

The first option is to zoom in on the screen:

☞ **Tap** Zoom

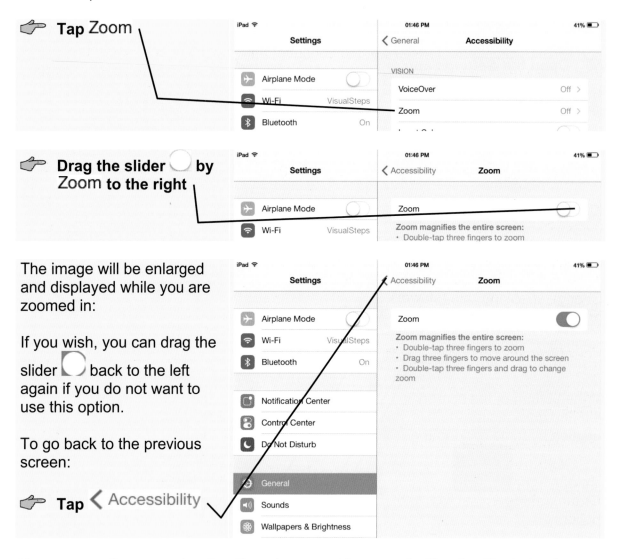

The image will be enlarged and displayed while you are zoomed in:

If you wish, you can drag the slider ⬭ back to the left again if you do not want to use this option.

To go back to the previous screen:

☞ **Tap** ‹ Accessibility

You can use the second option if you have problems controlling the iPad, due to vision impairments. You can let a VoiceOver read the text out loud. But keep in mind that you may need other gestures as well to use some of the additional features on the iPad.

☞ **Tap** VoiceOver

Read the operating instructions for VoiceOver

Drag the slider ⬭ by VoiceOver to the right

You will be asked whether you want to continue, and you will hear a voice (the VoiceOver) reading the text out loud. To set up the VoiceOver you need to tap twice in rapid succession:

Tap OK twice

In this screen you can edit various other settings for the use of the VoiceOver feature:

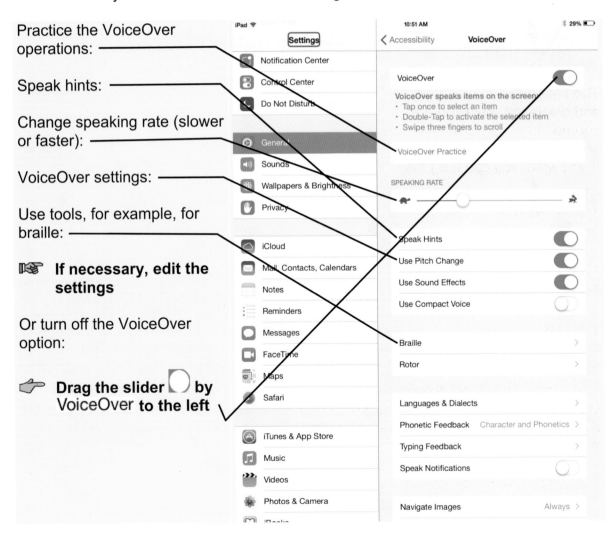

Practice the VoiceOver operations:

Speak hints:

Change speaking rate (slower or faster):

VoiceOver settings:

Use tools, for example, for braille:

If necessary, edit the settings

Or turn off the VoiceOver option:

Drag the slider ⬭ by VoiceOver to the left

1.21 Setting up Bluetooth

Bluetooth is a type of wireless connection that is frequently used to connect the iPad with other devices, such as a keyboard, printer or speaker.
This is how you connect your iPad to an external device using Bluetooth:

☞ **Turn on the external device**

☞ **Make sure that Bluetooth has been enabled on the external device**

☞ **Open the *Settings* app** 🐾¹

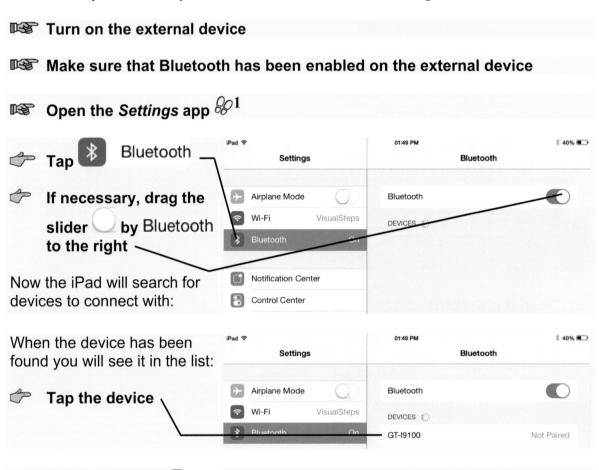

☞ **Tap** 🔷 Bluetooth

☞ **If necessary, drag the slider ◯ by Bluetooth to the right**

Now the iPad will search for devices to connect with:

When the device has been found you will see it in the list:

☞ **Tap the device**

☞ **If necessary, tap** 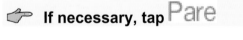Pare

Now the device is connected and can be used in combination with the iPad. The iPad will remember the Bluetooth connection information. You will not need to enter it again, as long as both devices are turned on and Bluetooth is enabled. If you do not want to connect the device automatically the next time you use it, you can do this:

☞ **By the device, tap** ⓘ

☞ **Tap** Forget this Device

☞ **Tap** OK

If you do not want to use Bluetooth for a short while, you can turn it off by tapping

⊞ **Bluetooth** and dragging the slider ◯ by Bluetooth to the left.

1.22 Find My iPad

The Find my iPad option will allow you to locate your iPad through an Internet browser, such as *Internet Explorer* or *Safari*. First you need to enable this option on your iPad. Then you can sign in with www.icloud.com and display your iPad on a map. This is not only handy if you misplace your iPad, but also useful if your iPad gets stolen. Keep in mind that the iPad should be turned on while you use this option. To set up the Find My iPad option:

☞ **Open the *Settings* app** 🦶¹

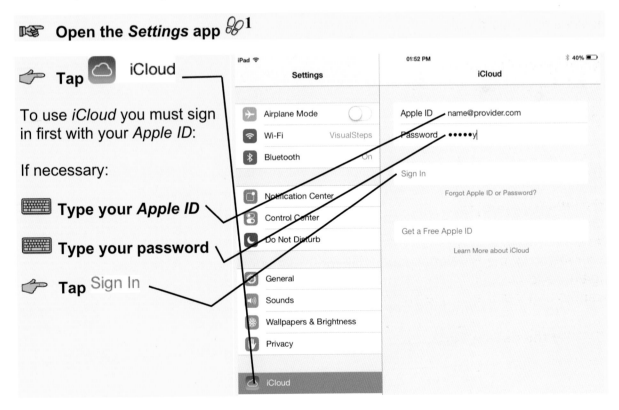

☞ **Tap** iCloud

To use *iCloud* you must sign in first with your *Apple ID*:

If necessary:

⌨ **Type your *Apple ID***

⌨ **Type your password**

☞ **Tap** Sign In

☞ **If necessary, drag the slider ⬭ by ⬤ Find My iPad to the right**

You may see this window:

☞ **If necessary, tap the desired option**

Merge with iCloud?

Your Safari data, contacts and calendars on this iPad will be uploaded and merged with iCloud.

Don't Merge | Merge

In order to use the Find My iPad option you will need to turn on the Location Services for this feature. You may see a message concerning this subject:

☞ **Tap** OK

If you have lost your iPad you can look for it with your computer, like this:

☞ **Open the www.icloud.com website on a computer** 𝒫𝒫4

⌨ **Type your *Apple ID***

⌨ **Type your password**

☐ **Click** ➡

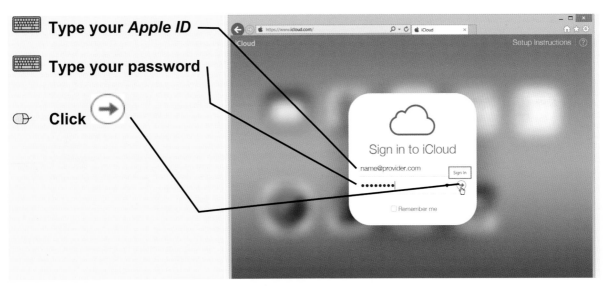

Your *iCloud* environment will be displayed:

☐ **Click** Find My iPhone

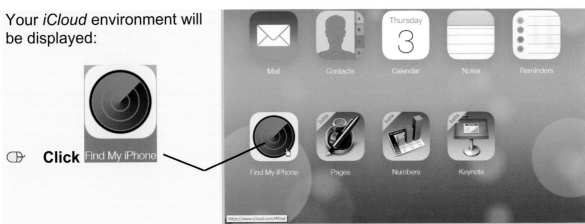

When you see this window:

⌨ **Type your password**

☐ **Click** Sign In

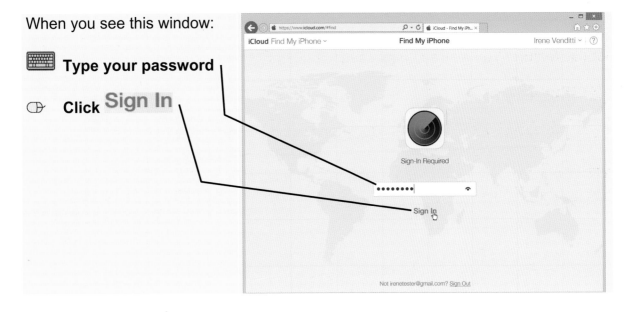

You will see a map on which the location of your iPad is indicated:

If you wish, you can zoom in or out by using the ⊞ and ⊟ buttons: —

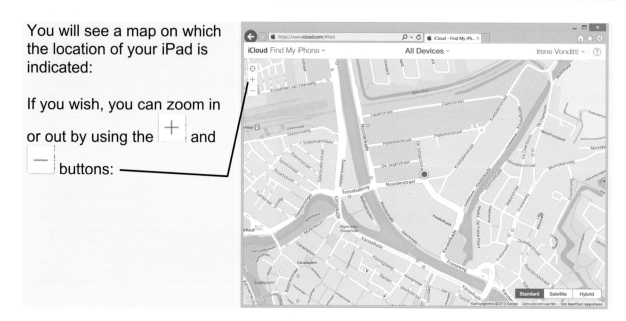

If you have lost your iPad somewhere in your own neighborhood, you can play a sound signal that will tell you where the iPad is located:

☞ **Click** ●

☞ **Click** ⓘ

☞ **Click** Play Sound

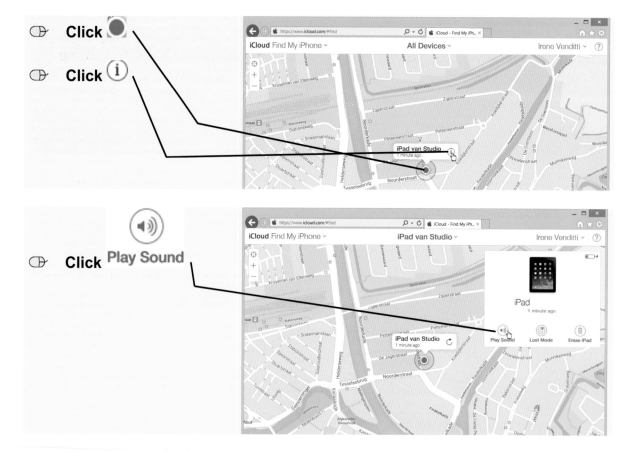

Now you will hear a sound on your iPad:

On your iPad you will see this message:

 Tip

Remotely locking an iPad
The Find My iPad option will also let you remotely lock the iPad with a passcode lock, so it can no longer be used. You will be able to track your iPad too, in case it is moved to a different location. In *section 1.9 Setting Up the Passcode Lock* you can read more about the passcode lock option.

 Click Lost Mode
 Follow the instructions in the windows

 Tip

Remotely remove data from an iPad
You can also remotely delete your personal data on your iPad with the Find My iPad option. If you ever want to use this option you should take precautions and create regular backups of the data on your iPad, so you will not lose important information.

 Click Erase iPad
 Follow the instructions in the windows

1.23 Creating and Restoring a Backup Copy on Your Computer Through iTunes

It is a good idea to create regular backups of the data stored on your iPad. You can use *iTunes* for this purpose:

 **Connect your iPad to the computer**

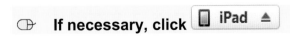 **If necessary, open *iTunes* on the computer** $\mathcal{QP}^2$

 If necessary, click [iPad ⏏]

By default, *iTunes* will automatically create a backup of the data on the iPad connected to your computer. But you can also manually create a backup copy:

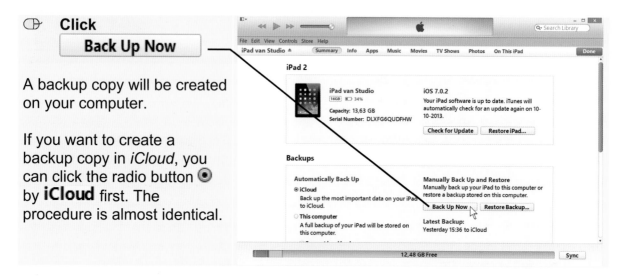

Click

Back Up Now

A backup copy will be created on your computer.

If you want to create a backup copy in *iCloud*, you can click the radio button ⦿ by **iCloud** first. The procedure is almost identical.

After the backup copy has been created:

☞ **Disconnect the iPad from your computer**

☞ **Close *iTunes* ✿³**

You can always restore a previously created backup copy. For instance, if you have lost important data on your iPad.

➥ **Please note:**

When you restore a backup copy to your iPad, the data that was created *after* you made the backup copy will be overwritten.

If you want to restore a backup copy to a blank iPad:

☞ **Follow the instructions in *section 1.28 Reset Factory Settings on the iPad*, in order to delete all the content and settings**

☞ **Set up your iPad all over again**

To restore the backup copy after the previous operation:

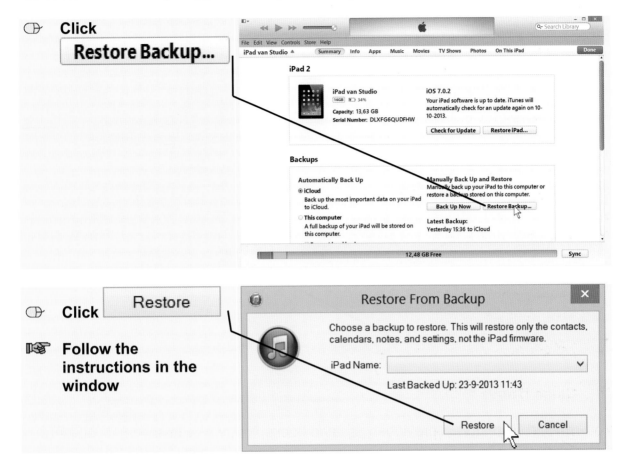

☞ **Click** **Restore Backup...**

☞ **Click** Restore

☞ **Follow the instructions in the window**

After a couple of minutes the backup copy will be restored to the iPad.

1.24 Creating and Restoring a Backup Copy on Your iPad through iCloud

It is recommended that you create regular backups of the data stored on your iPad. You can also use your storage space in *iCloud* for this purpose. This way, the backup copy will be sent directly from your iPad to your *iCloud* account through Wi-Fi.

The difference between restoring a backup from *iTunes* (on your computer) and one from *iCloud* is that the *iCloud* version requires you to erase all settings and information from your iPad. If you do not want to do this, then you should use *iTunes* for creating and restoring a backup copy.

Please note:

You must have *iCloud* set up first before doing the next few steps (if necessary, read the beginning of *section 1.22 Find My iPad* to find out how you set up *iCloud*).

 Please note:

If you use the *iCloud* automatic backup function, the automatic backup copy will no longer be created through *iTunes*. But you can still create a backup copy manually. See *section 1.23 Creating and Restoring a Backup Copy on Your Computer Through iTunes*.

☞ **Open the *Settings* app** 🦶¹

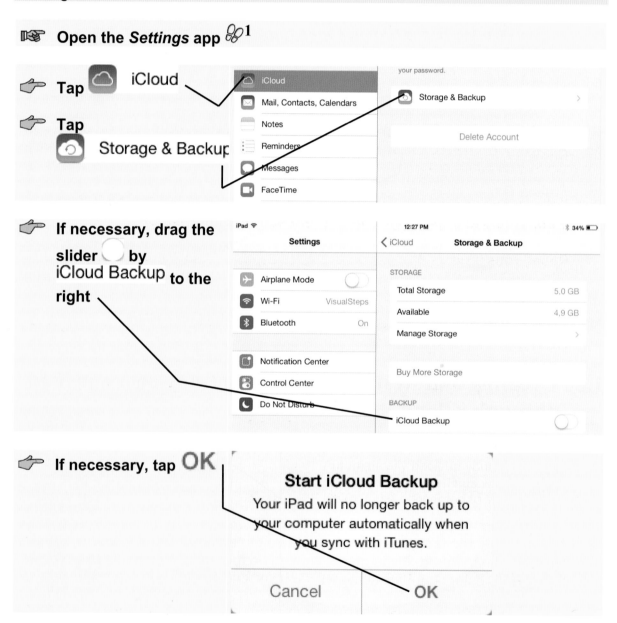

☞ **Tap** Back Up Now

Now the *iCloud* backup will be created.

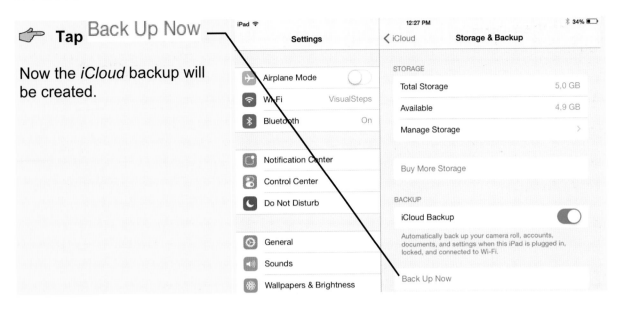

If you want to restore the backup copy from the *iCloud* to a blank iPad, you can follow the next few steps in this section. If you do not want to restore a backup copy, then just read through this section.

☞ **Follow the instructions in *section 1.28 Reset Factory Settings on the iPad*. This will erase your content and settings information.**

☞ **Reset your iPad**

When you see the *Configuration* screen:

☞ **Tap**
   Restore from iCloud E

At the bottom of the screen:

☞ **Tap** Next

⌨ **Type the *Apple ID* and the corresponding password**

☞ **Tap** Next, Agree, Agree

☞ **If necessary, tap the backup copy you want to use**

The backup copy will be restored as well as your app data and other content.

1.25 Managing the Storage of Backup Copies in iCloud

You can manage the storage of data in *iCloud*, and view and delete your backup copies as needed:

☞ **Open the *Settings* app** 𝒜𝒜¹

☞ **Tap** ☁ *iCloud*

☞ **Tap** ⟳ Storage & Backup

☞ **Tap** Manage Storage

☞ **By BACKUPS, tap your iPad**

Information on the backup copies:

Turn the creation of backup copies on or off for specific apps:

To delete a backup copy, you tap Delete Backup:

At the bottom of the screen you can see the available storage space of your *iCloud* account:

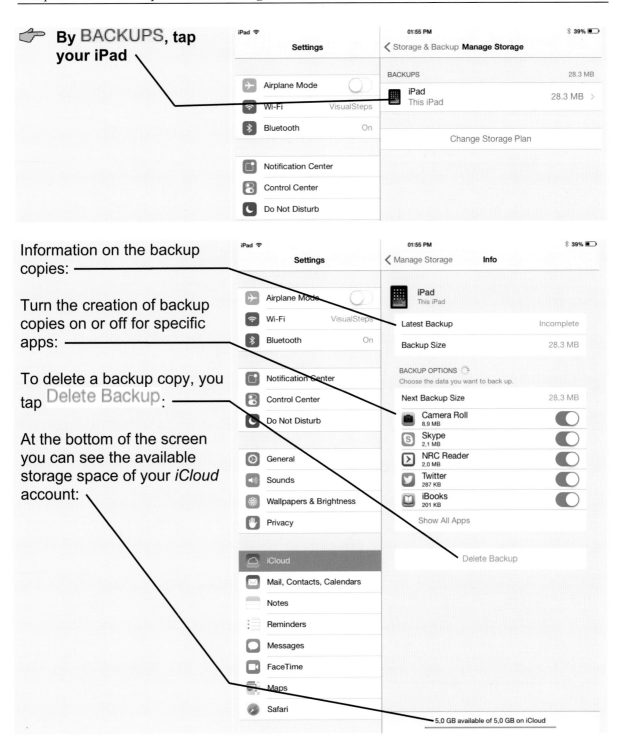

1.26 Settings for Synchronizing with iCloud

You can select the app data that you want to synchronize with the data in the *iCloud*:

☞ **Open the *Settings* app** 👣¹

👉 **Tap** ☁️ **iCloud**

Tap the sliders off or on to synchronize data in the apps shown:

Automatically upload photos to the *iCloud Photo Stream*. Tap off or on:

Save documents and data in the *iCloud.* Tap off or on:

☞ **Edit the desired settings**

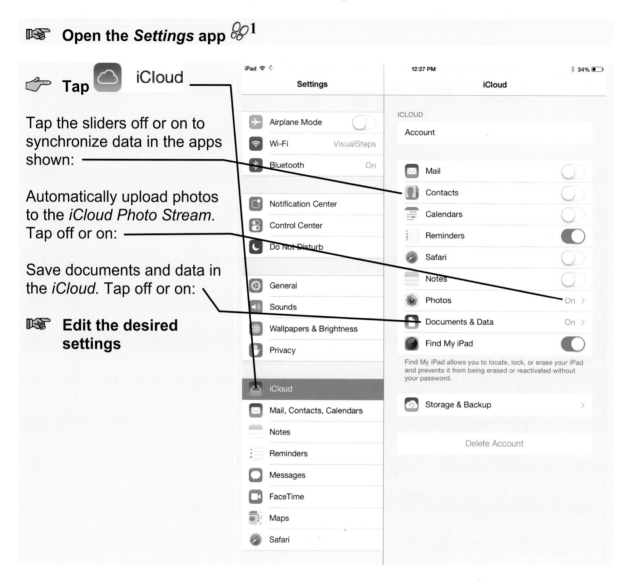

1.27 Resetting Various Settings

Most likely after using your iPad for a while you will have made changes to the settings. For example, you may have changed the opening screen of the iPad, and selected certain settings for using Wi-Fi networks. You may have also turned on Location Services for specific apps or perhaps you have added new words to the iPad's dictionary while typing. If you ever need to reset all these settings and revert back to their original values, you can do that like this:

☞ **Open the *Settings* app** ✂¹

☞ **Tap** ⚙ General

☞ **Drag upwards across the right side of the screen**

☞ **Tap** Reset

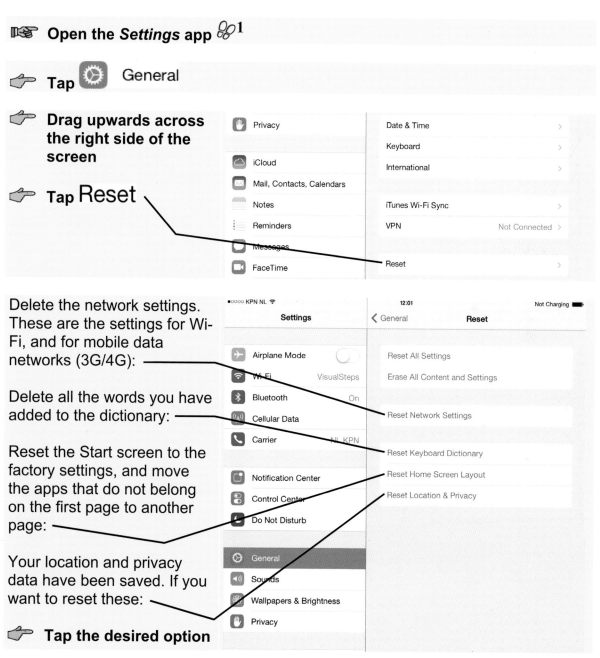

Delete the network settings. These are the settings for Wi-Fi, and for mobile data networks (3G/4G):

Delete all the words you have added to the dictionary:

Reset the Start screen to the factory settings, and move the apps that do not belong on the first page to another page:

Your location and privacy data have been saved. If you want to reset these:

☞ **Tap the desired option**

 **If necessary, enter your passcode**

You will be asked to confirm this action:

☞ **Tap** Reset

1.28 Reset Factory Settings on the iPad

It is always possible to reset your iPad to the original factory settings. You can use this option if you notice your iPad is no longer working properly, or if you want to lend or sell it to somebody else. If you wish you can make a backup copy, to be sure you can always access important data in case you need it.

☞ **Open the *Settings* app** 🦶**1**

☞ **Tap** ⚙ General

☞ **Drag upwards across the right side of the screen**

☞ **Tap** Reset

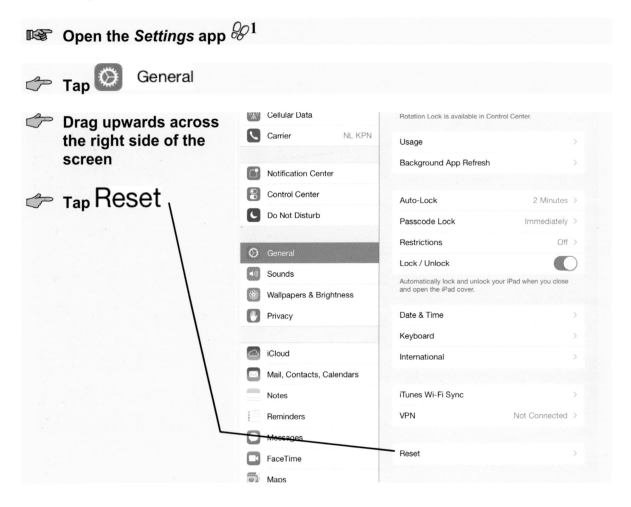

You can select various options for reverting back to the original settings and deleting your data:

Replace all of your edited settings with the original settings. Selecting this option will not delete your data:

☞ **Tap** Reset All Settings

You can also delete all of the settings you have made and the data as well (emails, music, photos, and other files). Then tap Erase All Content and Settings.

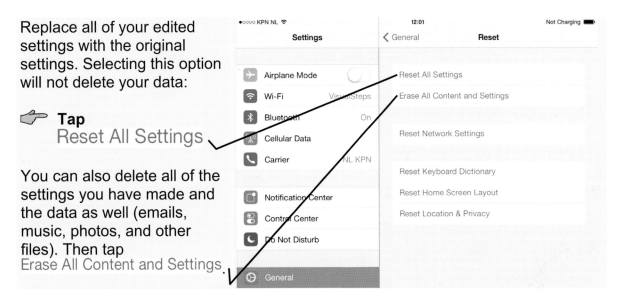

☞ **If necessary, enter your passcode**

☞ **Tap** Reset

If you want to cancel the operation, tap Cancel.

If you have decided to delete the content as well, you will see the Erase button.

You will need to confirm this action once more:

☞ **Tap** Reset

The settings will be deleted.

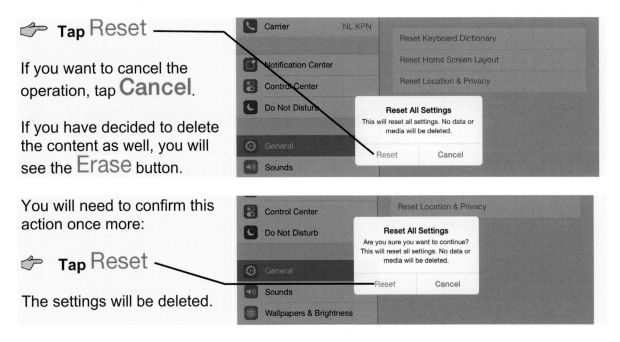

☞ **Set up the iPad all over again**

1.29 Printing with Your iPad

You can only print from the iPad on with printers that support *AirPrint*. If you want to print on other printers in your Wi-Fi network you will need to install an auxiliary program to your computer, such as the *Presto* program, for example. This program has the added advantage that it is suitable for both *Apple* and *Windows* computers. If you want to check if this program functions properly in your network, you can download a free trial version first.

You need to install the trial version of the *Presto* program on a computer that is connected to the same Wi-Fi network that is used by your iPad:

☞ **Open the www.collobos.com web page on your computer** &⁴

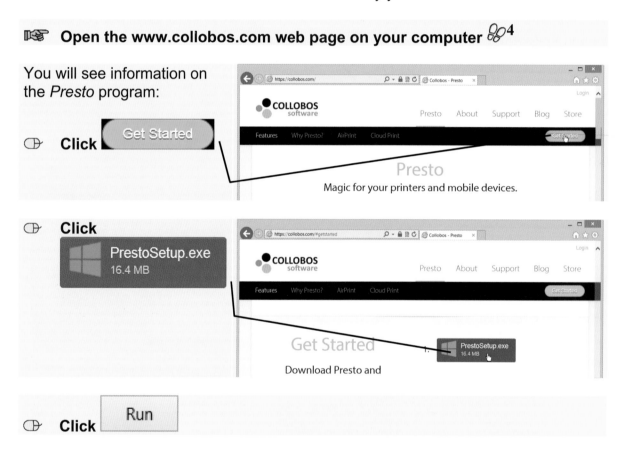

You will see information on the *Presto* program:

⏻ **Click** Get Started

⏻ **Click** PrestoSetup.exe 16.4 MB

⏻ **Click** Run

Your screen may turn dark and you will be asked for permission to continue:

☞ **Give permission to continue**

⏻ **Click** Next >

☞ **Click a radio button** ⦿ **by**
I accept the agreement

☞ **Click**

Next >

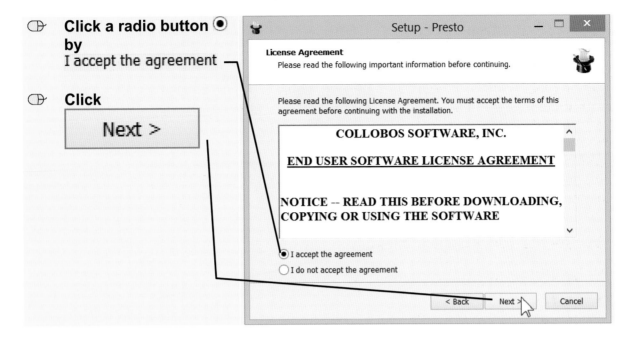

In the next two windows:

☞ **Click** Next >

☞ **Click** Install

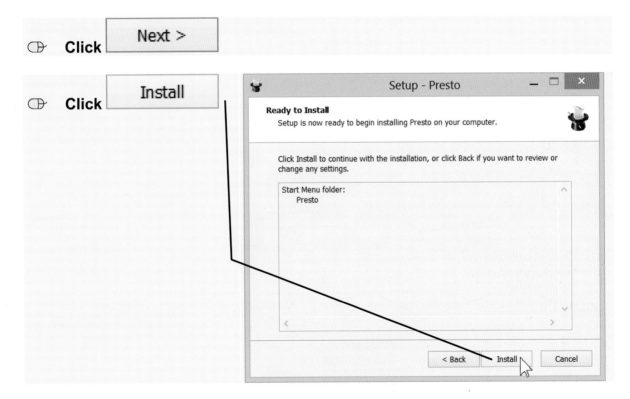

Click Finish

You will see the printers and printer drivers that have been found:

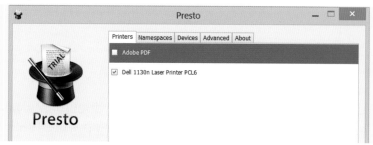

In this example we have printed a web page:

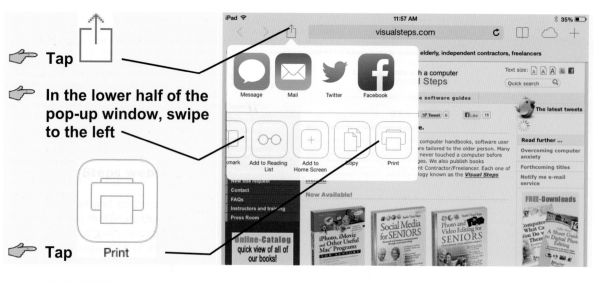

☞ **Tap**

☞ **In the lower half of the pop-up window, swipe to the left**

☞ **Tap** Print

☞ **If necessary, tap** Printer   Select Printer >

You will see the printers:

☞ **Tap the desired printer**

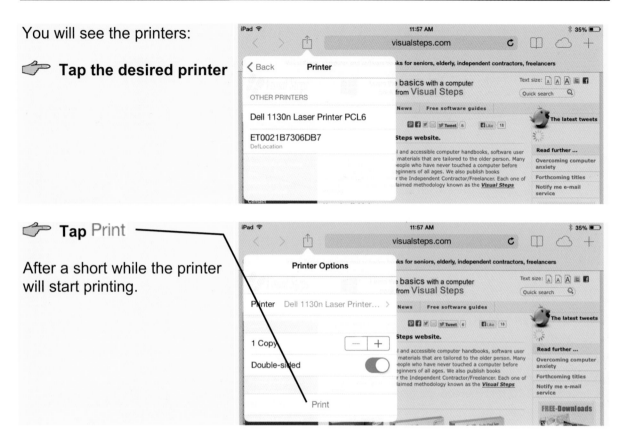

☞ **Tap** Print

After a short while the printer will start printing.

When using the trial version, the printed documents will display a message: 'Purchasing a license will make *Presto* stop watermarking your print jobs.'

💡 **Tip**

Other apps
You can also try to find your printer's brand name in the *App Store*. A number of printer manufacturers offer their own app that makes it possible to print wirelessly from an iPad.

1.30 GoToMyPC

Sometimes it can be easier to use your computer instead of your iPad. For instance, you may want to view a specific file, or use a certain program. You can do this with *GoToMyPC*. With this app you gain full access to your computer and you can use the remote desktop to operate your computer through your iPad. You will need to download the app from the *App Store* and you also need a subscription to *GoToMyPC*.
You can download a free trial version first and see if you like this app. You can use the free version for 30 days.

You need to install the program onto your computer. This is how you do that:

☞ **Open the www.gotomypc.com web page on your computer** ✂⁴

To download the trial version of the program:

⊕ **Click**

Try It Free

⊕ **If necessary, drag the scroll bar downwards a bit**

☞ **Enter the required data**

⊕ **Check the box ☑ by I agree to the Terms of Se**

⊕ **Click**

Continue ▸

Enter a password for *GoToMyPC*:

⌨ **Type your password for *GoToMyPC* and re-type it for confirmation**

⊕ **Click**

Continue ▸

To install the program onto your computer:

⊕ **Click**

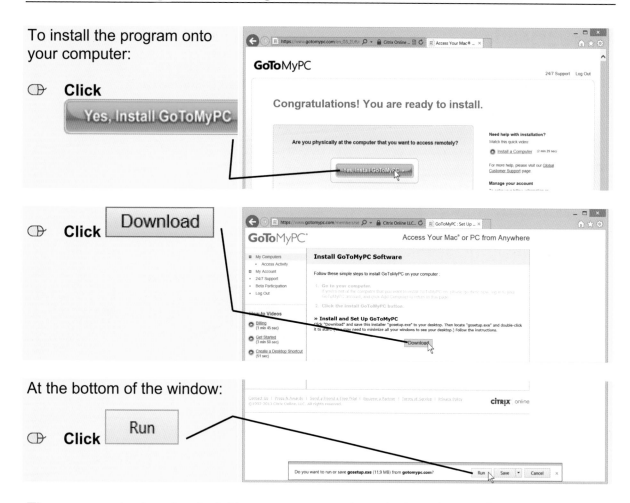

⊕ **Click** Download

At the bottom of the window:

⊕ **Click** Run

The program is downloaded. Your screen may turn dark and you will see the *User Account Control* window. Whether this happens, depends on the settings of your computer. In this window you will need to give permission to continue.

☞ **Give permission to continue**

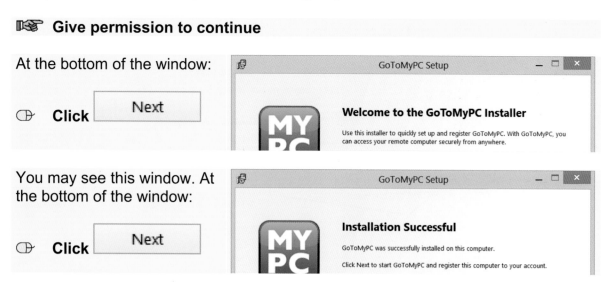

At the bottom of the window:

⊕ **Click** Next

You may see this window. At the bottom of the window:

⊕ **Click** Next

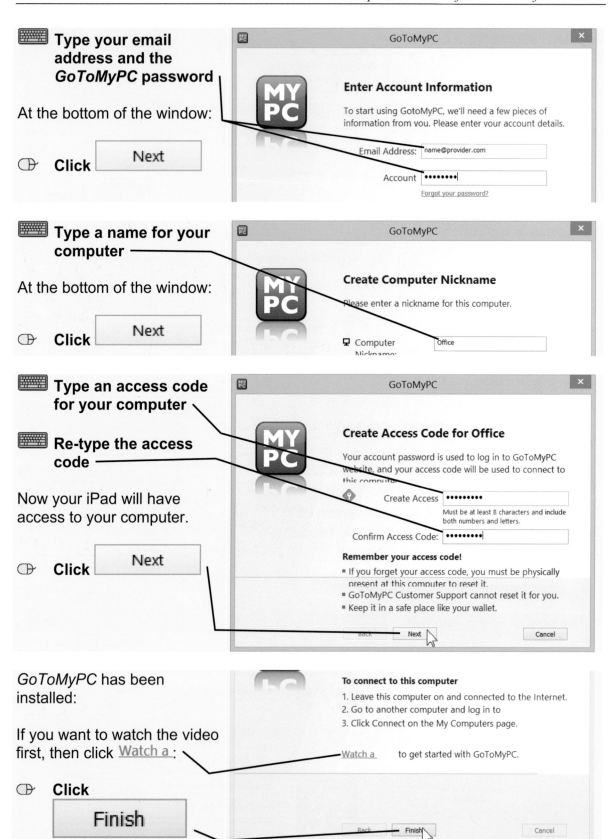

⌨ **Type your email address and the *GoToMyPC* password**

At the bottom of the window:

👆 **Click** Next

Enter Account Information

To start using GotoMyPC, we'll need a few pieces of information from you. Please enter your account details.

Email Address: name@provider.com

Account ••••••••

Forgot your password?

⌨ **Type a name for your computer**

At the bottom of the window:

👆 **Click** Next

Create Computer Nickname

Please enter a nickname for this computer.

💻 Computer Nickname: Office

⌨ **Type an access code for your computer**

⌨ **Re-type the access code**

Now your iPad will have access to your computer.

👆 **Click** Next

Create Access Code for Office

Your account password is used to log in to GoToMyPC website, and your access code will be used to connect to this computer.

Create Access ••••••••

Must be at least 8 characters and include both numbers and letters.

Confirm Access Code: ••••••••

Remember your access code!
- If you forget your access code, you must be physically present at this computer to reset it.
- GoToMyPC Customer Support cannot reset it for you.
- Keep it in a safe place like your wallet.

Back   Next   Cancel

GoToMyPC has been installed:

If you want to watch the video first, then click Watch a :

👆 **Click** Finish

To connect to this computer
1. Leave this computer on and connected to the Internet.
2. Go to another computer and log in to
3. Click Connect on the My Computers page.

Watch a   to get started with GoToMyPC.

Back   Finish   Cancel

☞ **Close the windows** ³

Now you can use your iPad to connect to your computer:

☞ **Open the *GoToMyPC* app** 👣¹

👉 **Tap** Sign In

⌨ **Type your email address and password**

👉 **Tap** Sign In

You will see the next window about saving your password:

👉 **Tap the desired option**

You will see your computer's name:

👉 **Tap** Connect

The connection will be established.

⌨ **Type the access code to access your computer**

👉 **Tap** Go

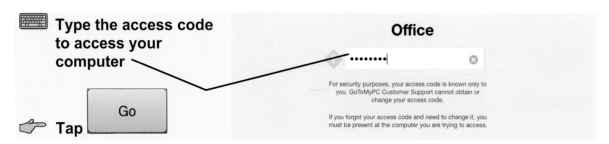

If you want to have a clearer image on your screen, it is recommended to lay down your iPad.

☞ **Lay your iPad flat**

In this image you can see how to execute the mouse operations:

☞ **Read the instructions**

👉 **Tap**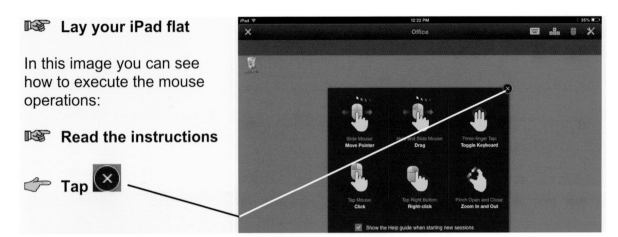

Now practice opening *Windows Explorer*:

👉 **Drag the pointer to**

👉 **Tap**

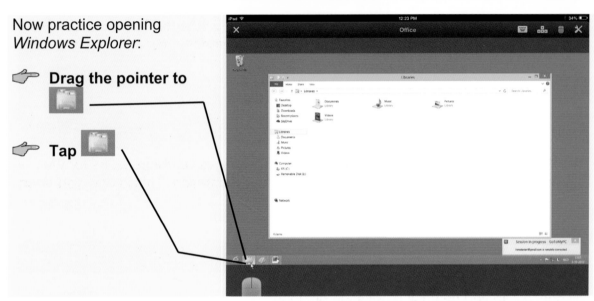

You will see *Windows Explorer*:

Close the window in the regular way:

👉 **Drag the pointer to**

👉 **Tap**

Tip

Keyboard

On your iPad you can also enter text with the keyboard:

Three-finger Tap:

☞ **Tap the screen of your iPad with three fingers at once** Toggle Keyboard

In the same way you can make the keyboard disappear again.

To break the connection you need to close the *GoToMyPC* app. The connection will also be broken automatically if you have not been active for a few minutes. You can reconnect by signing on with your computer again.

1.31 Siri

The iPad has a useful function with which you can give verbal instructions for the iPad to execute, and you can also use it to ask for information. This is how you open *Siri*:

 Press and hold the Home button

Siri opens and you can ask a question out loud:

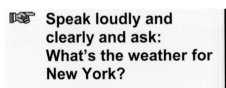 **Speak loudly and clearly and ask: What's the weather for New York?**

1:22 AM

What can I help you with?

 Please note:

This function might not be available on the iPad 2.

You will both see and hear the answer:

If you wish, you can tap the screen to open the weather forecast in the *Weather* app. For now this will not be necessary.

Pose another question:

☞ **Tap**

🖝 **Speak loudly and clearly and ask: Do I have any appointments today?**

You will both see and hear the answer:

You can ask many more questions in the same way.

🖝 **Go back to the home screen** 🦶**10**

2. Email

Your iPad comes equipped with a default email app called *Mail*. With *Mail* you can write, send, and receive email messages. Although sending emails is not a very difficult operation, you will find that the *Mail* app offers several other useful features. For example, you can create different folders to organize your mail and in this way get a better overview of all your email correspondence.

Nowadays people often have more than one email account. You may have a home account with your Internet service provider (ISP), an account with a web based service such as *Gmail* or *Outlook.* and perhaps another account from your work. You can manage all these accounts in *Mail*. You can select a specific account as your default email account, or delete the email accounts you no longer want to use on your iPad.

In this chapter we will give you tips on the following subjects:

- sending a copy of an email message;
- working with drafts;
- marking an email;
- working with folders;
- sending an email with an attachment;
- editing your signature;
- setting up a default account, when you have multiple email accounts;
- (temporarily) disabling an email account;
- saving a copy of an email on the mail server;
- receiving emails through fetch or push;
- deleting an email account.

2.1 Sending a Copy of an Email Message

When you compose an email to someone in *Mail*, you can also send a copy of it to one or more other email addresses. You can use either the "Cc" field (this stands for carbon copy) or the "Bcc" field (this stands for blind carbon copy). If you enter the email address in the Cc field, each recipient's email address is visible to all other recipients of the received message. If you prefer these addresses to be hidden, you can use the Bcc field which will display only the email address that is listed in the "To" field of the received message.

Here is how you add another recipient to an email message:

☞ **Open the *Mail* app**

In this example you are going to open a new email message:

☞ **Tap**

☞ **Tap** Cc/Bcc:

If you want to send a copy of the email to someone else:

⌨ **Type the email address by** Cc:

If you click ⊕, you can select an email address from the *Contacts* app.

If you want to send a blind copy of the email, type the email address by Bcc::

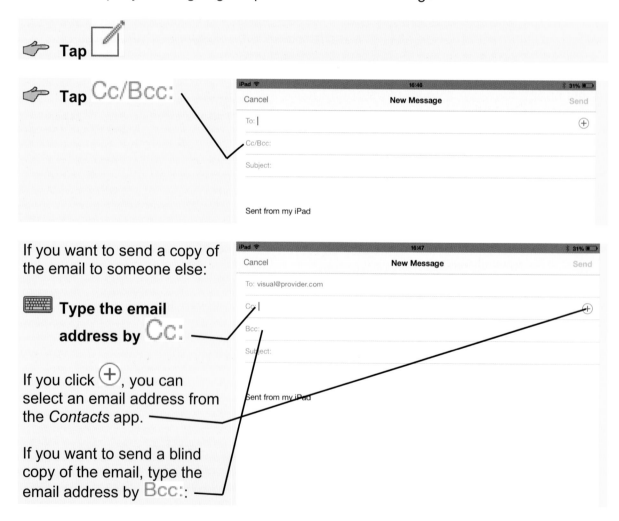

Tip

Send a copy to multiple addresses
You can use the Cc or Bcc option to send an email message to multiple addresses at once. In order to do this, you need to enter the email addresses one after the other and separate them by a ";" (semicolon). For example:
peter@mailaddress.com;anton@mailaddress.org

Tip

Sending a BCC of a sent email to yourself, by default
You can set your email app to send a copy of every email you send out to yourself. In this way you will be certain that the email has actually been sent:

☞ **Open the *Settings* app** ✇¹

☞ **Tap**
✉ Mail, Contacts, Ca

☞ **Drag the slider ⃝ by Always Bcc Myself to the right**

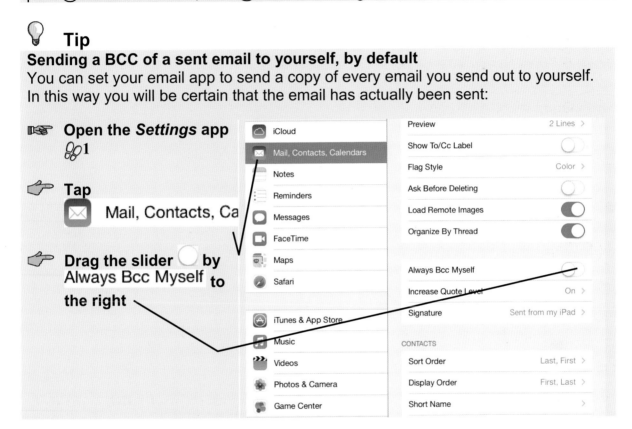

2.2 Working with Drafts

If you have written an email message but do not yet want to send it, you can save it as a draft:

☞ **Open the *Mail* app** ✇¹

☞ **Tap** ✎ **and type the email message**

On your iPad you can quickly see an overview of all your drafts:

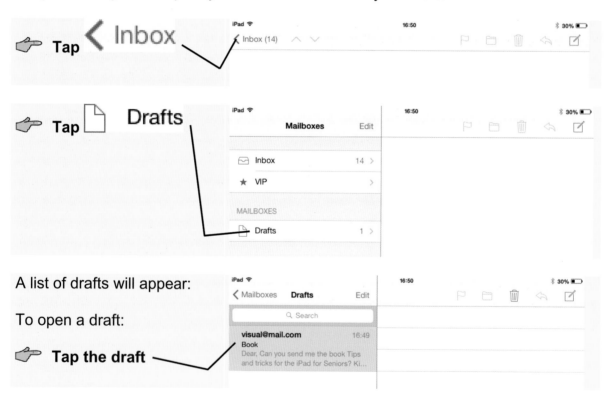

A list of drafts will appear:

To open a draft:

👉 **Tap the email message**

You will see the draft email:

👉 **Finish the email message**

👉 **Tap** Send

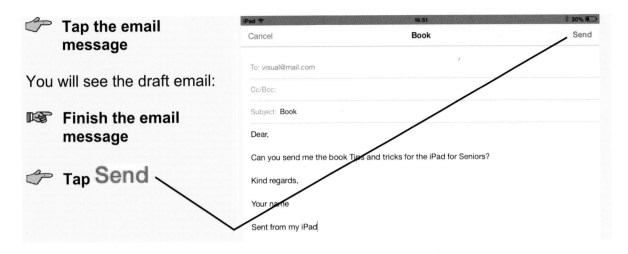

2.3 Marking an Email

Your email messages can be marked in several ways. For example, you can mark a message with a flag, indicating that it is important. It will stand out between all the other messages. Or you can mark a message as read or unread. This is how you mark an opened email message:

👉 **Tap** ⚑

To mark with a flag ⬤:

👉 **Tap** Flag

If you want to mark a previously read email as unread, you do this by tapping Mark as Unread.

If the email has not been read yet, you will see the Mark as Read option.

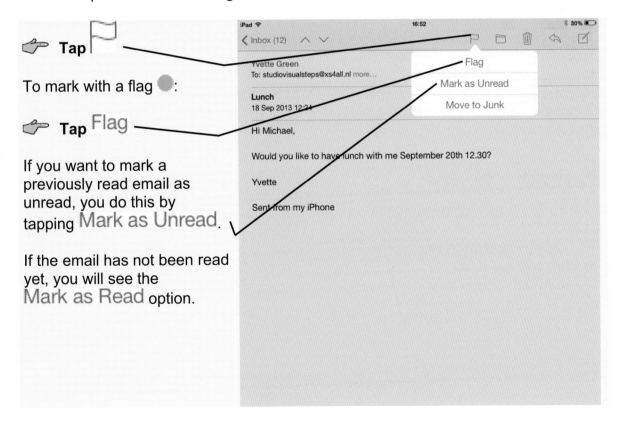

You can also mark an email within a mailbox:

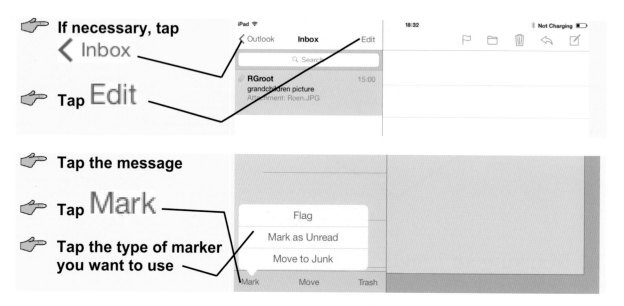

☞ **If necessary, tap**
   〈 Inbox

☞ **Tap Edit**

☞ **Tap the message**

☞ **Tap Mark**

☞ **Tap the type of marker you want to use**

2.4 Working with Folders

It can be useful to arrange your email messages in various folders or mailboxes. This will help you separate your private correspondence for example from your business emails.

You can use the button in the top left-hand corner of the screen to display the various mailboxes. You may see different mailboxes on your own screen, depending on the email accounts you use.

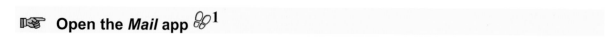

☞ **Open the *Mail* app** 🦶¹

If you have set up multiple email accounts:

☞ **Tap the button in the top left-hand corner; in this example it is**
   the 〈 Gmail button

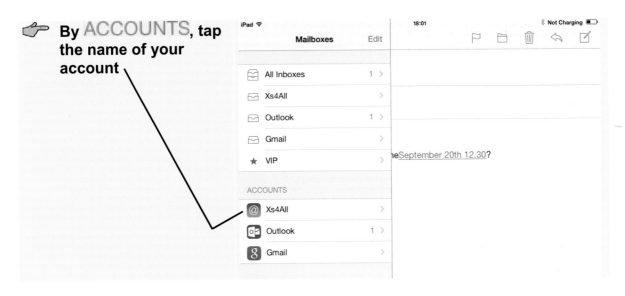

By ACCOUNTS, tap the name of your account

If you have a single email account:

Tap ❮ Mailboxes

You will see all the mailboxes in use:

To view the content of a mailbox:

Tap the desired mailbox

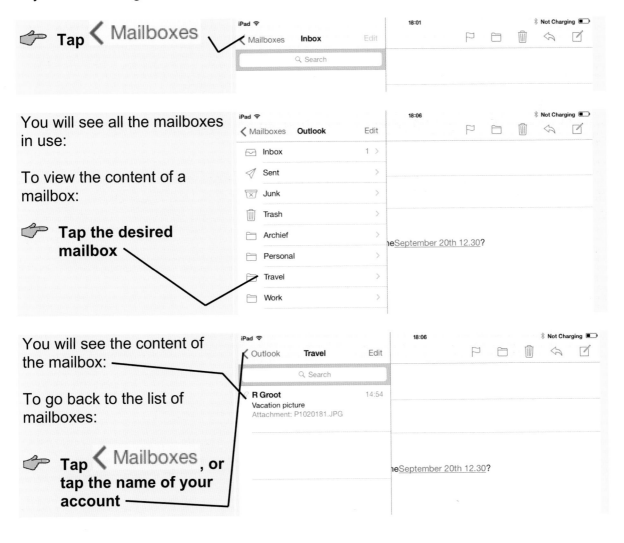

You will see the content of the mailbox:

To go back to the list of mailboxes:

Tap ❮ Mailboxes, or tap the name of your account

You can add new mailboxes yourself. If you do not see this option, creating a new mailbox may not be possible for your type of email account.

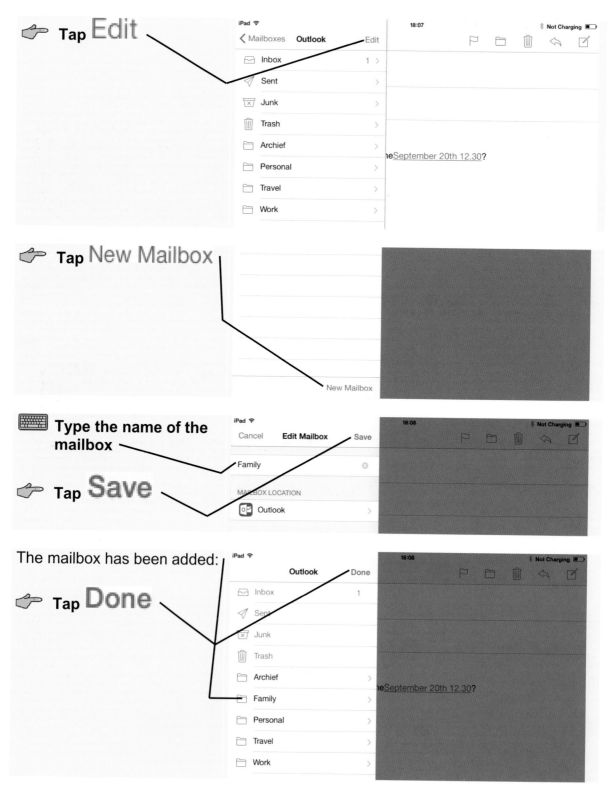

You can also move email messages from one folder to another. For example, from the *Inbox* to the new folder:

☞ **Open the email message**

👉 **Tap** 📁

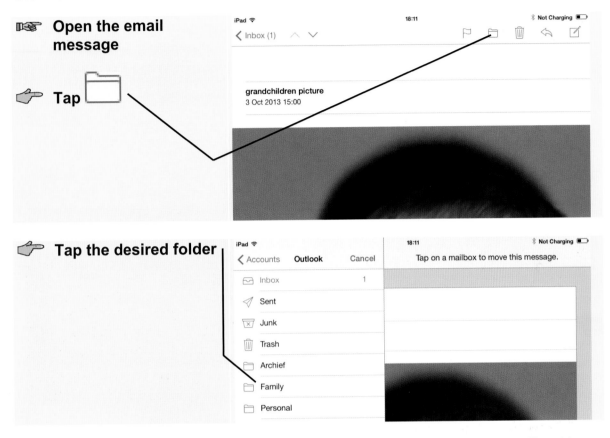

👉 **Tap the desired folder**

The email has been moved to the folder you selected. You can check that like this:

👉 **Tap the button in the top left-hand corner, for example** ❮ Inbox

👉 **Tap** ❮ Mailboxes **in the top left-hand corner, or tap the name of your account**

👉 **By** ACCOUNTS**, tap the name of your account**

👉 **Tap the mailbox**

You will see the message now in this mailbox.

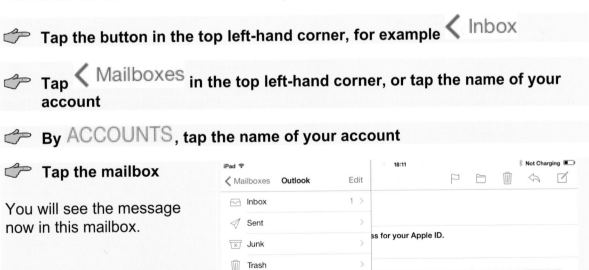

You can also delete a mailbox you have previously made. But bear in mind, that you will lose all email messages in this mailbox as well, when you delete it.

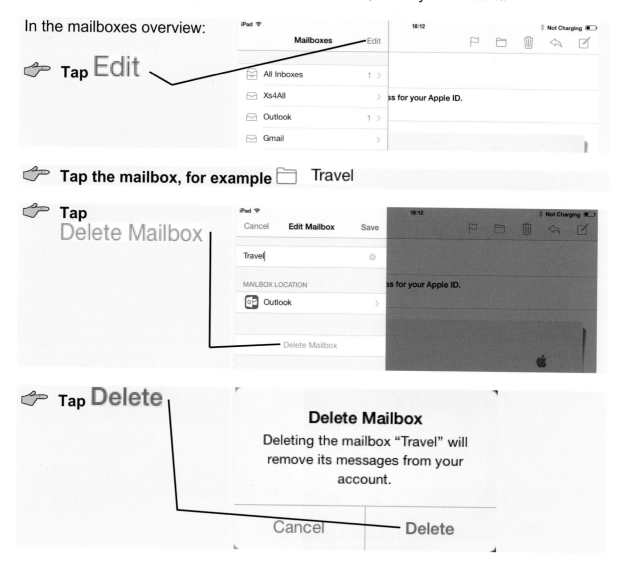

In the mailboxes overview:

☞ **Tap** Edit

☞ **Tap the mailbox, for example** 📁 Travel

☞ **Tap**
Delete Mailbox

☞ **Tap** Delete

Delete Mailbox
Deleting the mailbox "Travel" will remove its messages from your account.

Cancel | Delete

2.5 Sending an Email with an Attachment

On a regular computer or laptop you can use an email program to send a message and add an attachment to it. On the iPad this works differently. You cannot add an attachment to an email message in the *Mail* app. If you want to send an attachment, you will need to do this in the app where you have created or opened the file. If you want to send an image, for example:

☞ **Open the *Photos* app and open a photo** 👣[5]

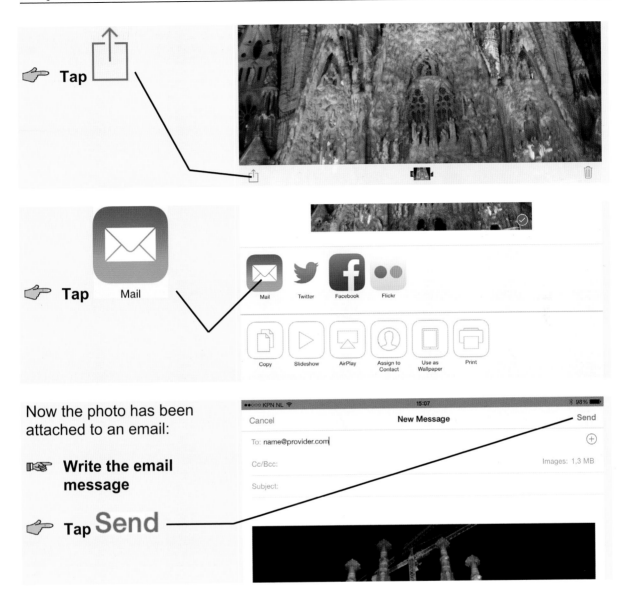

Now the photo has been attached to an email:

☞ **Write the email message**

☞ Tap **Send**

2.6 Editing Your Signature

By default, every email you send from an iPad is appended with the text 'Sent from my iPad'. This text is called a signature. You can replace this text easily with a text of your own, or you can remove it altogether. The text can contain your name and address for example. This is how you edit your email signature:

☞ **Open the *Settings* app** 🦶[1]

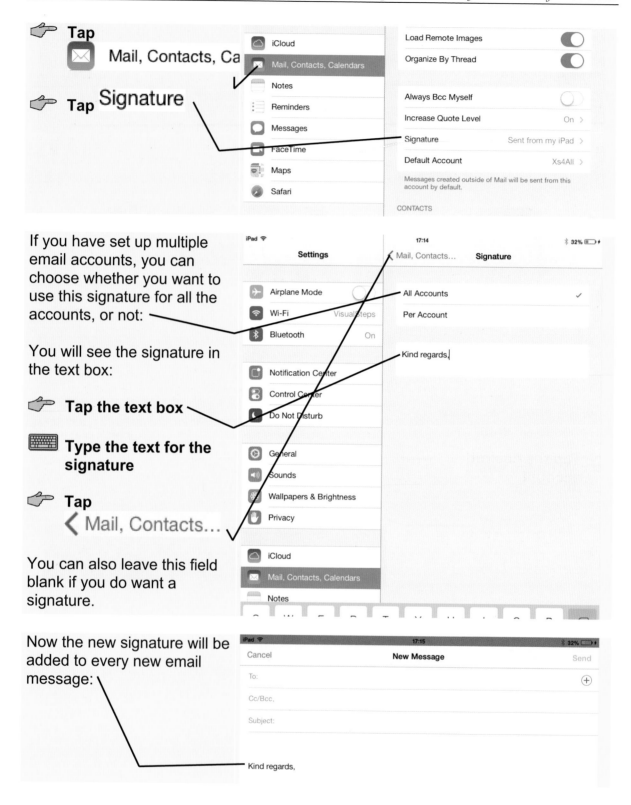

☞ **Tap**

Mail, Contacts, Ca

☞ **Tap** Signature

If you have set up multiple email accounts, you can choose whether you want to use this signature for all the accounts, or not:

You will see the signature in the text box:

☞ **Tap the text box**

⌨ **Type the text for the signature**

☞ **Tap**

❮ Mail, Contacts...

You can also leave this field blank if you do want a signature.

Now the new signature will be added to every new email message:

2.7 Set a Default Account when Using Multiple Email Accounts

If you have multiple email accounts set up on your iPad, you can set one of them as your default account. The emails will then be sent by default from that account. But you will still be able to send an email message from a different account by selecting a different sender for individual email messages.

☞ **Open the *Settings* app** 🦶**1**

👉 **Tap**
Mail, Contacts, Ca

👉 **Tap**
Default Account

👉 **Tap the desired account**

👉 **Tap**
‹ Mail, Contacts...

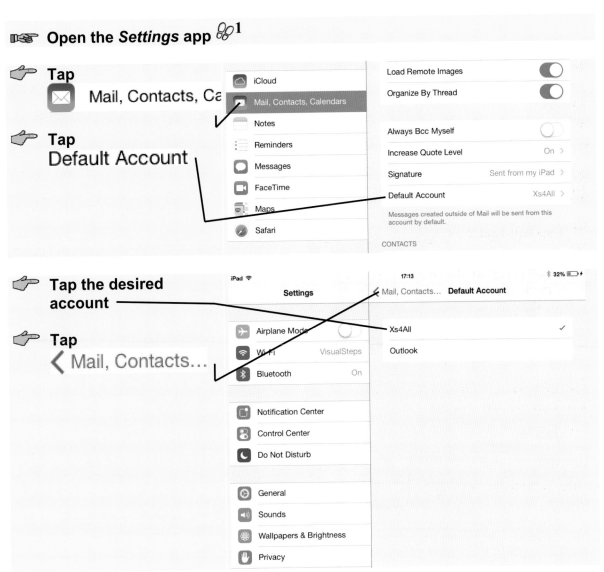

2.8 (Temporarily) Disable an Email Account

You can also temporarily disable an email account. This can be useful if you do not want to receive any email messages on your iPad for a while, for example when your iPad is connected to a mobile data network (3G/4G). This is how you set this option:

☞ **Open the *Settings* app** 👣¹

👉 **Tap** ✉ **Mail, Contacts, Calendars**

👉 **Tap the account**

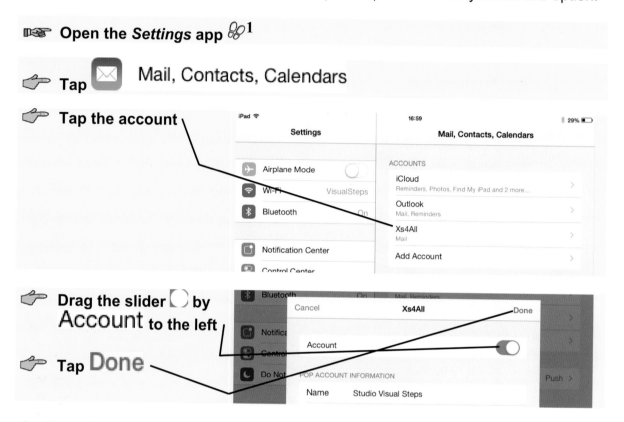

👉 **Drag the slider ◯ by Account to the left**

👉 **Tap Done**

Or, if you do not see this window:

👉 **Drag the slider ◯ by ✉ Mail to the left**

You can enable the account again using the same method.

2.9 Saving a Copy of Email Messages on the Mail Server

For POP email accounts, such as used by your Internet service provider, you can select an option to save a copy of the incoming emails on the mail server. If you save a copy on the server you will then be able to retrieve these messages on your computer as well, after you have received them on your iPad. This is how you change the settings:

☞ **Open the *Settings* app** 𝒮𝒮¹

☞ **Tap** ✉ Mail, Contacts, Calendars

☞ **Tap the account**

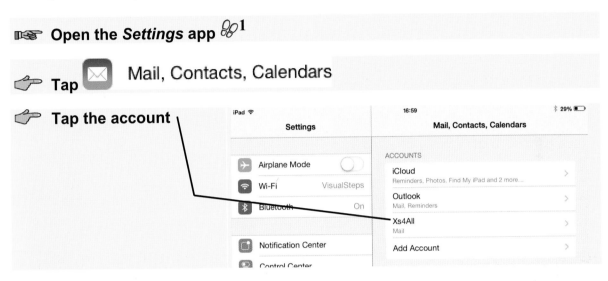

If the keyboard is blocking the option you need:

☞ **Swipe the window upwards**

You will see the account information, and the **Advanced** option:

☞ **Tap Advanced**

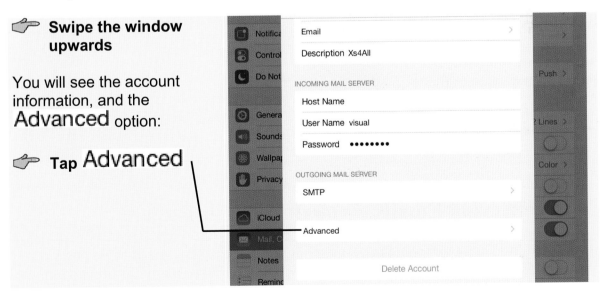

By default, this option is set in such a way that new messages are never deleted from the server.

This means that messages are only deleted from the server after you have received them in an email program that is set to delete messages from the server after they have been retrieved.

If none of the settings in various email programs are set to delete emails, all messages will remain stored on the mail server. This can be an advantage, because in this way you can retrieve all your emails on any computer that has an email program installed. However, it can also be a disadvantage, since you will continue to receive older emails stored on the server if you do not use a specific email program consistently. This may even lead to problems receiving new mail, if the account limit is reached.

To select the option for deleting emails on the server:

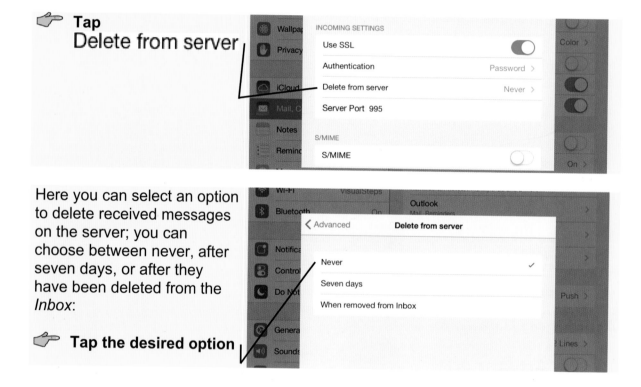

☞ **Tap**
Delete from server

Here you can select an option to delete received messages on the server; you can choose between never, after seven days, or after they have been deleted from the *Inbox*:

☞ **Tap the desired option**

2.10 Retrieving Emails through Fetch or Push

If you open and send your emails on a computer, you will be used to retrieving your email messages through the fetch function: you open your email program, it connects to the mail server and then new messages are received. You can also set up your email program to automatically check for new messages at regular intervals, after the email program has been opened.

On the other hand, the push function will immediately send new email messages to your email program, after they have been received on the mail server. Even if your *Mail* app has not been opened and your iPad is locked.

 Please note:

If you connect to the Internet through a mobile network, and you do not have an unlimited subscription for data traffic at a fixed rate, it is recommended to turn off the push function. This is because in such a case you will be paying for the amount of data you use. If any email messages containing large attachments are pushed to your iPad, you can expect high costs. In this case it is better to manually retrieve your email when you connect with Wi-Fi. Remember that you cannot disable the push function for *Hotmail* accounts.

This is how to view the push or fetch settings:

☞ **Open the *Settings* app** 👣¹

👉 **Tap**
✉️ Mail, Contacts, Ca

By default, the push function is set for all email accounts
Push:

👉 **Tap**
Fetch New Data

If you want to turn off push:

👉 **Drag the slider** ⬭ **by** Push **to the left**

If push is turned off or not supported by your provider, fetch will automatically be used. You can choose how often you want to get new messages, or whether you want to do this manually:

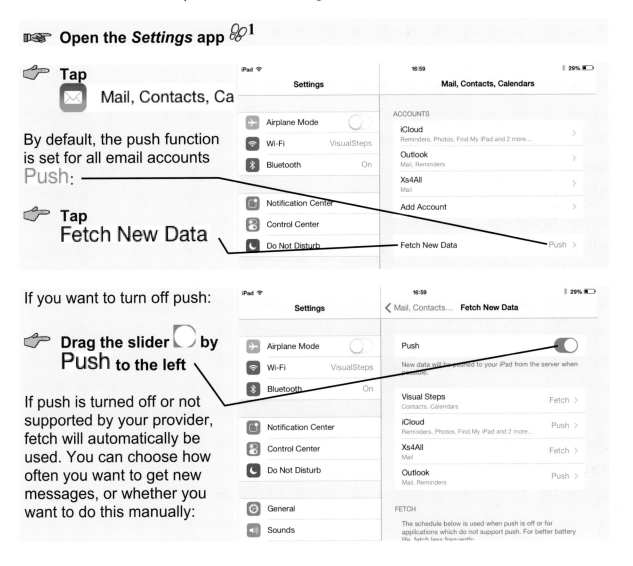

2.11 Deleting an Email Account

If you do not want to use a particular email account any longer on your iPad, you can delete it. Keep in mind that deleting an email account means that all the emails belonging to this account will be deleted from your iPad.

☞ **Open the *Settings* app** 🦶¹

👉 **Tap** ✉️ **Mail, Contacts, Calendars**

👉 **Tap your account**

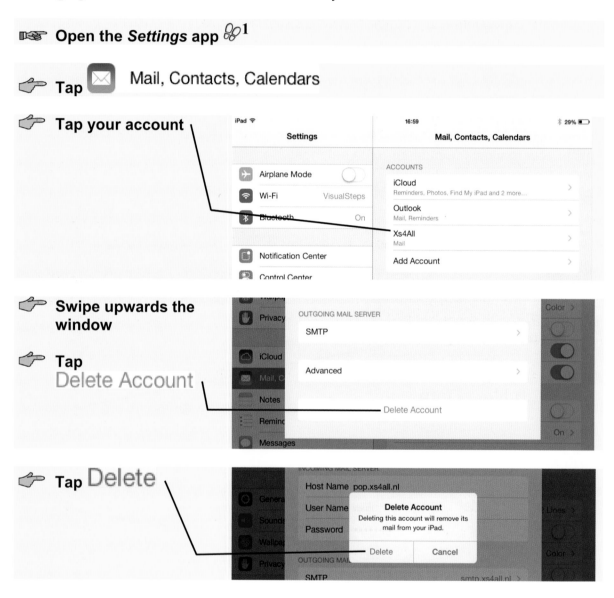

👉 **Swipe upwards the window**

👉 **Tap Delete Account**

👉 **Tap Delete**

Now the email account has been deleted, along with its emails.

3. Surfing the Internet

You can use the *Safari* app on your iPad to surf the Internet. *Safari* is the default web browser provided by *Apple*. In this chapter, we will show you a number of extra options, settings and tips that help to make surfing the Internet on your iPad easier.

For example, you can save websites as a bookmark. You can neatly arrange these bookmarks on the Favorites Bar or in folders, and you can share your bookmarks with others. You can also save a web page to read later on when you are offline.

From time to time, you have probably come across a nice image on a website. You can save a copy of this image with your iPad.

The default search engine in *Safari* is *Google*. But if you prefer, you can select a different search engine and set it as the default.

Security and privacy are important issues to consider when you surf the Internet. In this chapter we will give you several tips on how to protect your privacy while you surf and after you have finished surfing. You will also see how your iPad handles cookies and fraudulent websites.

In this chapter we will provide you with tips on the following subjects:

- adding bookmarks to the Favorites Bar;
- arranging bookmarks in folders;
- deleting bookmarks;
- adding a bookmark to the Home screen;
- sharing a web address;
- saving an image you have found on a website;
- saving a web page to read later;
- reading web pages without the advertisements;
- setting up a default search engine;
- deleting the browser history;
- autofill function for filling in personal data;
- using *Do Not Track*;
- handling cookies;
- phishing and pop-up windows;
- using an Access point or a Wi-Fi enhancer.

3.1 Adding Bookmarks to the Favorites Bar

Setting a bookmark means saving a link to a particular website. The bookmark allows you to jump quickly to the website whenever you want without any typing.
A bookmark is usually added to the bookmarks list but you can also add a bookmark to the Favorites Bar in *Safari*. By placing a bookmark on this bar you can open the website even quicker.

This is how you set *Safari* to display the Favorites Bar by default:

☞ **Open the *Settings* app** 👣¹

👆 **Tap** 🧭 Safari

👆 **Drag the slider ◯ by Show Favorites Bar to the right**

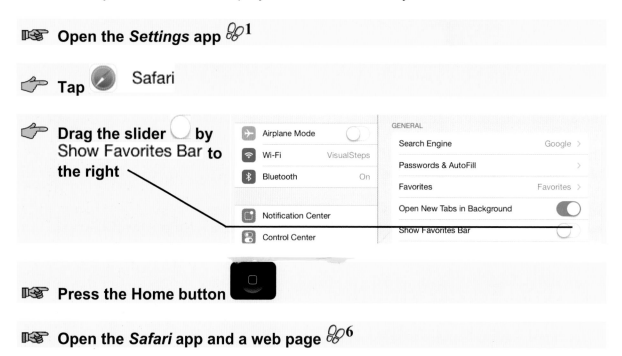

☞ **Press the Home button** ⬜

☞ **Open the *Safari* app and a web page** 👣⁶

This is how you add a bookmark to the Favorites Bar:

👆 **Tap** ⬆️

👆 **In the lower half of the pop-up window, tap**

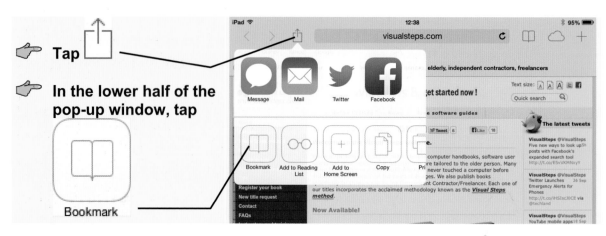

In the *Add Bookmark* window you can edit the name of the web page. This is handy in the case of a very long name.

⌨ **Type the desired name for the website**

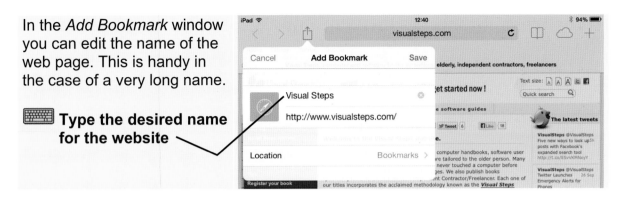

To add the bookmark to the Favorites Bar:

☞ **Tap** Location

☞ **Tap** Favorites

☞ **Tap** Save

Now the bookmark has been added to the Favorites Bar. This is how you open the bookmark:

👉 **Tap the bookmark**

The corresponding website will be opened.

You can add multiple bookmarks to the Favorites Bar in the same manner.

3.2 Arranging Bookmarks in Folders

If you have saved a lot of bookmarks, the list of bookmarks will eventually become too long and muddled. To solve this problem you can arrange the bookmarks in various folders, for instance, according to their subject.

☞ **Open the *Safari* app** 👣1

This is how you create a new bookmarks folder:

👉 **Tap** 📖

👉 **If necessary, tap Favorites**

👉 **Tap Edit**

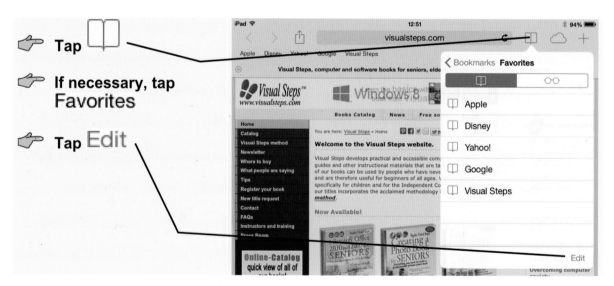

Tap New Folder

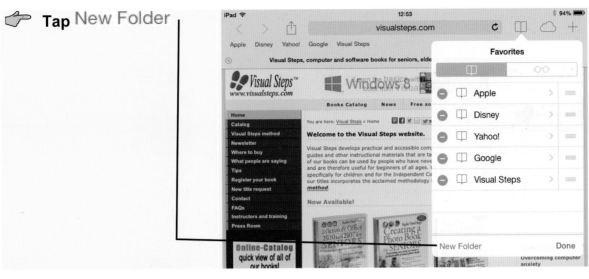

Type the name of the folder

In this example the folder will be added to favorites list.

If you want to add the folder to the bookmark list, you tap Location and select Bookmarks.

Tap ‹ Favorites

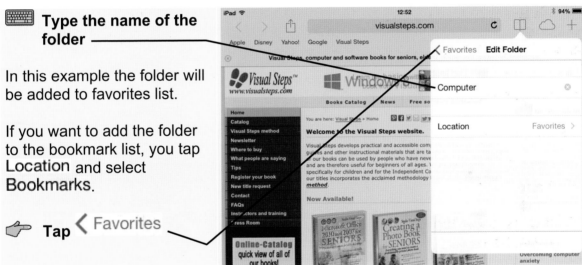

Tap Done

Tap ❮ Bookmarks

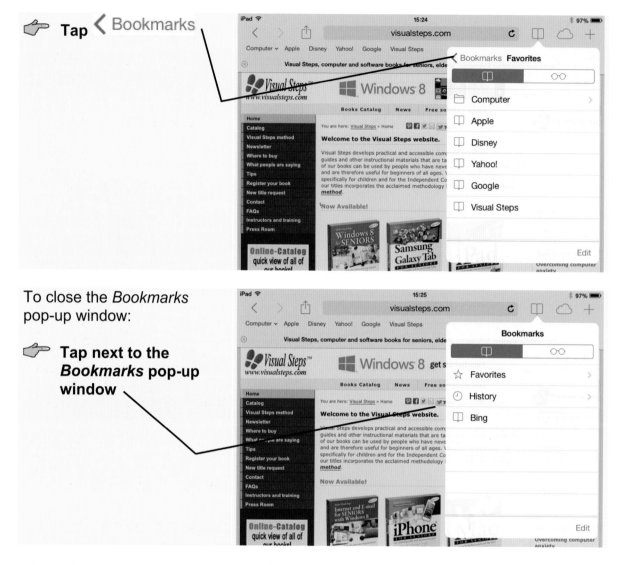

To close the *Bookmarks* pop-up window:

Tap next to the *Bookmarks* pop-up window

This is how you add a new bookmark to a folder:

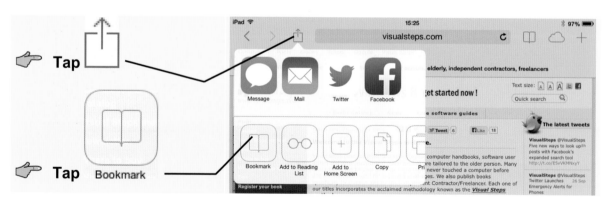

Tap

Tap Bookmark

If you have created a folder in the bookmarks list:

☞ **Tap** Favorites

☞ **Tap the folder**

⌨ **Type a different name, if you wish**

☞ **Tap** Save

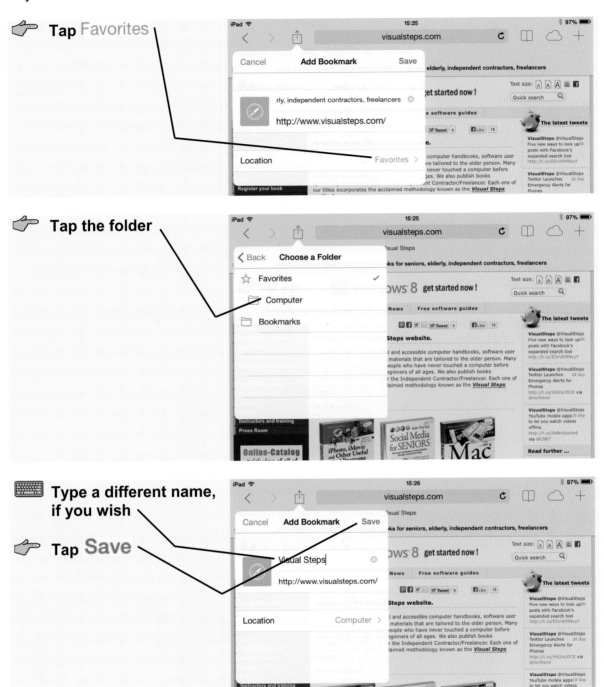

This is how you add an existing bookmark to a folder:

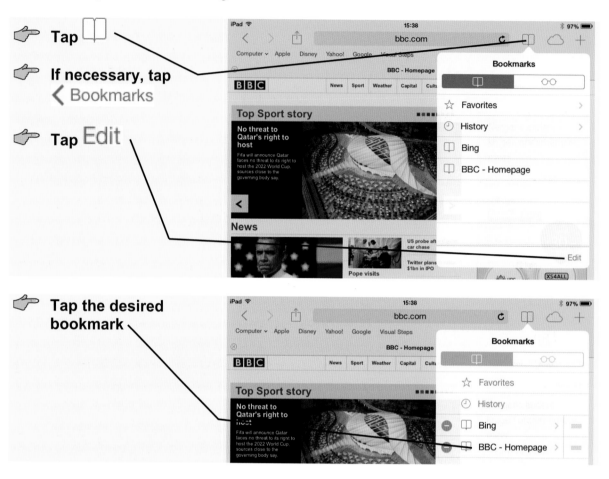

☞ **Tap** 📖

☞ **If necessary, tap**
  ‹ Bookmarks

☞ **Tap Edit**

☞ **Tap the desired**
  bookmark

If you want to save the bookmark in a folder in the bookmarks list:

☞ **Tap Bookmarks**

Tap the folder

Now the bookmark has been saved in the folder:

Tap ❮ Bookmarks

Tap Done

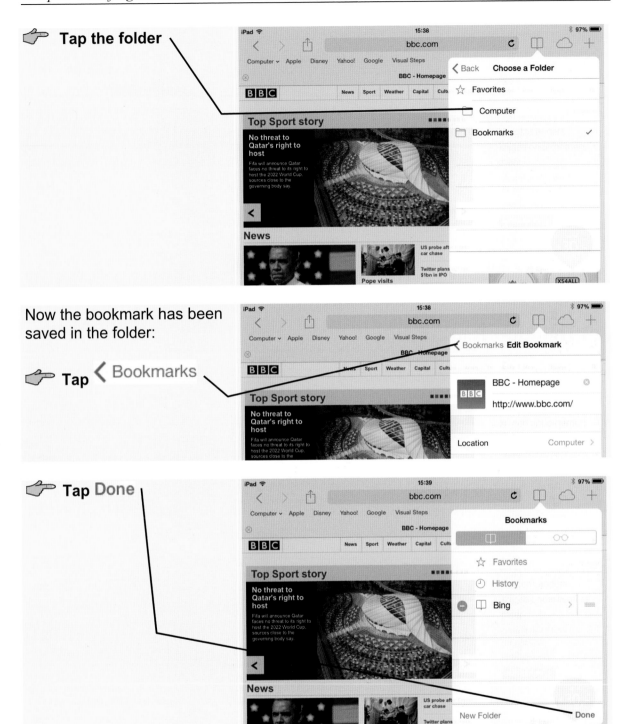

☞ **Tap next to the**
Bookmarks pop-up
window

3.3 Deleting Bookmarks

If you no longer use a particular bookmark you can delete it, like this:

☞ **Open the** *Safari* **app** ⌚¹

☞ **Tap** 📖

☞ **If necessary, tap**
    📖

☞ **Tap** Edit

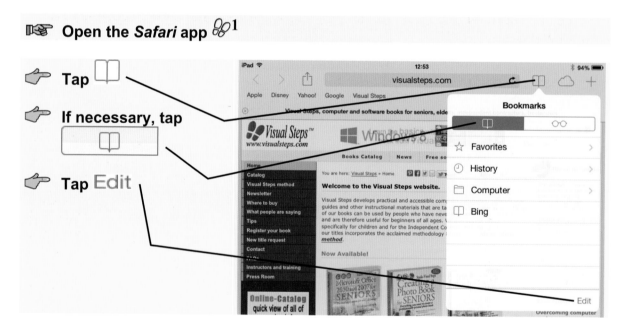

👉 **If necessary, tap a folder**

👉 **Tap ⊖ by the bookmark**

👉 **Tap Delete**

👉 **Tap Done**

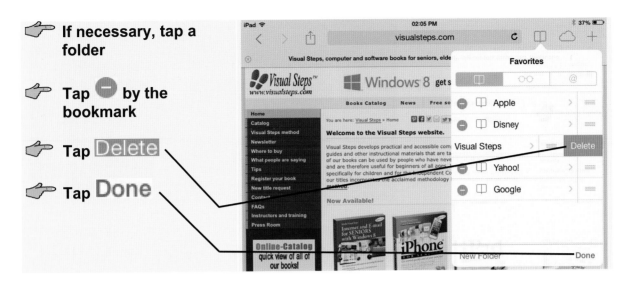

3.4 Adding a Bookmark to the Home Screen

There are also other ways of saving bookmarks as favorites. For example, you can add a web address to your iPad's Home screen. It will become a new icon, much like all the icons representing apps. In this way you will always have quick access to a favorite website:

👉 **Open the *Safari* app and a web page** ℘⁶

👉 **Tap** ⬆️

👉 **Tap Home Screen**

👉 **Tap Add**

Now the bookmark has been added to the Home screen as a new icon:

To open the corresponding website:

☞ **Tap the icon**

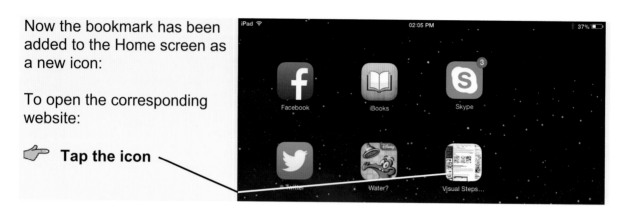

3.5 Copying Bookmarks from Your Computer to the iPad

If you have saved lots of favorite websites (bookmarks) on your computer, either in *Internet Explorer* or *Safari*, you can synchronize these with your iPad. To do this you need to use *iTunes*:

🖙 **Open the *iTunes* program on your computer** ℘℘²

🖙 **Connect your iPad to the computer**

☞ **Click** 📱 **iPad** ⏏

☞ **Click Info**

☞ **Drag the scroll box downwards**

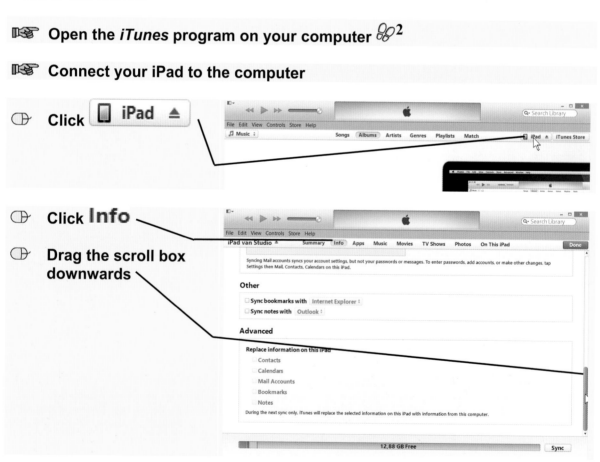

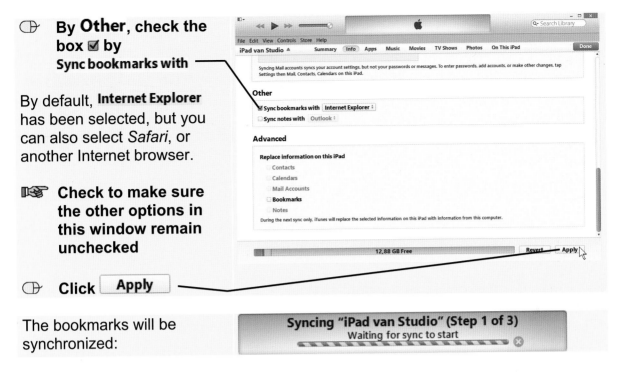

⊕ **By Other, check the box ☑ by Sync bookmarks with**

By default, **Internet Explorer** has been selected, but you can also select *Safari*, or another Internet browser.

☞ **Check to make sure the other options in this window remain unchecked**

⊕ **Click** **Apply**

The bookmarks will be synchronized:

Now the bookmarks have been transferred to the *Safari* browser on your iPad.

3.6 Sharing a Web Address

☞ **Open the *Safari* app and a web page** ⅋⅋6

There are several ways to share a favorite web address with others:

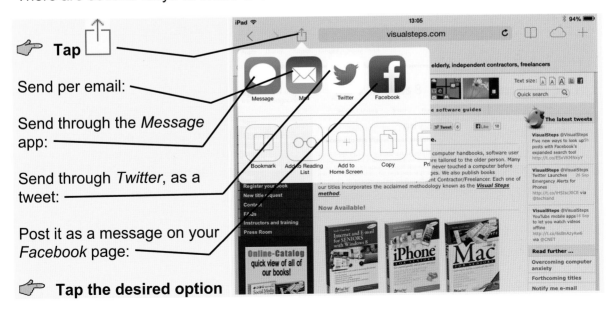

☞ **Tap** ⬆️

Send per email:

Send through the *Message* app:

Send through *Twitter*, as a tweet:

Post it as a message on your *Facebook* page:

☞ **Tap the desired option**

HELP! I do not see a specific option.

If you cannot see a specific option for sharing a web address, you may be working on an iPad that has not been updated to *iOS 7*, or your *Safari* app itself has not been updated.

The corresponding app will be opened and you can send the web address.

3.7 Saving an Image from a Website

You can save images you have found on a website, such as a photo or illustration. These saved images are stored in the *Photos* app:

☞ **Open the *Safari* app and a web page** 𝒥⁶

👆 **Set your finger on the photo for a while, and then release it** ——

A pop-up window appears. To save the image in the *Photos* app:

👉 **Tap** Save Image

You can also copy the photo and paste it directly into an email message.

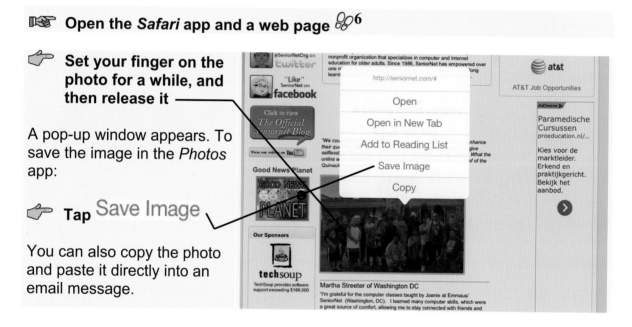

3.8 Reading Web Pages Later

In *Safari* you can create a reading list. In the reading list you can save entire web pages offline, and then read them later on. You do not need to be connected to the Internet to read a web page that has been saved in this manner. This is how you add a web page to the reading list:

☞ **Open the *Safari* app and a web page** 𝒥⁶

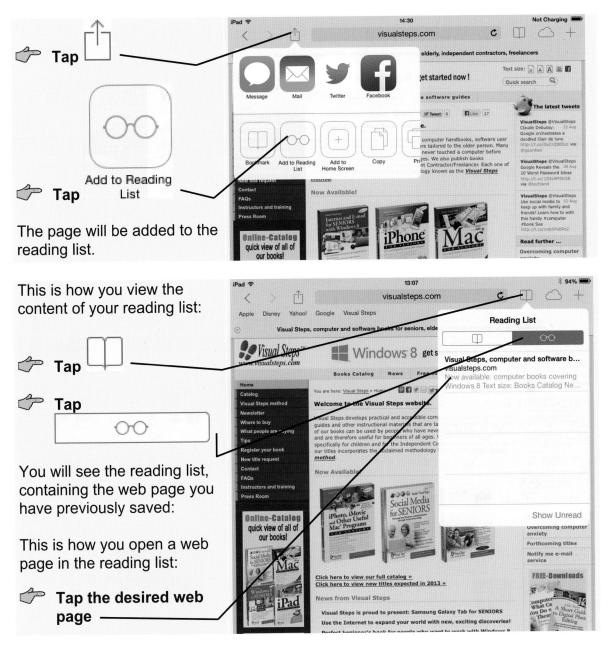

Tap

Tap Add to Reading List

The page will be added to the reading list.

This is how you view the content of your reading list:

Tap

Tap

You will see the reading list, containing the web page you have previously saved:

This is how you open a web page in the reading list:

Tap the desired web page

You will also see the Show Unread list, where you can view all the web pages you have saved and not yet read, after you saved them.

3.9 Reading Web Pages Without the Advertisements

Safari Reader will remove any advertisements and other merchandising elements that can distract you while you are reading (newspaper) articles online. This option is only available for web pages that contain articles.

☞ **Open the *Safari* app and a web page that contains an article, such as you find on www.newyorker.com** 🕮⁶

In this example you will see all sorts of ads above and next to the article:

Safari has noticed that an article is displayed on this web page. You can tell this by the ☰ icon in the address bar:

☞ **Tap ☰**

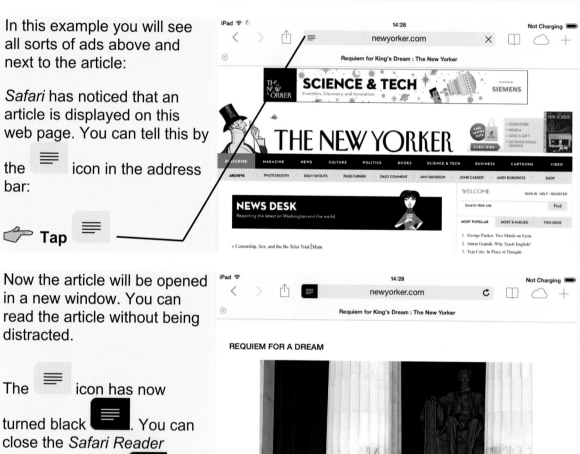

Now the article will be opened in a new window. You can read the article without being distracted.

The ☰ icon has now turned black ☰. You can close the *Safari Reader* screen by clicking ☰:

3.10 Setting Up a Default Search Engine

When *Safari* searches the Internet, it will use *Google* as a default search engine. If you prefer to use a different search engine, you can set it up, like this:

☞ **Open the *Settings* app** 🐾¹

👉 **Tap** 🧭 Safari

👉 **Tap** Search Engine

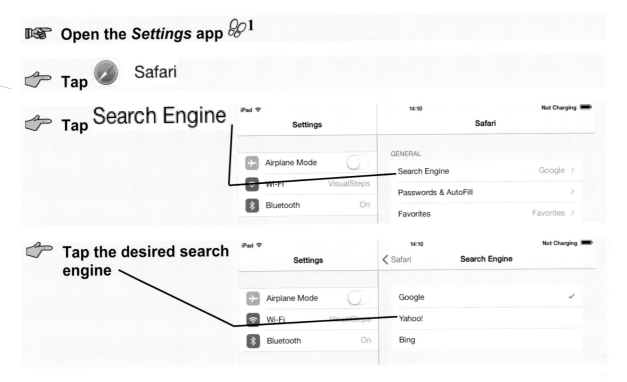

👉 **Tap the desired search engine**

3.11 Delete the Browser History

When you are surfing the Internet it is important to pay attention to privacy and security issues. You can set various options to ensure your safety while surfing the net.
For example, the browser history saves the links to all the websites you recently visited. You can use these links to quickly find a website you have previously visited. If you do not want others to see which sites you have visited, you can delete the browser history:

☞ **Open the *Safari* app and a web page** 🐾⁶

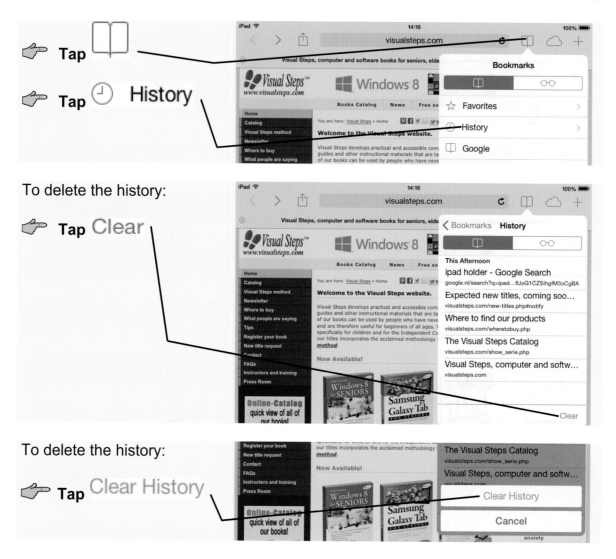

☞ **Tap** 📖

☞ **Tap** History

To delete the history:

☞ **Tap** Clear

To delete the history:

☞ **Tap** Clear History

The history will be deleted.

3.12 Autofill Data

If you have entered your own data in the *Contacts* app, you can automatically fill any forms on the Internet with your own personal information. This way, you do not need to enter this data each time you want to fill in a form. This is how you set up this option:

☞ **Open the *Settings* app** ✍¹

☞ **Tap** 🧭 Safari

☞ **Tap**
Passwords & AutoFill

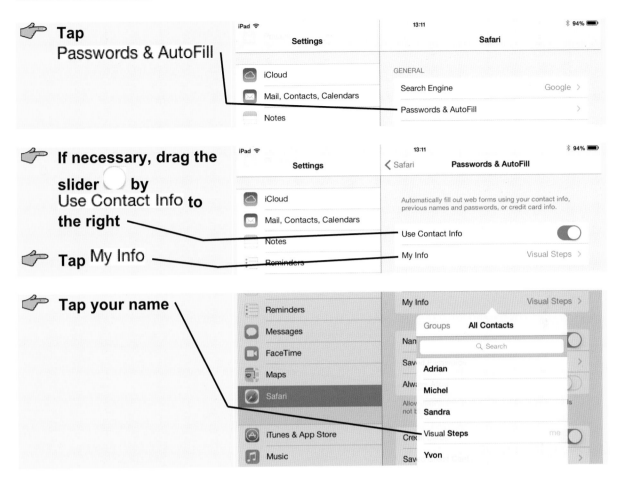

☞ **If necessary, drag the slider ○ by**
Use Contact Info **to the right**

☞ **Tap** My Info

☞ **Tap your name**

You can also automatically fill in names and passwords you have used previously, for example, when you signed in to certain websites.

☞ **If necessary, drag the slider ○ by**
Names and Passwords **to the right**

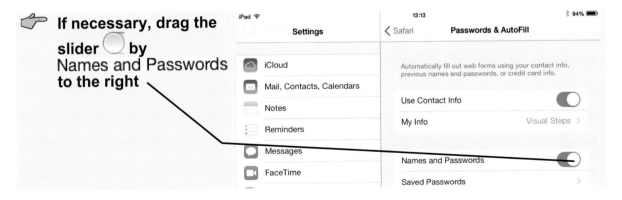

☞ **Please note:**
If you set up the system to automatically fill in names and passwords, this means that other people who use your iPad will also be able to sign in this way. You need to keep this in mind if you want to use this option.

If you have turned on the *Always Allow* option, you can delete the saved passwords as follows:

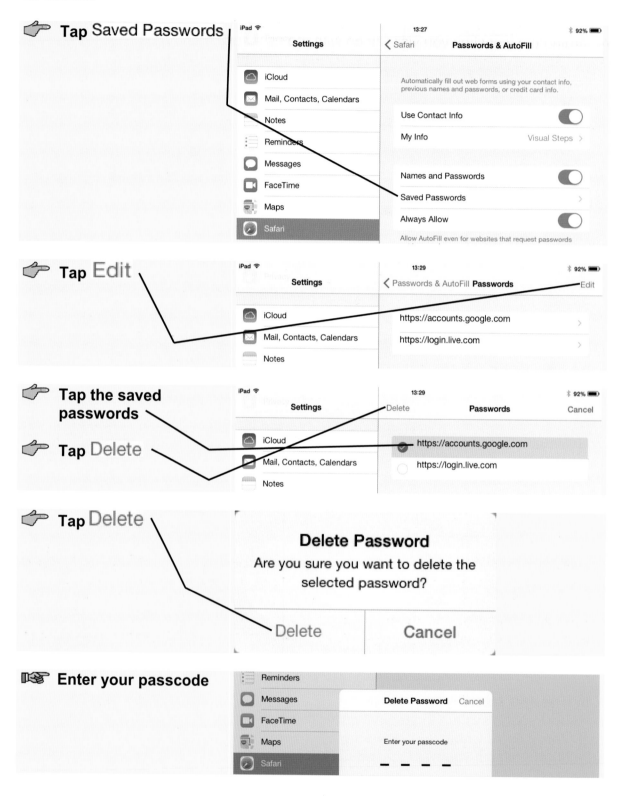

3.13 Using Do Not Track

While you are surfing the Internet, the system will automatically save information regarding the websites you visit, along with the user names and passwords you enter. Basically, this data can also be accessed by the other people who use your iPad. If you turn on *Do Not Track*, this data will not be saved:

☞ **Open the *Settings* app** 🐾¹

👉 **Tap** Safari

👉 **Drag the slider ⬭ by Do Not Track to the right**

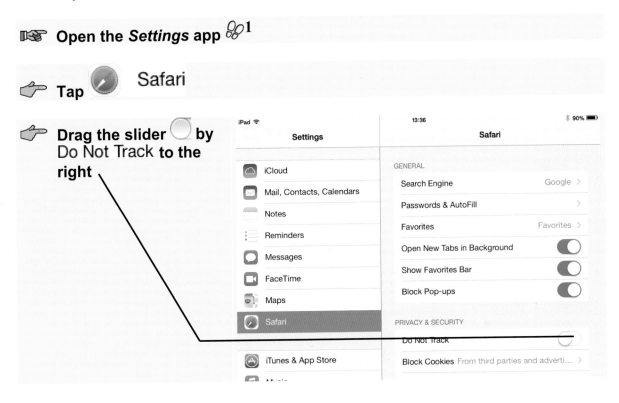

3.14 Handling Cookies

Cookies are small files that are stored on your computer by websites in order to make it easier to surf these websites and take advantage of extra services that may be offered. But these cookies may also collect information regarding your surfing behavior. It is up to you to decide whether you want to store cookies on your iPad. But remember that nowadays many websites will not work properly without the use of cookies.

☞ **Open the *Settings* app** 🐾¹

👉 **Tap** Safari

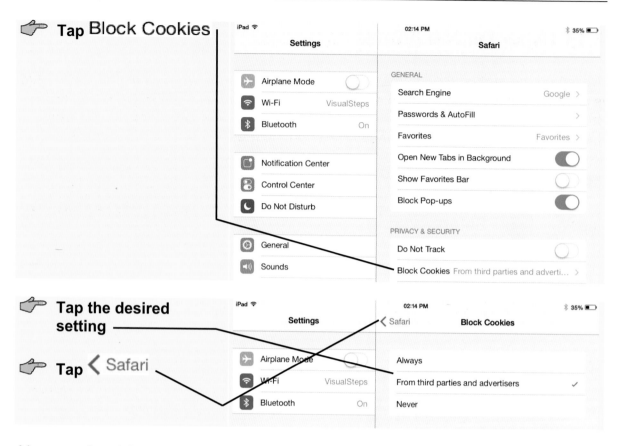

You can also delete the cookies and other website information:

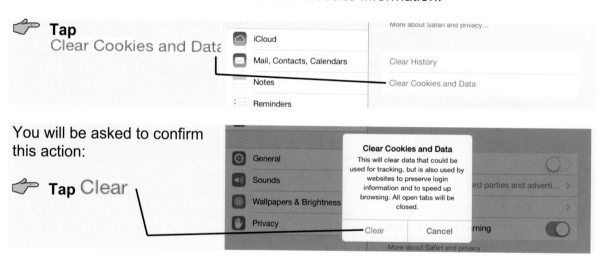

3.15 Phishing and Pop-up Windows

By default, you will always receive a message when you visit a phishing website. This is a website that is disguised as a regular website, such as a banking website, with the intention of getting you to enter your login information and use this information later on for all sorts of fraudulent activities. On the iPad this is called a fraudulent website.

Pop-ups are windows that are automatically opened when you visit certain websites. These windows often contain unwanted ads and messages. The default setting is to block these pop-ups.

This is how you view and change the relevant settings:

☞ **Open the *Settings* app** 🦶¹

👉 **Tap** 🧭 Safari

👉 **Drag the slider ⬤ by Fraudulent Website War or Block Pop-ups to the opposite side, if you wish**

🖐 **Please note:**
No matter which setting you select, you always need to be on the lookout for fraudulent activities. The iPad is just a device and there is always a possibility that it may fail to detect a fraudulent website.

3.16 Using an Access Point or a Wi-Fi Enhancer

If you do not have a separate Internet subscription for your iPad, you can use the Internet through Wi-Fi, at home as well as when you are away. Wireless Internet connections can be quite good when you do not stray too far from the router. If you are too far away, the connection will be poor and lead to a slower Internet connection with your iPad. You may notice this when you are up on the second floor or down in the basement of your house or perhaps out in the garden.

You can easily solve this problem by using some extra equipment. A Wi-Fi enhancer (also called a booster or range extender) is a device that receives the wireless signal, enhances it, and passes it on. Because of this, your iPad will receive a more powerful network signal.

If you already have set up a wired Internet connection in a room where the signal is weak, you can connect an Access point. This device will work as a switch for your wired Internet connection, and will let you connect your devices through a network cable. Apart from that, you can also use the Access point to connect your wireless devices, such as the iPad, to your home network. An Access point provides a more powerful Internet signal than a Wi-Fi enhancer.

You can buy Wi-Fi enhancers and Access points in various shapes and sizes. The type of device you choose may look different from the images in this book.

4. Tips for Various Apps

In this chapter we discuss some of the standard apps that are already installed on your iPad. They can be used to perform a variety of tasks. The *Contacts* app, for example, lets you manage all your contacts while the *Calendar* app will allow you to keep a calendar and record your appointments and other activities. These apps also have useful options to make it even easier to use the iPad.

In the *Maps* app, you can view maps from around the whole world, and plan trips. This app even offers the possibility of using it as a GPS system, if you have an iPad with a GPS receiver (3G or 4G versions).

We will also show you how to manage your apps. For example, how to move them to another screen, how to combine them into a folders, or delete them.

In this chapter we will provide you with tips on the following subjects:

- working with *Contacts*;
- settings for viewing contacts;
- contact data in other apps and synchronizing contact information;
- working with *Calendar*;
- synchronizing calendars in *Outlook*, *Gmail*, and *iCloud*;
- creating a new calendar and setting a default calendar;
- a default time for notifications;
- adding an event from an email message to a calendar;
- viewing *Calendar* and *Contacts* in *iCloud*, on the computer;
- the *Maps* app;
- the *Clock* app;
- finding apps in the *App Store*;
- moving apps, saving apps in a folder and deleting apps;
- updating apps;
- viewing apps you have purchased;
- transferring apps you have purchased to the computer;
- transferring apps from *iTunes* to the iPad;
- transferring apps from other devices to the iPad;
- viewing the apps settings and the memory usage of apps;
- setting up *Spotlight*;
- further suggestions for useful apps.

4.1 Working with Contacts

The *Contacts* app is used to manage your contacts on the iPad.

☞ **Open the *Contacts* app** 🥾**1**

You will see all the contacts you have entered on the left-hand side of the window, in alphabetical order:

If you want to edit the contact data, tap the contact and then tap Edit:

This is how you add a new contact:

👉 **Tap ✚**

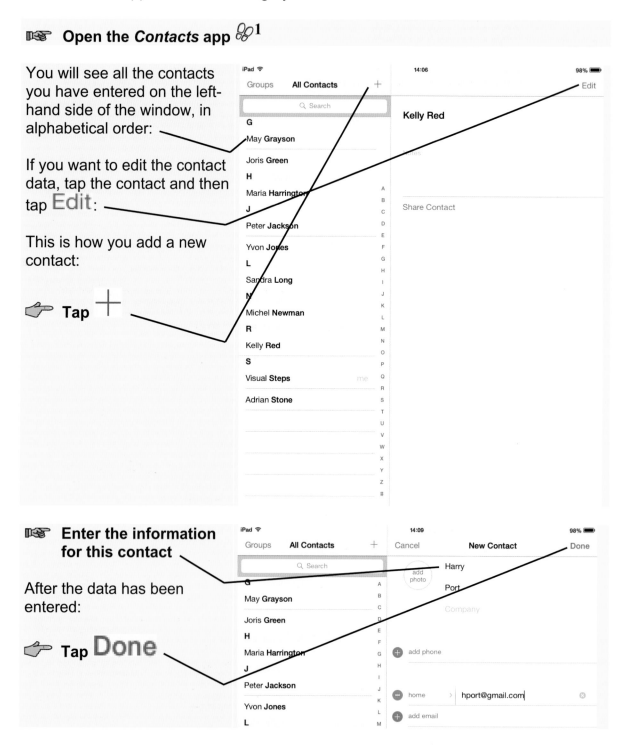

☞ **Enter the information for this contact**

After the data has been entered:

👉 **Tap Done**

Through the letters in the middle you can directly access the contact you need, if the list of contacts is very long: ————

You can also search for contacts: ————

And you can forward the contact data in the form of a business card (a VCF file), along with an email or message: ————

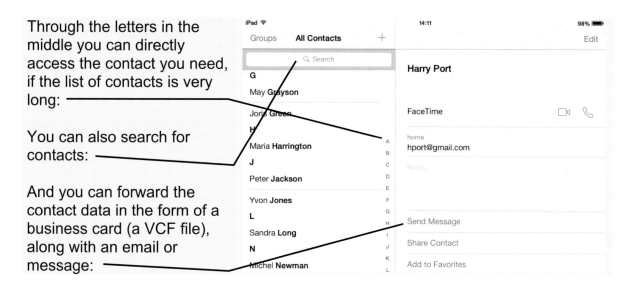

4.2 Settings for Viewing Contacts

By default, the names of the contacts are displayed in the FirstName, LastName format, for example: Charles Hudson. But you can display the names in reverse order if you prefer: Hudson Charles. Here is how you do that:

☞ **Open the *Settings* app** ✌¹

☞ **Tap** ✉ **Mail, Contacts, Calendars**

☞ **Drag upwards across the right side of the screen** ————

By default, the contacts are displayed in alphabetical order, by their last names. You can change the order here, if you wish: ————

You can also change how the first and last name are diaplayed:

☞ **By** CONTACTS, **tap** **Display Order** ————

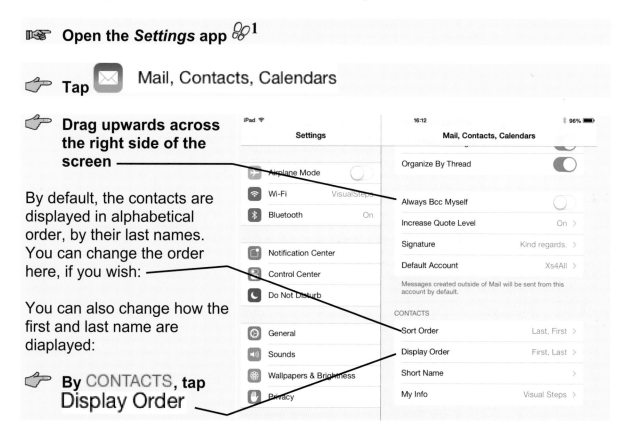

👉 **Tap the desired display order**

4.3 Contact Data in Other Apps

Contact information can also be accessed from several other apps. You can use a contact's home address to look them up on a map with the *Maps* app:

☞ **Open the** *Maps* **app** 𝒫¹

👉 **Tap** Bookmarks

👉 **Tap the desired contact**

You will see the contact's address appear on the map:

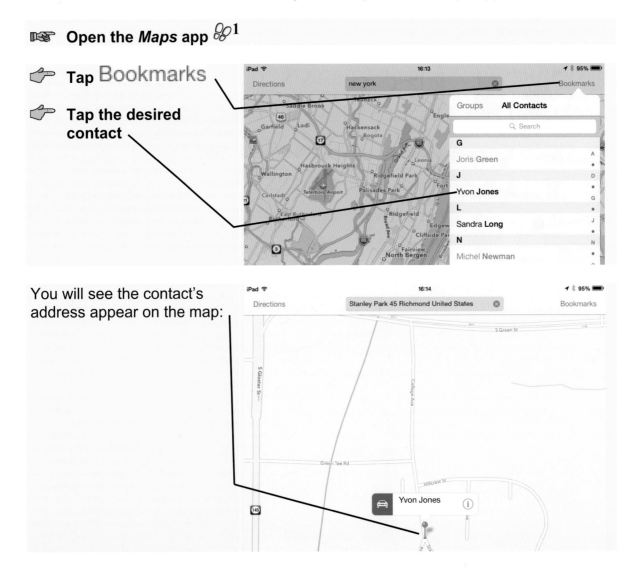

4.4 Synchronizing Contact Information

If you use a *Outlook* email account on your iPad (one ending with hotmail.com, outlook.com, or live.com), you will also see that account's corresponding contacts in the *Contacts* app. These are the contacts you previously entered on your computer, for instance.
This works the other way around too. When you add a new contact, you can also save the contact data in the *Outlook* contact list.

☞ **Open the *Contacts* app** 🐾¹

☞ **Enter a new contact**

👉 **Tap the contact**

👉 **Tap Edit**

👉 **Drag upwards across the right side of the screen**

👉 **Tap**
 ⊕ link contacts...

👉 **Tap Groups**

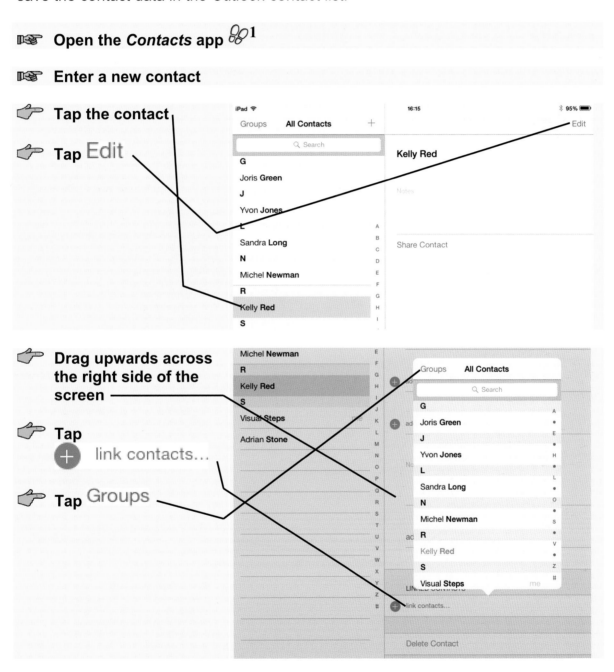

Here you can see in which groups the contact is stored:

If necessary, you can delete the checkmarks ✔.

☞ Tap Done

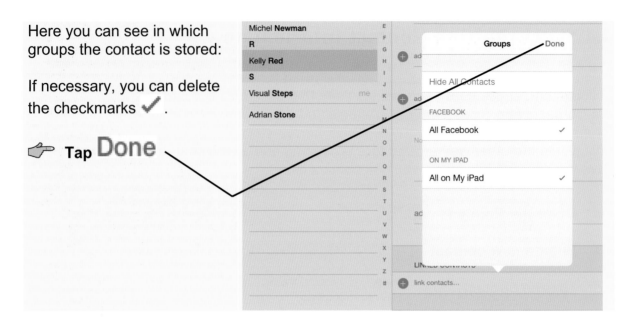

🐦 Please note:

When you open an existing contact you have entered on your iPad and you view all the groups to which this contact has been added, you will also see a checkmark ✔ by All Outlook. However, if you view your *Outlook* (*Hotmail*) contacts on the Internet, you might not see all the contacts in this list. The synchronization procedure does not seem to work consistently all the time. This problem will hopefully be addressed in the future.

If you do not want to display your *Outlook* contacts on your iPad, you can do this:

🖝 Open the *Settings* app 🐾¹

☞ Tap ✉ Mail, Contacts, Calendars

☞ Tap your *Outlook* account

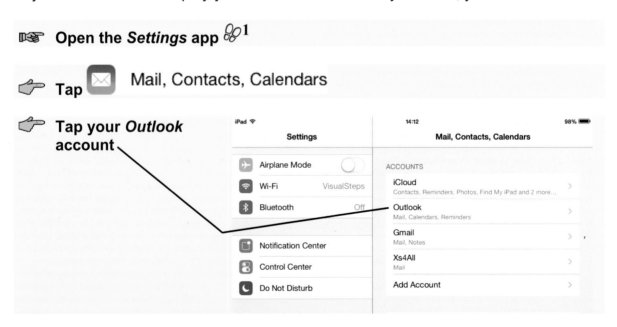

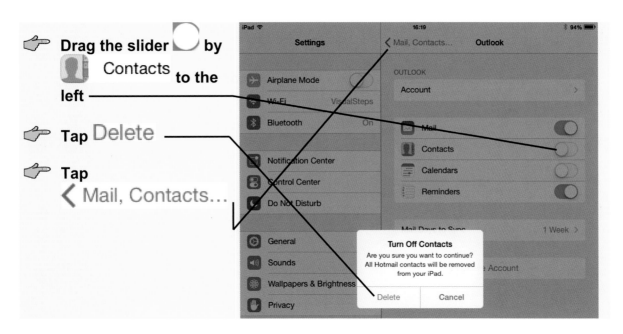

☞ **Drag the slider** by
Contacts **to the**
left

☞ **Tap** Delete

☞ **Tap**
❮ Mail, Contacts...

If you use *iCloud* you can store contact data there as well. You can view and manage this contact data on other devices, such as an iPhone, desktop computer, or laptop.

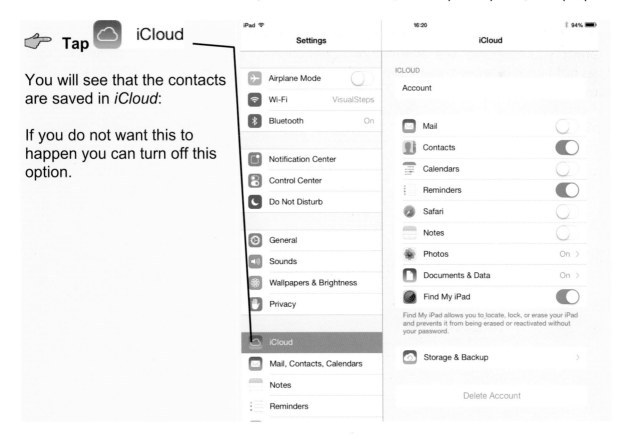

☞ **Tap** iCloud

You will see that the contacts are saved in *iCloud*:

If you do not want this to happen you can turn off this option.

4.5 Working with the Calendar app

With the *Calendar* app you can manage your appointments. In the *Calendar* app an appointment is called an *event*.

☞ **Open the *Calendar* app** 🦶¹

The calendar will be opened on the current day.

You can display the calendar in several ways:

To add a new event, you click ➕:

After you have added events you can view, edit, or delete them:

👉 **Tap the event**

You will see additional information in a frame that pops up by the event:

To edit the event:

👉 **Tap** Edit

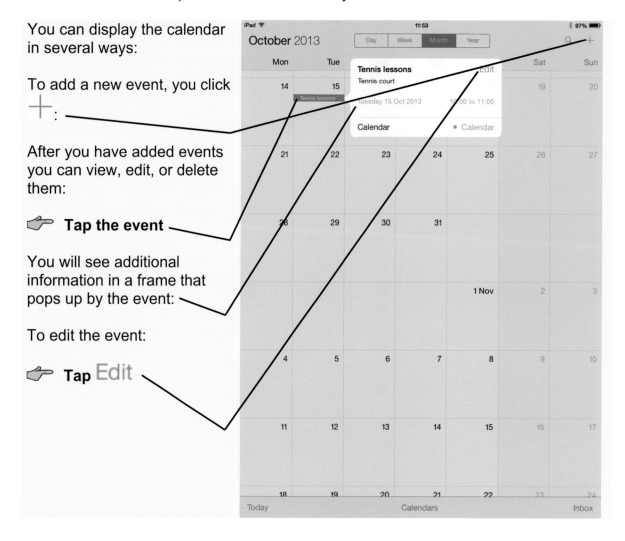

You will see the event settings:

You can select various options. You can change these settings, if you wish:

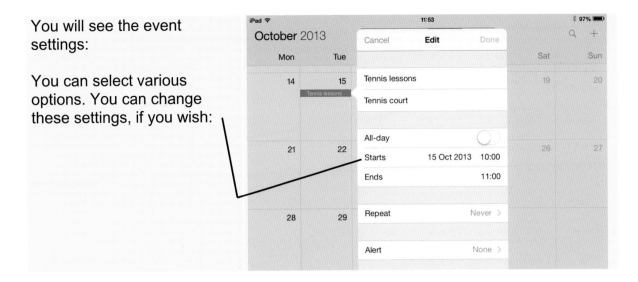

4.6 Synchronizing Calendars in Outlook, Gmail, and iCloud

Some email accounts, such as *Outlook* and *Gmail*, will also let you manage a calendar. If you have *iCloud* set up, you can use the *iCloud* calendar too. Here is how you display these calendars:

☞ **Open the *Settings* app** 👣¹

👆 **Tap** ✉ **Mail, Contacts, Calendars**

👆 **By ACCOUNTS, tap the email account**

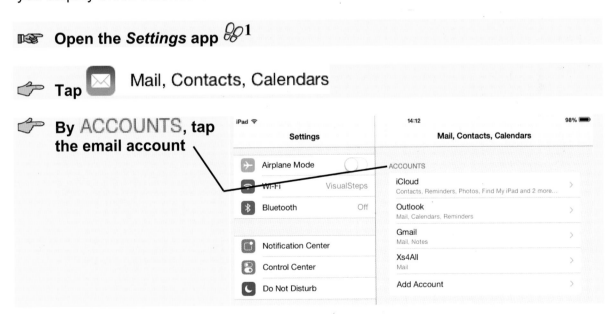

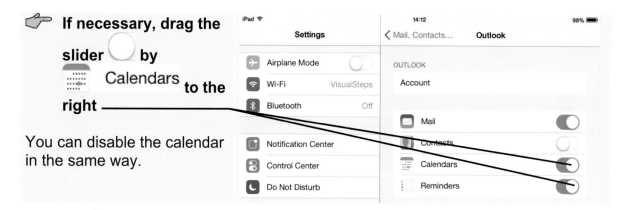

If necessary, drag the slider ⬭ by 🗓 Calendars to the right ——

You can disable the calendar in the same way.

🩹 HELP! I see a message regarding existing calendars.

You may see a message asking you what to do with the existing calendars. To save the current calendars on the iPad you tap Keep on My iPad and Keep.

If you want to turn the *iCloud* calendar on or off, you open the ☁ iCloud section in the *Settings* app, and drag the slider ⬭ by 🗓 Calendars and tap Merge.

You can also indicate the period over which older events will be synchronized:

If necessary, tap ‹ Mail, Contacts...

Drag upwards across the right side of the screen

By CALENDARS, tap Sync

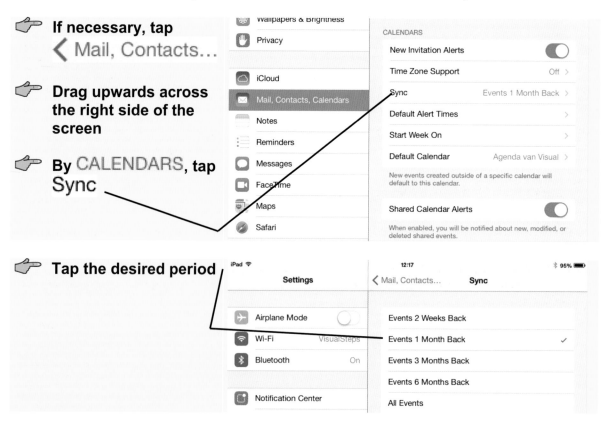

Tap the desired period

This is how you display or hide a calendar:

☞ **Open the *Calendar* app** 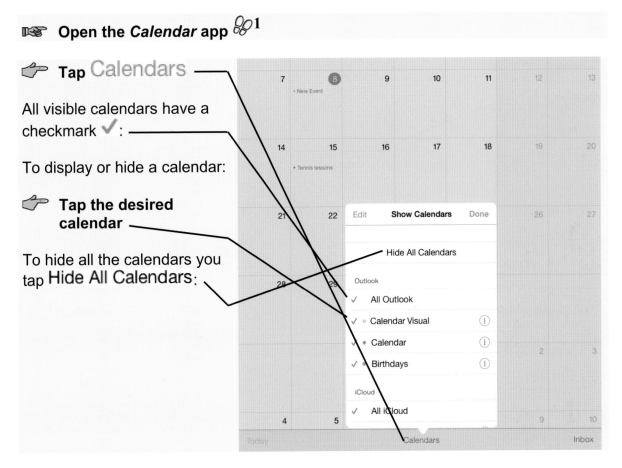¹

👉 Tap Calendars ——

All visible calendars have a
checkmark ✔ : ————

To display or hide a calendar:

👉 **Tap the desired
calendar** ———

To hide all the calendars you
tap **Hide All Calendars**:

You will see that multiple calendars are available for some of the accounts. In this
way you can choose which calendars are displayed on your iPad.
You can recognize the calendars by their color.

4.7 Creating a New Calendar

It is possible to create a new calendar. That can be useful if you want to subdivide
your appointments and keep a separate calendar for your sports events, for instance.
In this example we have added a calendar to an *iCloud* account. If you do not use
any *iCloud* calendars but you do use the default calendar on the iPad, you can add a
new calendar too.

☞ **Open the *Calendar* app** ¹

👉 **Tap** Calendars

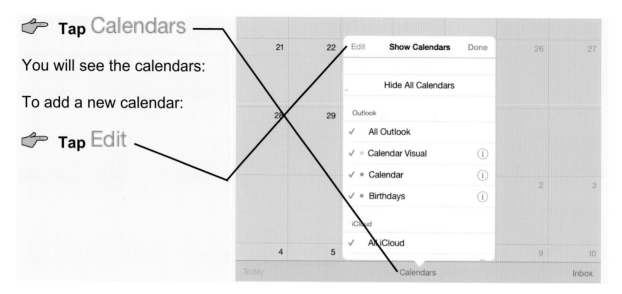

You will see the calendars:

To add a new calendar:

👉 **Tap** Edit

👉 **Tap** Add Calendar...

⌨ **Type a name**

👉 **Tap a color**

👉 **Tap** Done

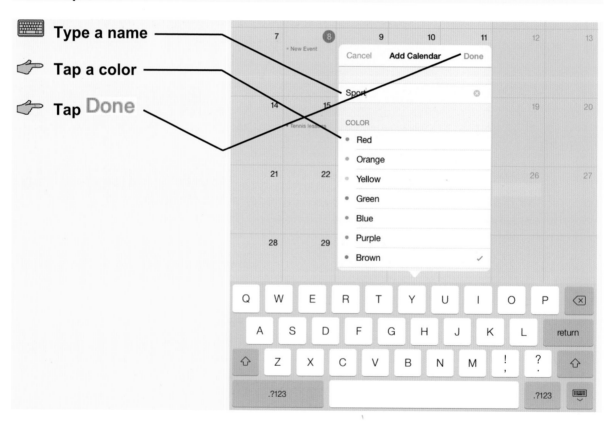

In the next window:

👉 **Tap** Done

Tip

Delete a calendar
It is possible to delete a calendar.
Please note: all the events in this calendar will then be deleted as well.

☞ **Tap** Calendars

☞ **Tap** Edit

☞ **Tap the desired calendar**

☞ **Drag upwards across the window**

☞ **Tap** Delete Calendar

☞ **Tap** Delete Calendar

4.8 Setting a Default Calendar

If your iPad contains more than one calendar you can set one of the calendars as a default calendar. This will then be the calendar that is displayed first when you open the *Calendar* app.

☞ **Open the** *Settings* **app** 🦶¹

☞ **Tap** ✉ Mail, Contacts, Calendars

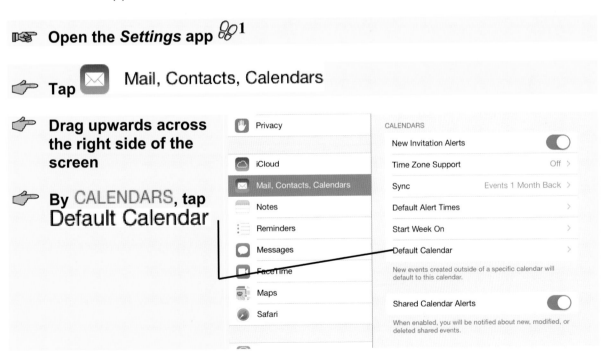

☞ **Drag upwards across the right side of the screen**

☞ **By** CALENDARS, **tap** Default Calendar

☞ **Tap the desired calendar, for example** Calendar Visual

4.9 Default Notification Time

You can set a default time for notifications such as birthdays or specific events. A notification for this type of event will then be displayed at a specific interval:

☞ **Open the *Settings* app** 👣¹

☞ **Tap** ✉ Mail, Contacts, Calendars

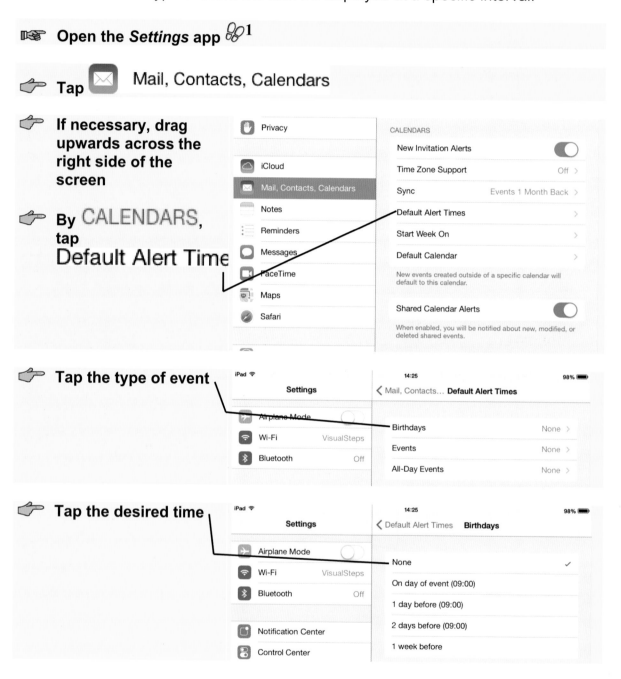

☞ **If necessary, drag upwards across the right side of the screen**

☞ **By CALENDARS, tap Default Alert Times**

☞ **Tap the type of event**

☞ **Tap the desired time**

4.10 Adding an Appointment From an Email To a Calendar

The *Mail* app is able to identify dates in email messages. You can use this feature to quickly add such a date to your calendar:

☞ **Open the *Mail* app and open an email message** ℘⁷

👉 **Tap the date**

👉 **Tap** Create Event

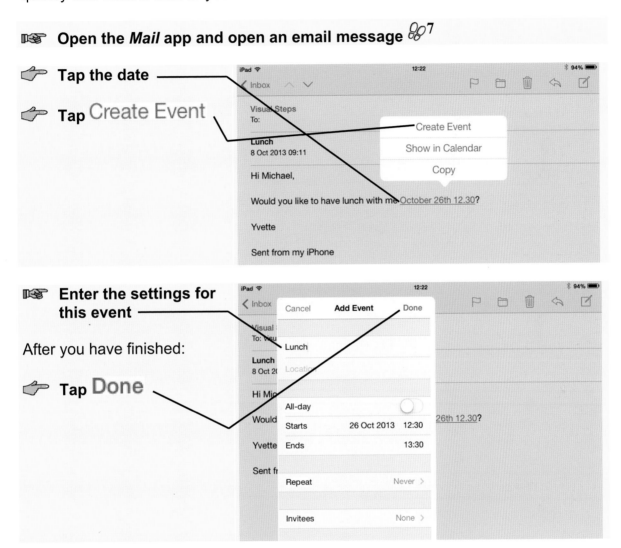

☞ **Enter the settings for this event**

After you have finished:

👉 **Tap** Done

Now the event has been added to the calendar.

4.11 Viewing the Calendar and Contacts in iCloud on the Computer

If you have *iCloud* set up on your iPad you can use your computer to view and edit your contacts and calendar. You do this using the www.icloud.com website:

☞ **Open the www.icloud.com web page on your computer** ✂4

You will see the *iCloud* website. You will need to sign in with your *Apple ID*:

⌨ **Type your *Apple ID* and password**

🖱 **Click** ➡

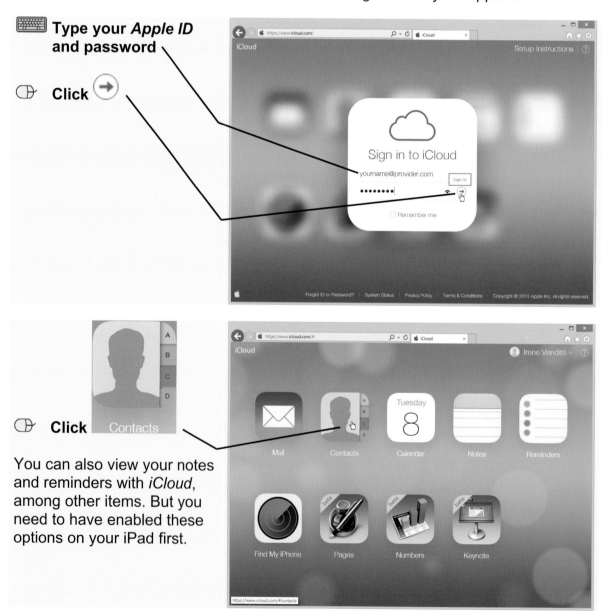

🖱 **Click** Contacts

You can also view your notes and reminders with *iCloud*, among other items. But you need to have enabled these options on your iPad first.

You will see your contact information:

You can add a new contact:

Here you can change the data:

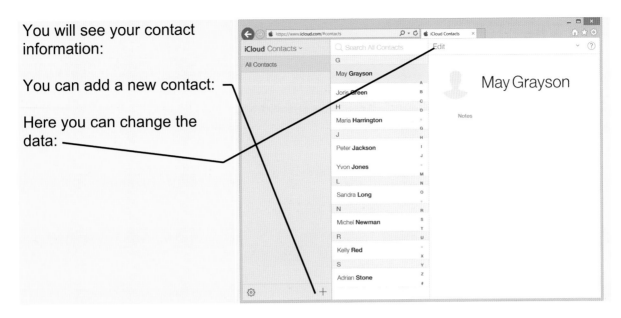

You can also view the *Calendar* app on your computer:

Click iCloud

Click Calendar

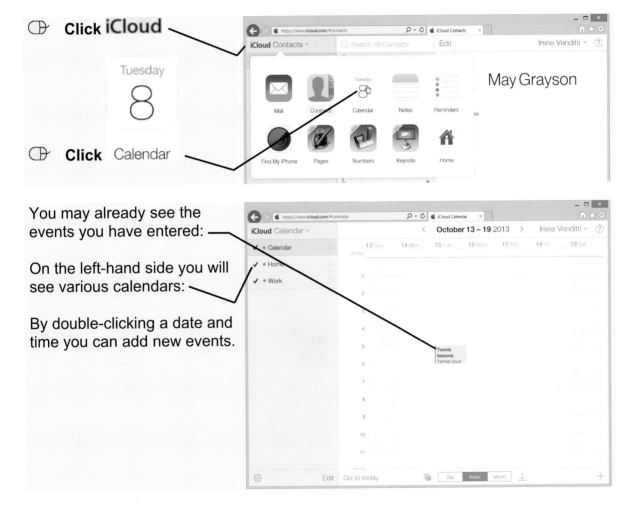

You may already see the events you have entered:

On the left-hand side you will see various calendars:

By double-clicking a date and time you can add new events.

4.12 The Maps App

With the *Maps* app on your iPad, you can view certain locations on a map, plan trips and get directions.

☞ **Open the *Maps* app** 👣**1**

You will see a map of your own country. First, you need to determine your current location:

In the bottom left-hand side of the screen:

☞ **Tap** ⓘ

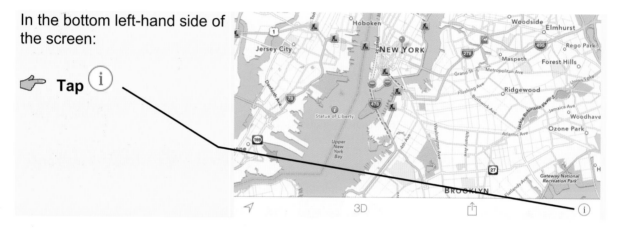

You may be asked for permission to use your current location (Location Services):

☞ **If necessary, tap** OK

Your current location is indicated by a blue dot. If you wish, you can zoom in or out by spreading two fingers, or pinching them together across the screen.
This is how you change the map view:

☞ **Tap the bottom right-hand corner of the screen to turn the page**

☞ **Tap** Standard **or** Hybrid

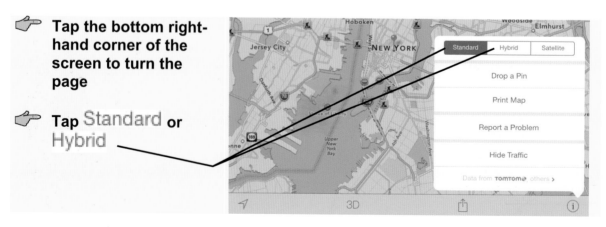

There is a very useful option that will prevent you from getting stuck in traffic jams:

Any obstructions are indicated by a dotted line:

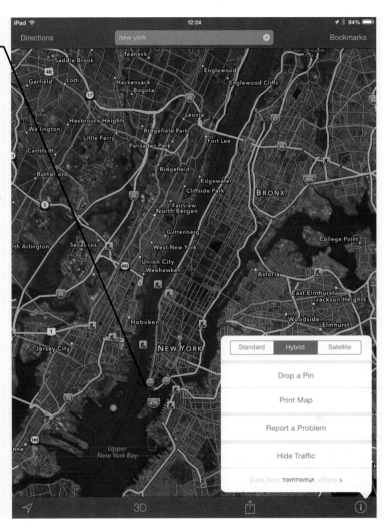

![roadworks icon] indicates there are road works in progress.

![no entry icon] means the road is blocked.

![accident icon] indicates an accident has happened.

If you tap an icon you can read more about these problems.

In *Maps* you can search for certain locations:

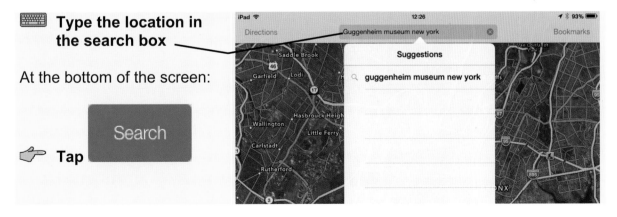

![keyboard icon] **Type the location in the search box**

At the bottom of the screen:

☞ **Tap** Search

The location is indicated on the map by a red pin :

You can use the window to view additional information on the location you found, and to share or save this information:

You can also get directions:

☞ **Tap Directions**

By default, the trip from your current location to the location you just found is set for travel by car, but you can change this. With ↻ you can reverse the starting and destination locations:

With 🚌 and 🚶 you can get directions for travelling by public transport, or on foot:

Get directions for this trip:

☞ **Tap Route**

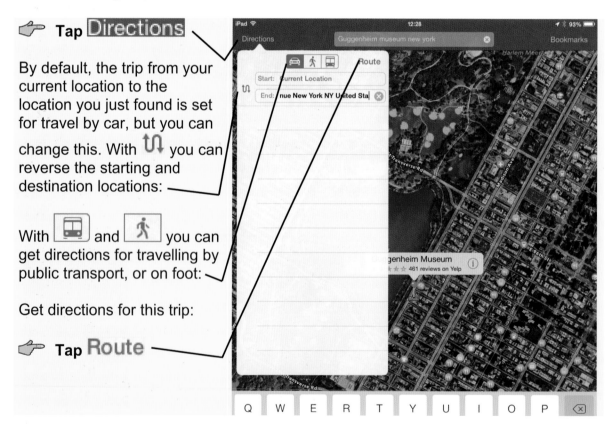

A car trip will be computed, starting at your current location. The blue line indicates the route:

Here you see the distance to be travelled in kilometers or miles, and the estimated time:

In this example, two alternative routes have been computed,  and

1 hr 5 min :

This is how you view the directions for the entire route:

👉 **Tap** ▤

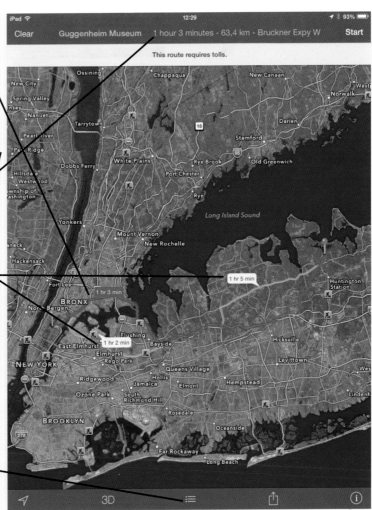

Tap the map to close the instructions window:

You can also display the route one step at a time:

👉 **Tap**

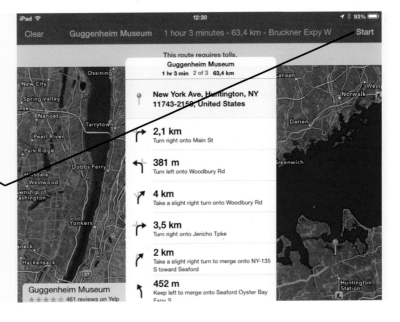

An iPad that is only equipped with Wi-Fi will display the first step of the route. You will also see the instructions in the highlighted box:

Tap the next box to display the next step:

 Tap the box

Now you can follow the route step by step, by constantly tapping the next box.

However, on an iPad with Wi-Fi + 3G/4G the screen will look different. This type of iPad has a built-in GPS receiver that can be used as a navigational system.

You will hear verbal instructions and you can view your current location at the bottom of the screen. As soon as you change position, the arrow will move too, and you will see and hear the next instruction.

If the speaker's voice is too loud or too soft, you can change the volume using the *Settings* app.

You can even view several cities and places of interest in 3D. This function is called *Flyover*. This function may not be available for each area or place of interest. In this example we will take a look at the Golden Gate Bridge in San Francisco:

☞ **Tap ℹ️ in the bottom right-hand corner of the map**

☞ **Tap Hybrid or Satellite**

☞ **Go to the desired location and zoom in until you have a good view**

☞ **Tap 🏢 in the bottom left-hand corner**

Now you will see the Golden Gate Bridge in 3D:

You can zoom in on the bridge and move the map by dragging it. You can rotate the view by rotating your thumb and index finger.

To turn off 3D again, tap 🏢.

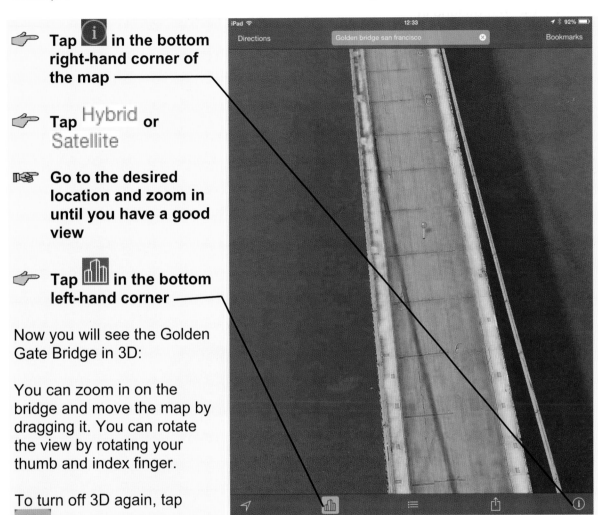

4.13 The Clock App

The *Clock* app on your iPad tells the time. But did you know that it can also be used as an alarm clock, a stopwatch or a timer?

☞ **Open the *Clock* app** 👣¹

The first component of the *Clock* app is the world clock. Here you can see at a glance what the time is in other time zones. A number of clocks have already been set up by default, such as the one for New York. If you wish, you can add a new clock yourself:

At the bottom of the screen:

☞ **If necessary, tap**

World Clock

Add a new clock by tapping:

➕

Add

You can delete or move a clock with Edit:

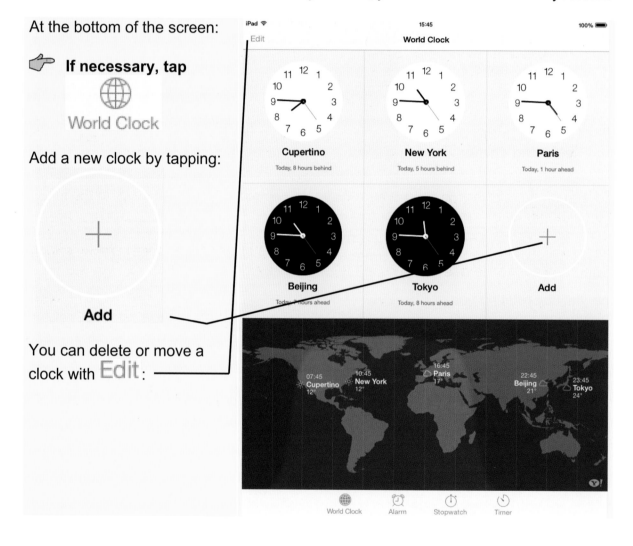

You can use the *Clock* app as an alarm clock:

At the bottom of the screen:

☞ **Tap** Alarm

To add an alarm clock:

☞ **Tap** +

You will see that you can set various options, just like on a regular alarm clock:

☞ **Set the alarm clock**

☞ **Tap** Save

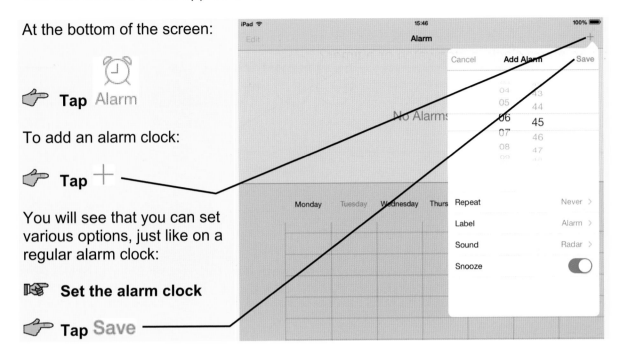

To turn off the alarm clock you drag the slider ⊂⊃ next to the alarm clock to the left. To delete an alarm clock you use the Edit button.

A stopwatch can come in handy if you need to keep track of time, for example, during a sporting event. Here is how to use the *Clock* app as a stopwatch:

At the bottom of the screen:

☞ **Tap** Stopwatch

To start the stopwatch running:

☞ **Tap** Start

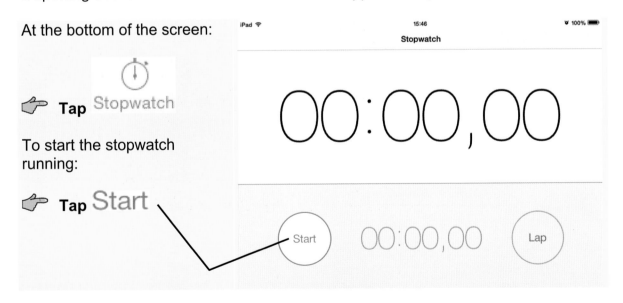

If you want to record lap times, you tap **Lap**:

To stop the time, you tap **Stop**.

After you have stopped the time, you can reset the time to 0 and delete the lap times by tapping **Reset**.

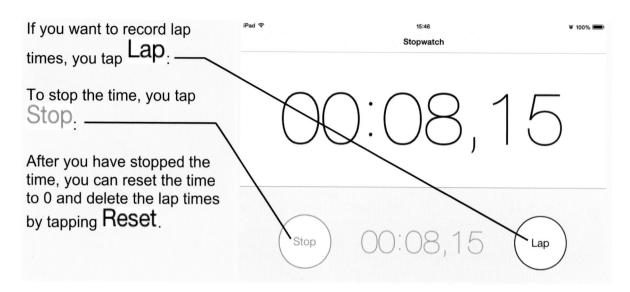

The timer in *Clock* can be useful when you need an egg-timer or something like that:

At the bottom of the screen:

👉 **Tap** Timer

👉 **Spin the wheels to set the time**

👉 **Tap** Start

After the time has expired you will hear a sound signal. You can adjust the sound you hear by tapping 🎵 **Radar**:

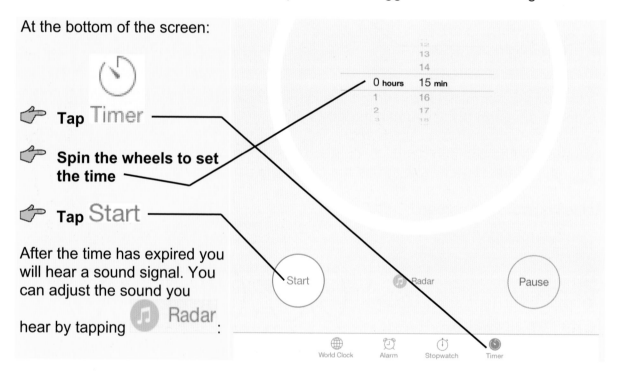

4.14 Finding Apps in the App Store

The *App Store* contains a huge amount of apps. How do you find an app when there are so many available? In this section we will give you some tips:

☞ **Open the *App Store*** ✂¹

When you have opened the *App Store* you will see the Featured page, where the most recent and popular apps are highlighted.

If you drag from right to left across the rows of apps, you will see even more apps:

On this page you can also view the apps per category:

☞ **Tap** More

To display more categories:

☞ **Drag upwards across the menu**

☞ **For example, tap** Food & Drink

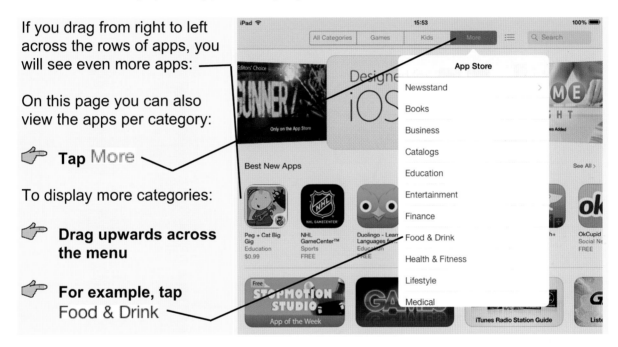

Now you will see the apps in this category. If you already know (part of) the app's name, you can search for the app directly:

⌨ **Type the name of the app in the search box**

☞ **If necessary, tap** Search

After the app has been found, you will see it on the screen and you can download it by tapping $\boxed{^+\text{FREE}}$:

To quit this screen:

☞ **Tap** Cancel

You can also look for apps in the charts containing the most popular apps:

☞ **Tap** Top Charts

You will see the general charts showing free apps and top paid apps:

You can also view these charts per category:

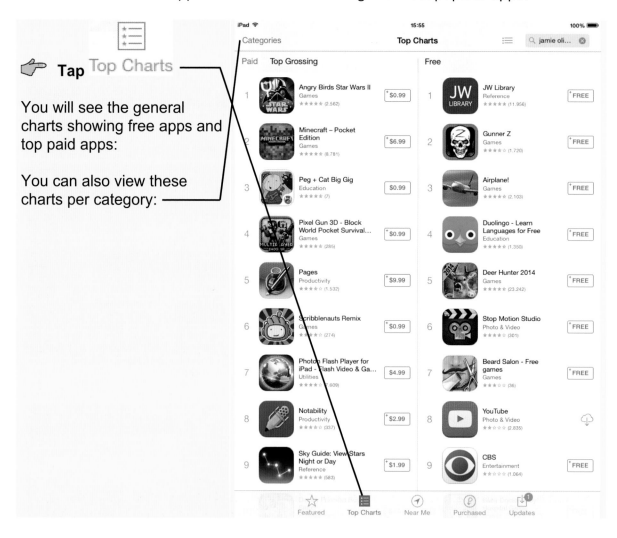

If you have already installed various apps on your iPad, you can allow the *App Store* to look for popular apps used by people in your current location. You do this with *Near Me* option:

☞ **Tap** Near Me

For the *Near Me* function to work, you need to turn on Location Services first:

You will see the suggestions offered by *Near Me*:

If you tap the app icon, you will see information about the suggested app:

Additional chapters in this book include tips for other interesting or useful apps. These are mentioned at the end of the chapters. These are just a few suggestions from the hundreds of apps available in the *App Store*. But the tips in this section will hopefully assist you in searching for an app that matches your interests.

4.15 Moving Apps

You can change the order of the apps on your iPad by moving them around:

👉 **Practice by going to a page with apps you have purchased**

👉 **Press your finger lightly on one of these apps**

The apps will start jiggling and some may display a little cross . Now the app can be moved:

👉 **Hold your finger down on top of the app and drag it to a different location**

Now the app has been moved:

You can also move an app to a different page. Here is how you move an app to the Home screen:

 Press down lightly on the jiggling app you want to move and carefully drag it to the left edge of the screen

When the Home screen appears, you can continue to drag the app until it is positioned where you want it:

 Release your finger from the app

Now the app is placed between other apps on the Home screen: ───

You can move an app from the Home screen to another screen in the same way.

To stop the apps from jiggling:

 Press the Home button

4.16 Saving Apps in a Folder

You can save multiple apps in the same folder. In this way you can neatly arrange the apps on your iPad to make them easier to find later on. You can put all the media-related apps together in the same folder, for instance.

☞ **Practice with an app you have purchased**

👉 **Press your finger lightly on the desired app until it jiggles**

👉 **Drag the app you want to combine on top of another app**

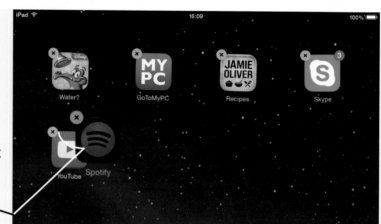

A name will be suggested for the new folder:

⌨ **If you prefer a different name, type the name you want to use**

👉 **Tap outside the folder**

You will see the new folder:

To stop the apps from jiggling:

☞ **Press the Home button**

Now the apps have stopped moving. To view the content of a folder:

👉 **Tap the folder**

You will see the apps in the folder:

You can put a lot of apps into a single folder. You do this by dragging the apps on top of the folder of your choosing.

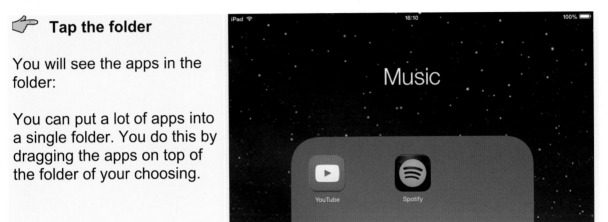

This is how you remove an app from the folder:

👉 **Press your finger on the app**

It will start to jiggle:

👉 **Drag the app outside the folder**

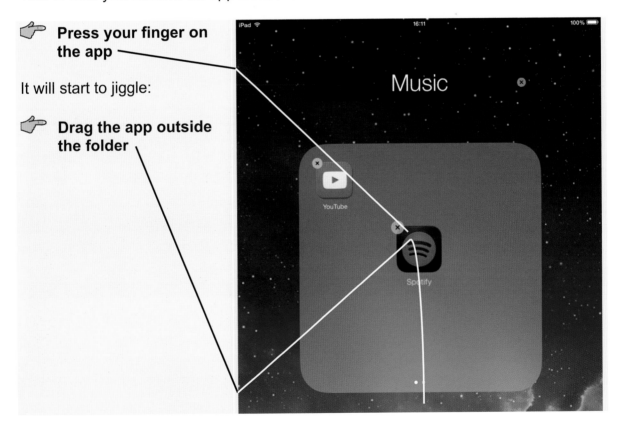

Now the app is displayed on the screen again as a separate app:

If you remove the other app from the folder as well, the folder will disappear.

To stop the apps from jiggling:

 Press the Home button

4.17 Deleting Apps

Have you downloaded an app that you no longer want to use? You can free up some memory space on your iPad by deleting the app.

 Please note:
You can only do this with the apps you have acquired in the *App Store*.

☞ **Press your finger on the app until it jiggles**

☞ **If you want to delete the app, tap** ⊗

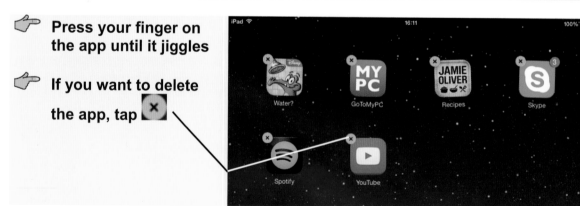

If you are really sure you want to delete the app:

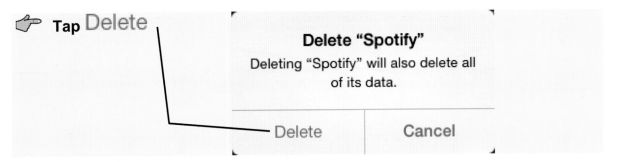

☞ **Tap** Delete

The app will be deleted. To stop the apps from jiggling:

☞ **Press the Home button**

4.18 Viewing the Apps You Purchased

In the *App Store* you can quickly see an overview of all the free and paid apps you have ever downloaded with your *Apple ID*. This overview also contains apps you have deleted from your iPad. You can reinstall one of these apps to your iPad, if desired. You will not be charged twice for the same app:

☞ **Open the *App Store*** 👣¹

At the bottom of the screen:

☞ **Tap** Purchased

By default, you will see all of the apps you have acquired:

To view the apps that have not been installed on this iPad:

☞ **Tap** Not on This iPad

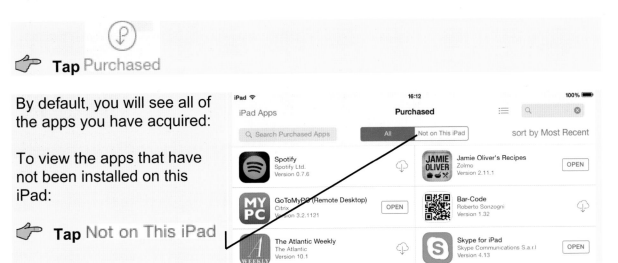

If you want to reinstall an app:

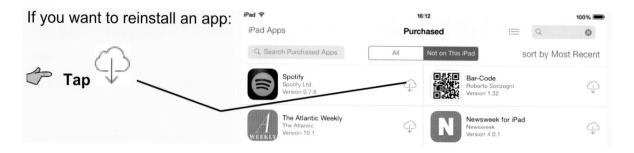

☞ Tap

4.19 Transferring Purchased Apps to the Computer

In *iTunes* you can copy the apps you have purchased (or acquired for free) to your computer. This way, you will always have a backup of your purchased apps, and you will be able to synchronize them with other devices, such as an iPhone. This is how you copy your purchases:

☞ **Open the *iTunes* program on your computer** 👣²

☞ **Connect your iPad to the computer**

First, you will need to authorize your computer to use the content you have downloaded with your iPad. If you have already done this previously, you will not need to do it again. In the upper left corner of your screen:

🖰 **Click** ▣ ▾

🖰 **Click** iTunes Store

🖰 **Click** Authorize This Computer...

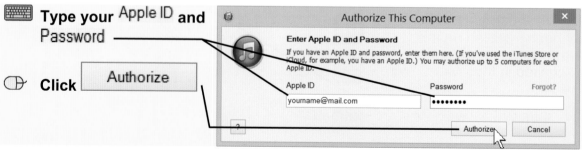

⌨ **Type your** Apple ID **and** Password

🖰 **Click** Authorize

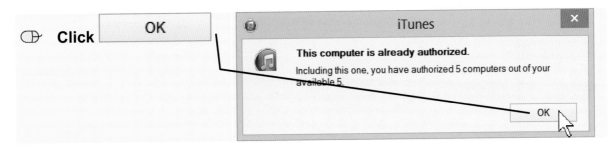

⊕ Click [OK]

Now you can transfer the apps from your iPad to your computer. First, you need to display the menu bar in *iTunes.* In the upper left corner of your screen:

⊕ Click □ ▾

⊕ If necessary, click Show Menu Bar

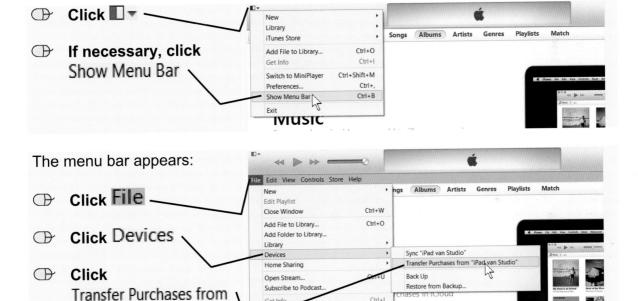

The menu bar appears:

⊕ Click File

⊕ Click Devices

⊕ Click Transfer Purchases from

The purchased apps on the iPad will be copied to the computer.

4.20 Transferring Apps to the iPad using iTunes

You can transfer the apps you have copied to *iTunes* and the apps you have purchased in the *iTunes Store* to your iPad:

☞ **Open *iTunes* on your computer** 🦶²

☞ **Connect your iPad to the computer**

If necessary, sign in with your *Apple ID*. In the upper left corner of your screen:

Click ▣▾

Click iTunes Store

Click Sign In...

⌨ Type your Apple ID and Password

Click Sign In

Click 📱 iPad ⏏

Click Apps

You will see the available apps:

If you want to copy an app, you need to select the screen where you want to put it:

Click the desired screen

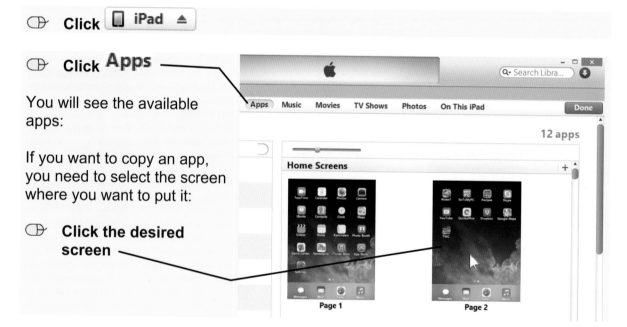

Drag the app to the screen

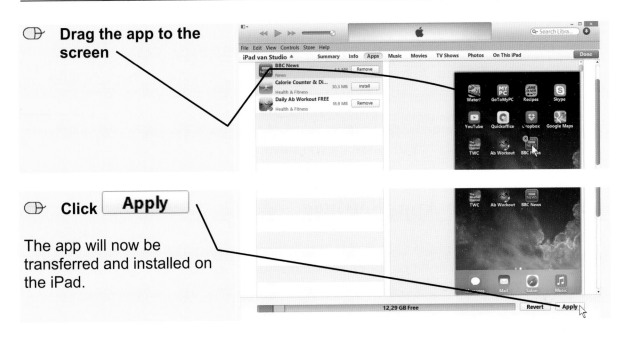

Click Apply

The app will now be transferred and installed on the iPad.

4.21 Transferring Apps from Other Devices to the iPad

If you use other *iOS* devices, such as an iPhone or an iPod touch, you can automatically download the apps you purchase in the *iTunes Store* or *App Store*, as well as books and music to all of your devices. In order to do this, you need to change a setting on each device:

☞ **Open the *Settings* app** 📖¹

☞ **Drag upwards across the left side of the screen**

☞ **Tap** 🅐 iTunes & App Store

☞ **If necessary, sign in with your *Apple ID***

☞ **Drag the slider by Apps to the right**

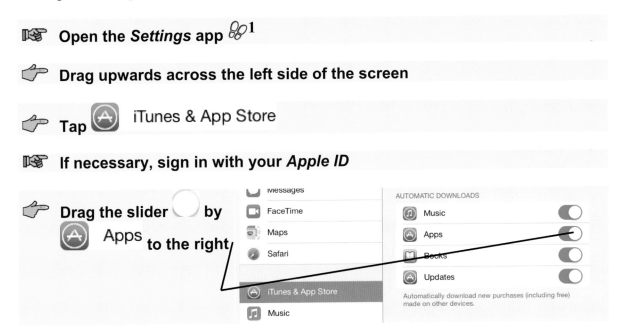

On the iPad Wi-Fi + 3G/4G it is better not to turn on Cellular Data. If you just use the Wi-Fi connection, the automatic downloads will only occur when a Wi-Fi connection is established. Automatic downloads processed through a mobile data network can lead to unexpected high costs.

If you have enabled automatic downloads on all of your devices, your purchases will be downloaded automatically as soon as you have a Wi-Fi connection.

4.22 Viewing the Apps Settings

The iPad allows you to make changes to the settings for many different functions. You can also adjust the settings for various individual apps. Selecting the proper setting can make it easier for you to use a certain app.

☞ **Open the *Settings* app** 🐾¹

👉 **Drag upwards across the left side of the screen**

In the column on the left-hand side you will see a list of all the apps, including the standard apps: ⎯⎯

Here you see the apps you have downloaded from the *App Store*: ⎯⎯

To display the settings for a specific app:

👉 **Tap the app**

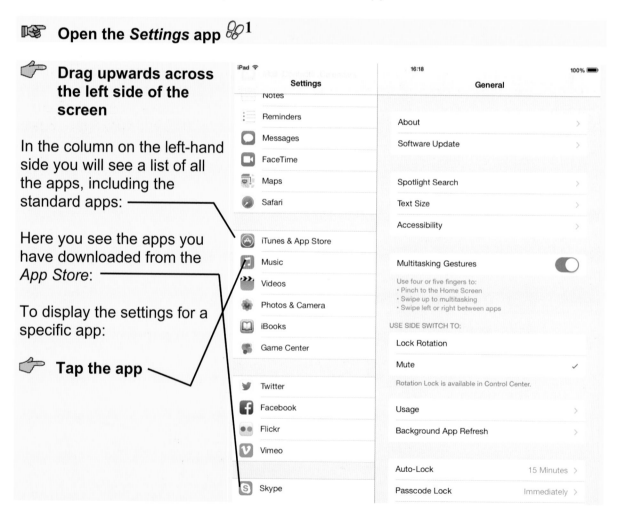

You will see the settings for this app:

Some apps offer more settings options than others. We recommend you carefully check these settings before you start using the app.

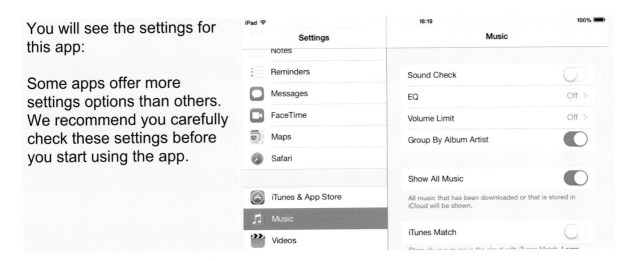

4.23 Viewing the Memory Usage of the Apps

Each time you open an app, it takes up memory space and some apps will take up memory space even if they are not open. For example, if you use the *Music, Photos* or *iBooks* app, they will have files stored on your iPad.
You can check to see how much memory space these apps are using on your iPad. This can be useful if your iPad becomes full. Typically, it will be the *Photos* and *Music* app that take up a lot of storage space:

Open the *Settings* app ❦¹

Tap General

Tap Usage

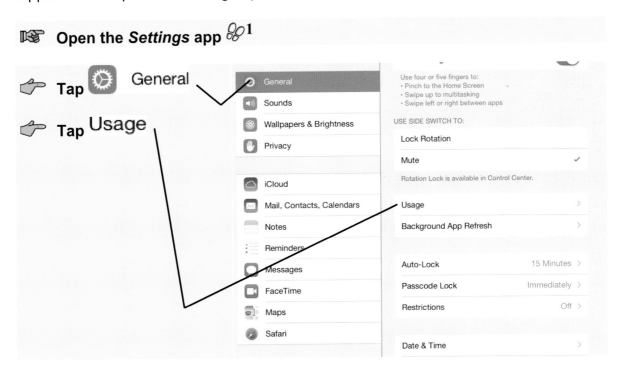

You will see the memory usage of various apps and components: ——————

You can view more detailed information for some of the apps:

👉 **Tap the desired app**

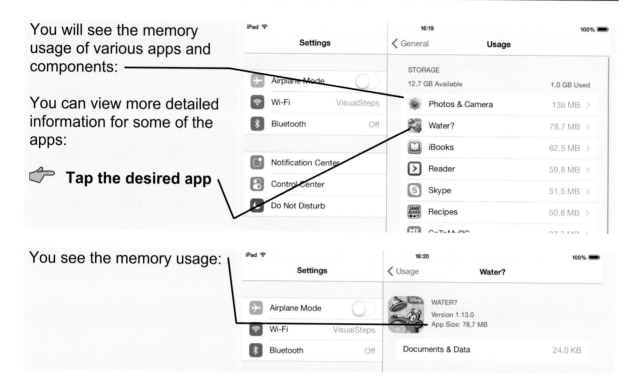

You see the memory usage:

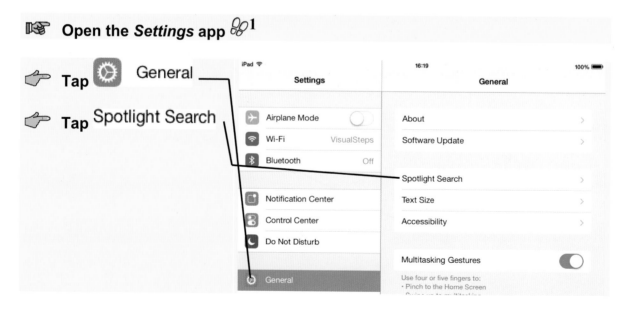

4.24 Setting Up Spotlight

Spotlight is the name of the iPad's search function. By default, *Spotlight* will search all the items on the iPad. If you wish, you can select the components that are to be searched by *Spotlight* yourself:

👉 **Open the *Settings* app** 👣 **1**

👉 **Tap ⚙ General** ——————

👉 **Tap Spotlight Search**

You will see the various components that are searched by *Spotlight*:

A checkmark ✔ means that the corresponding component is searched.

To add or remove components for *Spotlight* to search:

☞ **Tap the component**

If you want to change the order in which the various components are searched, just drag the component upwards or downwards by ▤ :

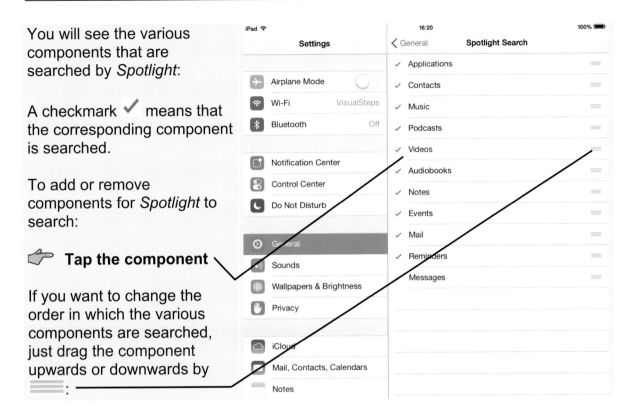

4.25 QuickOffice for Office Applications

The *QuickOffice* app is a simple Office suite (not from *Microsoft*) that lets you create files on your iPad that are compatible with *Microsoft Office*, and with other Office programs. The app does not offer the extensive options of the Office suites on a *Windows* computer or a Mac, but will allow you to work with the basic functions. In this way you can create a basic document on your iPad, and work out the details and formatting on your computer later on. You will need a *Google* account in order to use this app.

☞ **Tap**

Type your email address and password

Tap **Sign in**

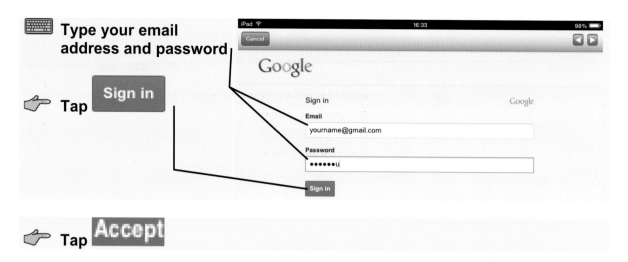

Tap **Accept**

The suite consists of a text editing app, a spreadsheet app and an app for creating presentations.

The home screen shows several options to help get you started:

You can create various types of files:

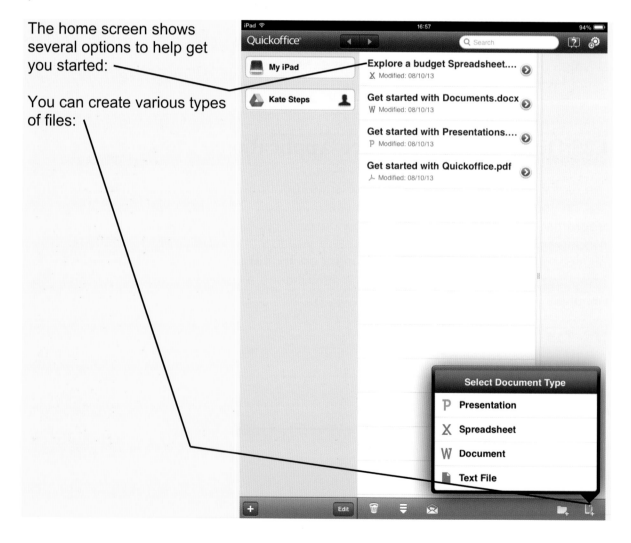

Here is an example of a *Quickword* file:

There are various options that allow you to format the text. One of these options is selecting a different font:

The other apps in this suite use the same type of screen. The apps are easy to use.

4.26 Dropbox

With the *Dropbox* app you can manage and share files with different computers and other devices. This app is the most popular of its kind, mainly because it is so easy to use. The app gives you 2 GB of free storage space on a *Dropbox* server. You can store a photo in the *Dropbox* folder on your computer and then view, save, and edit it on your iPad.

It makes no difference whether you have added a file to *Dropbox* on your iPad or on your computer.

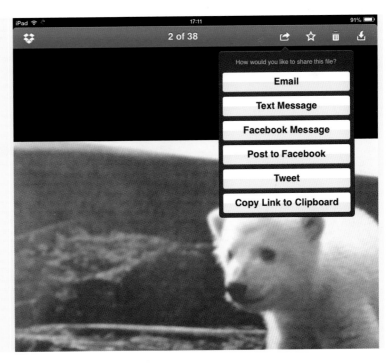

4.27 Google Maps

The free *Google Maps* app lets you view maps and get directions for places you want to visit. The app is an adequate substitute for *Maps,* one of the standard apps installed on the iPad.

 HELP! I cannot find the app in the App Store.

You may not immediately see the *Google Maps* app in the *App Store*. In that case, you can open the *Safari* app and go to the https://itunes.apple.com/app/id585027354?mt=8 web page. The *App Store* will be opened and you can download the app from there.

Google Maps will ask you if it can use your current location. If you allow this, you will see it appear on the map:

If you want to look for a specific location:

Search for the desired location by Q Search:

You can also get directions by entering the data after tapping the icon:

Once the location has been found you can display additional information by tapping the name of the location:

Next, you can open the *Google Street View* feature which will let you virtually 'walk' through the streets of the selected location.

If you tap ☰ you will see extra options, such as displaying the traffic conditions, or satellite photos:

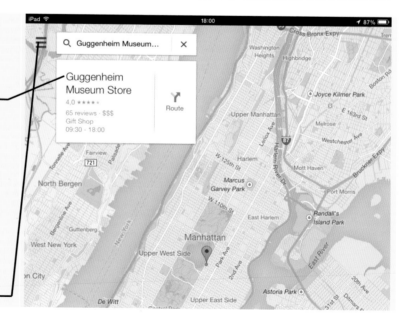

4.28 Money Journal HD

Money Journal HD is a personal finance app that will help you keep an overview of your income and expenses. The app is a paid app and can be downloaded in the *App Store*. You can enter your earnings and expenses, and view the result in various charts. Useful extra functions include an option to save data in *Dropbox*, an option to export data in the CSV or TSV formats which can then be imported into the *Excel* program on your computer, and various synchronizing options.

The home page displays a summary of recent expenses and your financial situation:

You will see various components of this app, such as the option for viewing charts:

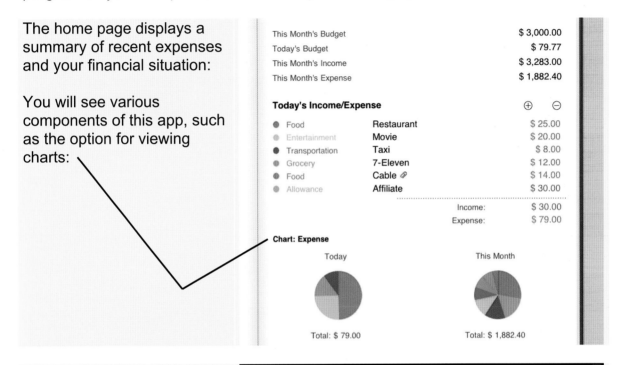

By tapping the + or − signs ⊕ ⊖ in the Income/Expenses section you can add new income and expenses:

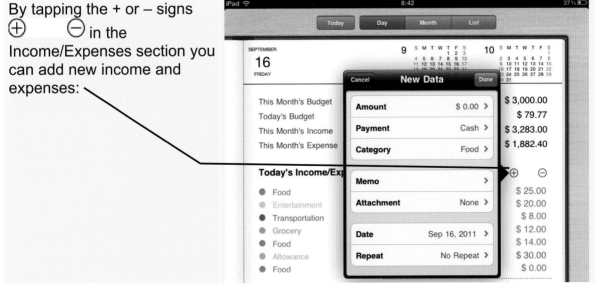

4.29 Weather Channel

The weather is always one of the most popular topics of conversation and as you may expect, there are many weather apps available in the *App Store*. One of the free apps is *The Weather Channel* app. You can quickly view the weather conditions and weather forecast on your iPad with this app. *The Weather Channel* also reports wind speeds and pollen forecasts, and offers beautiful photos.

Here you see *The Weather Channel* app:

In this view, you see a photo of a cloudy day. You also see lots of other weather information, such as the current temperature, humidity, wind speed and more.

You can view various components of the app and enter you own location, to find out what the weather will be like:

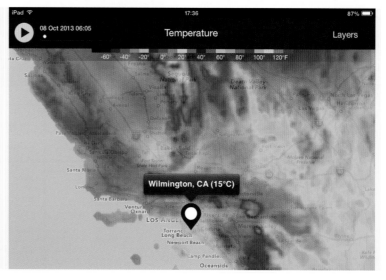

5. Photo and Video

It is not difficult to take pictures and record videos on the iPad. You can use either one of the cameras to do this. But there are some extra options you may not know about. For example, you can quickly take a picture by using the volume control button. And you can easily transfer photos and videos from the Internet to your iPad.

To arrange these photos and videos in an orderly way you can use albums. This chapter gives you tips on how to create, edit or delete albums in the *Photos* app.

There are some photo editing options available on your iPad. We will discuss these options and show you how to display your photos in a slideshow.

Do you already know about *Photo Stream*? This is a nice feature that lets you save your photos in the cloud and makes it possible to view your photos on other devices.

In this chapter we will provide you with tips on the following subjects:

- quickly take a picture with the volume control button;
- storing photos directly onto the iPad;
- transferring photos from the computer to the iPad;
- a photo as a background picture;
- a slideshow with music;
- deleting photos and videos;
- making a screen shot;
- working with albums;
- photo editing with the *Photos* app on your iPad;
- other photo editing apps;
- *Photo Stream* on your iPad;
- *Photo Stream* on your computer;
- Apple TV.

5.1 Taking a Picture with the Volume Control Button

In the *Camera* app you can take pictures by tapping a button on the touchscreen. But you can also do this by briefly tapping the volume control button. The advantage of using this button is that it will be easier for you to keep the iPad still while you are taking the picture.

☞ **Open the *Camera* app** 👣[1]

☞ **Point the camera to the object you want to photograph**

☞ **Press the volume button**

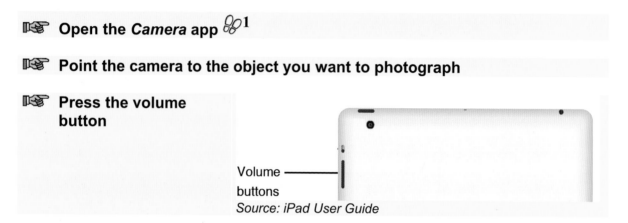

Volume ———
buttons
Source: iPad User Guide

The picture is taken and you will find it in the *Photos* app.

5.2 Storing Photos Directly onto the iPad

The *Camera Connection Kit* is a nice addition to your iPad. This is a set of two connectors that lets you transfer photos directly from your digital camera to your iPad, quickly and easily. The Camera Connection Kit costs about $25 or £24.50 (prices October 2013). It can be purchased from your Apple retailer and online from the Apple store. For the newest iPad and the iPad mini you can use a lightning to SD Card Camera Reader:

One of the connectors connects to your camera's USB cable: ———

If you do not have one, you can insert your SD card into the other connector: ———

☞ **Connect the wide connector to your iPad**

☞ **Connect your camera's USB cable or insert the SD card into the connector**

☞ **If necessary, open the *Photos* app** 🦶¹

With the Import All button you can import all the photos from the camera or the SD card to your iPad. You can also select just the photos you want:

👉 **Tap the photos you want to import** ——

You will see a checkmark ✓ appear by these photos:

👉 **Tap**

👉 **Tap** Import Selected

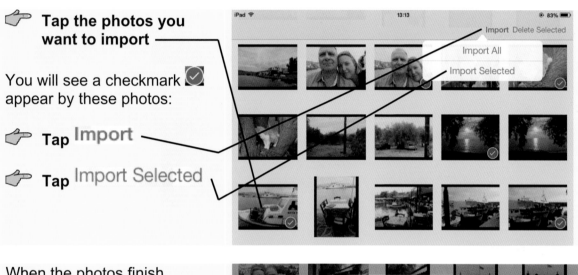

When the photos finish importing, you can decide whether you want to delete the photos on the camera:

👉 **Tap**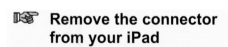

☞ **Remove the connector from your iPad**

You will see the imported photos on your iPad:

👉 **Tap** Albums

The imported photos have been put in a separate album:

The Camera Roll album contains all the pictures you have taken with your iPad:

Here you see the Last Import and All Imported albums:

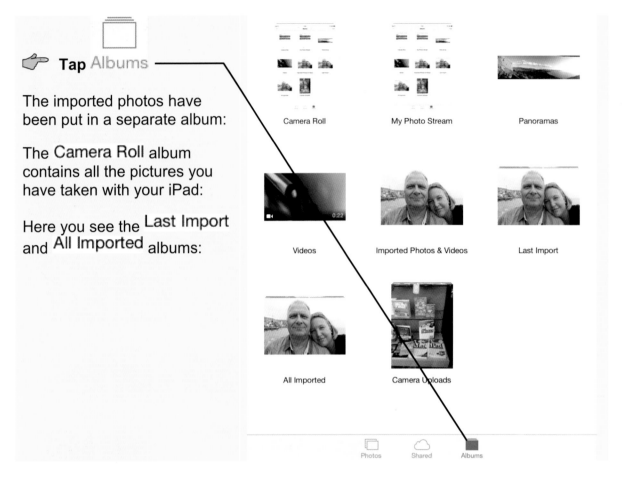

You can learn more about albums in *section 5.9 Working with Albums*.

5.3 Transferring Photos from the Computer to the iPad

Your iPad can come in handy when you want to show your favorite photos and videos to others. You can also display the photos and videos from your computer. You do this by synchronizing a folder with photos (and/or videos) with your iPad using *iTunes*.

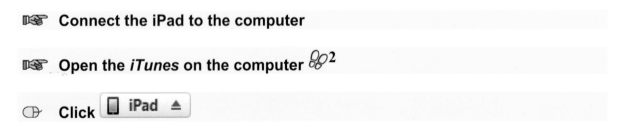

Look for the *Photos* tab in the top menu:

☞ **Click** **Photos**

In this example the photos that will be synchronized are stored in a subfolder of the *(My) Pictures* folder. You can select your own folder:

☞ **Check the box ☑ by Sync Photos from**

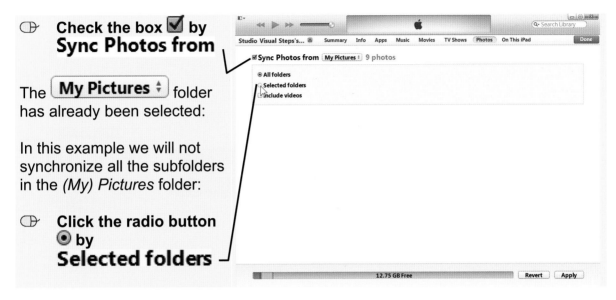

The **My Pictures ♦** folder has already been selected:

In this example we will not synchronize all the subfolders in the *(My) Pictures* folder:

☞ **Click the radio button ⦿ by Selected folders**

💡 **Tip**

Videos
If you want to synchronize the videos in this folder too:

☞ **Check the box ☑ by** **Include videos**

Now you select the folder(s) you want to synchronize with your iPad. You will see different folders than the folders in this example, of course:

☞ **Check the box ☑ by the desired folders, for example,** 📁 **Barcelona**

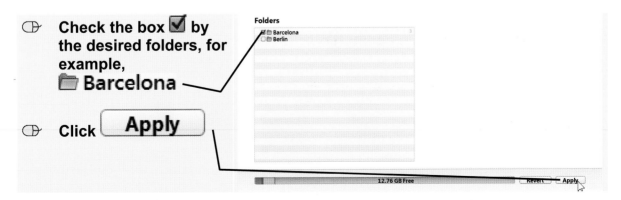

☞ **Click** **Apply**

The synchronization will start:

This area shows you the sync is in progess. When the syncing has finished:

☞ **Safely disconnect the iPad** 👣⁸

Now the photos will appear on your iPad.

☞ **Open the *Photos* app** 👣¹

👉 **If necessary, tap**

Albums

The stack of synchronized photos has been given the same name as the folder on your computer:

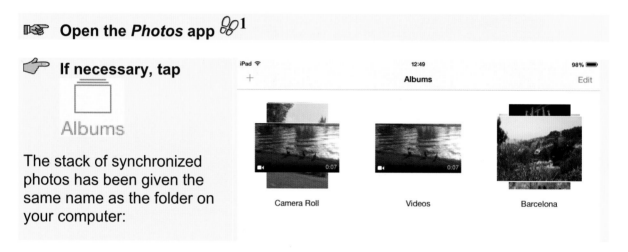

5.4 Showing the Location of a Photo or Video

If you had the location setting enabled while taking pictures or filming videos, you can look them up on the map:

☞ **Open the *Photos* app** 👣¹

👉 **Tap a location**

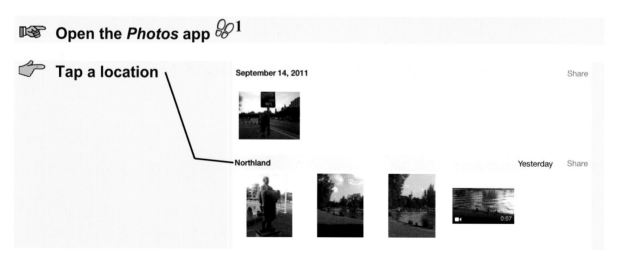

In this view you will see a map showing the locations where the photos were taken:

To go back to the recent view:

☞ **Tap** ‹ Moments **or** ‹ Collections

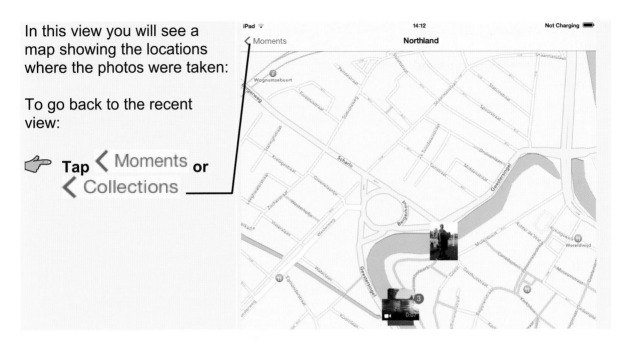

If you do not see any locations, then the Location Services for the *Camera* app have been turned off. See *section 1.7 Selecting Location and Privacy Settings*.

5.5 Using a Photo as a Background Picture

You can use a photo as a background picture (wallpaper) for the lock screen or the Home screen of your iPad. You do this using the *Photos* app:

☞ **Open the *Photos* app and open a photo** 𝄞5

☞ **Tap** ⬆️

☞ **Tap** Use as Wallpaper

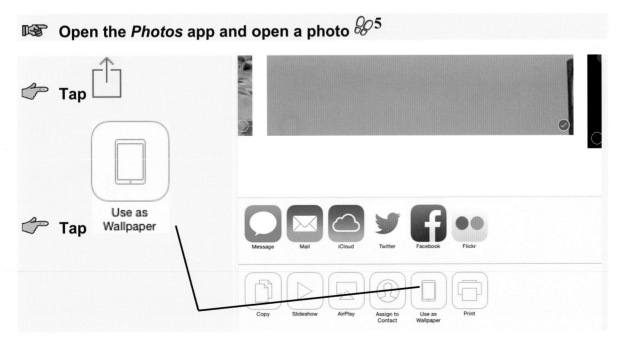

You can choose whether you want to use this background for the lock screen, the Home screen or both:

☞ **Tap the desired option**

Move and Scale

Cancel   Set Lock Screen   Set Home Screen   Set Both

5.6 A Slideshow with Music

You can also play your photos in a slideshow and if you want, you can even include background music. The music you have copied to your iPad or downloaded from the Internet can be used as the background music:

☞ **Open the *Photos* app and open a photo** 🦶**5**

☞ **Tap** 📤

☞ **Tap** Slideshow

To play the music:

☞ **Drag the slider ⬭ by** Play Music **to the right**

☞ **Tap** Music

Slideshow Options

Transitions   Dissolve >

Play Music

Music   None >

Start Slideshow

A list of songs will appear:

You can use the buttons at the bottom of the window to select a playlist, artist, or an album:

☞ **Select the desired song**

☞ **Tap ⊕**

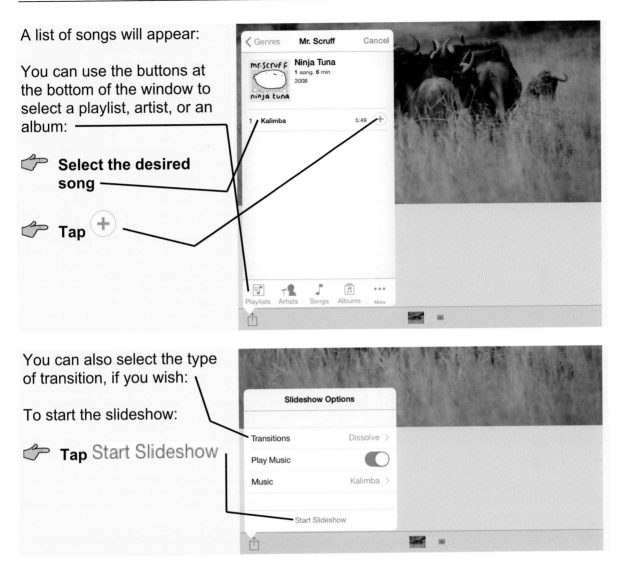

You can also select the type of transition, if you wish:

To start the slideshow:

☞ **Tap** Start Slideshow

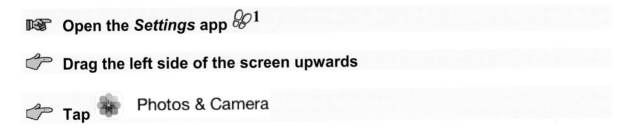

In the *Settings* app you can change some additional settings for playing the slideshow:

☞ **Open the *Settings* app** 🦶[1]

☞ **Drag the left side of the screen upwards**

☞ **Tap** 🌸 Photos & Camera

You will see the various slideshow settings that can be edited:

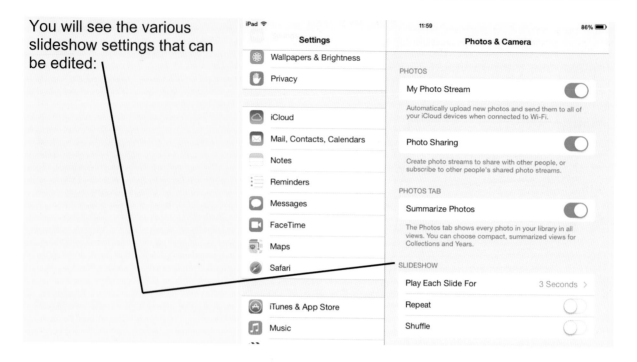

5.7 Deleting Photos and Videos

There are several ways of deleting photos and videos with the *Photos* app. This is how you delete an individual photo or video:

☞ **Open the *Photos* app and open a photo or a video** 🐾⁵

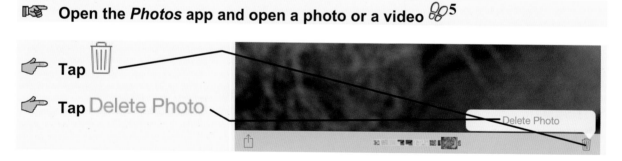

☞ **Tap** 🗑

☞ **Tap** Delete Photo

You can also delete multiple photos and videos at once. You can do this in the photos and videos overview screen:

☞ **If necessary, tap** ‹ Camera Roll

☞ **Tap** Select

Now you select the photos and videos you want to delete:

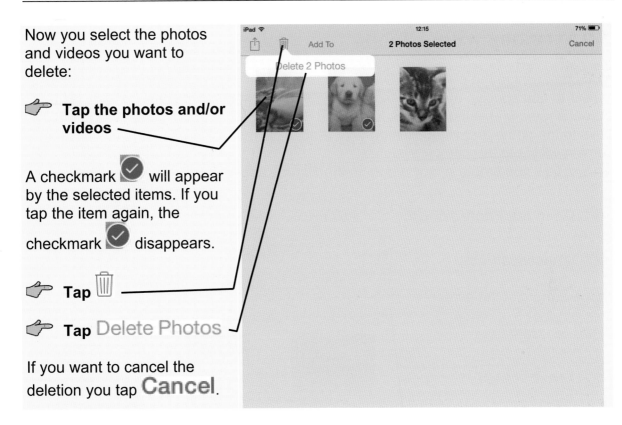

👉 **Tap the photos and/or videos**

A checkmark ✅ will appear by the selected items. If you tap the item again, the checkmark ✅ disappears.

👉 **Tap**

👉 **Tap** Delete Photos

If you want to cancel the deletion you tap Cancel.

🔖 **Please note:**

If you have used *iTunes* to transfer photos to your iPad you can only delete these photos from your iPad by using *iTunes* again. In *section 5.3 Transferring Photos from the Computer to the iPad* you can read how to transfer photos using *iTunes*.

5.8 Taking Screen Shots

You can use your iPad to take a screen shot. You can use such an option, among other things, to convert a specific image in a video to a photo and then save it. You can also capture the screen of a web page. Here is how to do that:

👉 **Simultaneously press the power button and the Home button**

You will hear the sound of a photo camera. Now the screen shot has been added to the *Photos* app and you can view it there.

5.9 Working with Albums

You can arrange the photos and videos in the *Photos* app into albums. This makes it easier to find specific photos or videos, and you can keep your collection tidy. The actual photos and videos will not be moved to the album, but the album will contain links to the photo and video files on your iPad. This means that the photos will also remain visible in the photos overview.

This is how you create a new album in the *Photos* app:

☞ **Open the *Photos* app** ⚇**1**

☞ **If necessary, tap ‹ Albums**

At the bottom of the screen:

☞ **Tap Albums**

This is how you create a new album:

☞ **Tap +**

⌨ **Type a name for the album**

☞ **Tap Save**

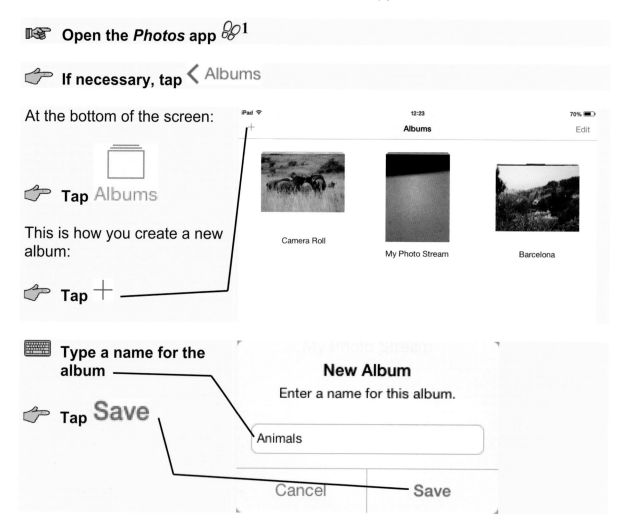

Now you select photos and videos to add to the album:

👉 **Tap the photos and/or videos**

A checkmark ✓ appears by the selected items. If you tap the item again, the checkmark disappears.

If you want to add all the photos, tap Select All.

👉 **Tap Done**

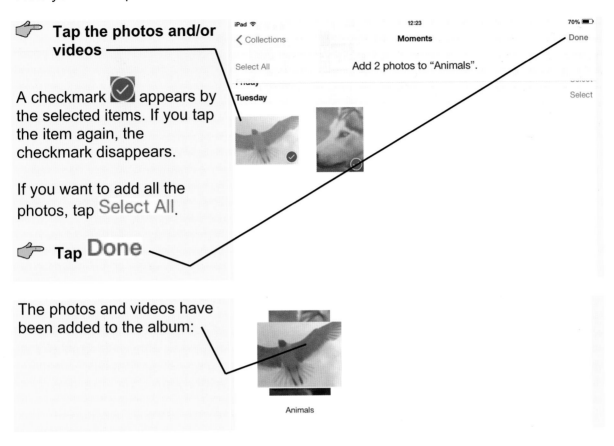

The photos and videos have been added to the album:

Animals

You can also add photos and videos to an existing album:

👉 **Tap Albums**

👉 **Tap the desired album**

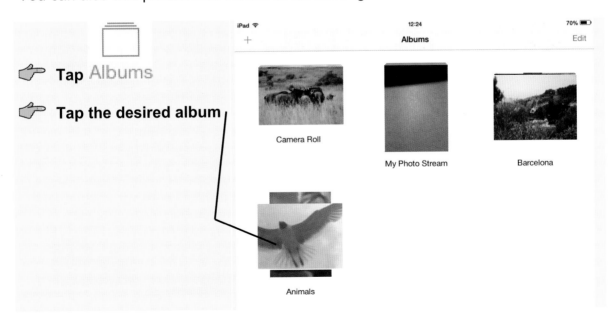

Select the photos/videos:

👉 **Tap** Select

👉 **Tap the photos and/or videos**

👉 **Tap** Add To

👉 **Tap the album**

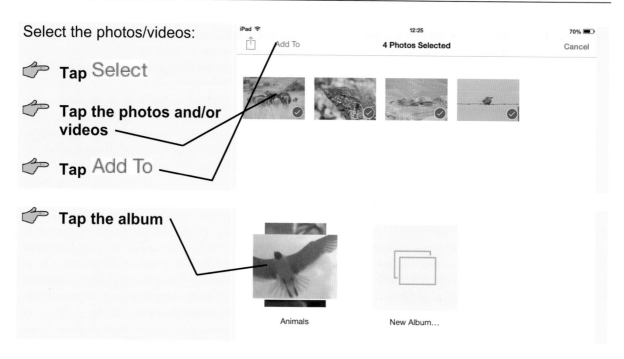

If you decide to put the photo in a new album, you tap New Album..., type a name for the album and then tap Save.

If you no longer need an album you can delete it. The photos and videos will not be deleted and will still remain stored on your iPad:

👉 **If necessary, tab** ‹ Albums

👉 **Tap** Albums

👉 **Tap** Edit

👉 **By the desired album, tap** ⊗

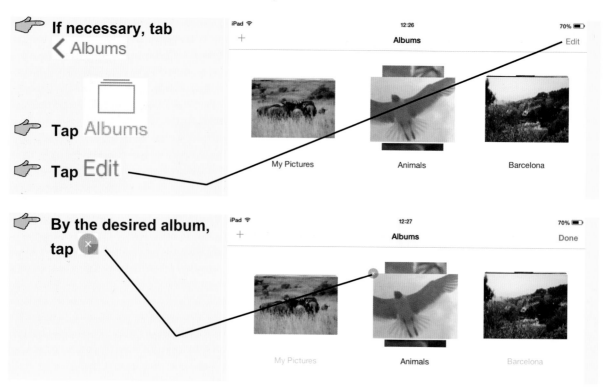

☞ **Tap** Delete Album

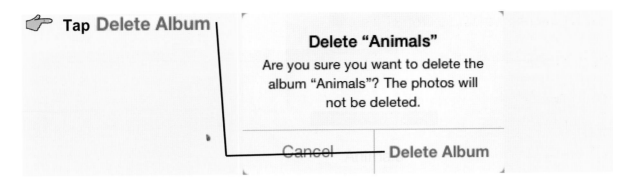

Delete "Animals"
Are you sure you want to delete the
album "Animals"? The photos will
not be deleted.

Cancel — Delete Album

5.10 Photo Editing on Your iPad using the Photos App

The *Photos* app gives you various options for enhancing your photos. You can rotate a photo, remove red eye, apply the auto-enhance option, crop a photo or use a filter. In this section we will give you an example of how to crop a photo.

☞ **Open the** *Photos* **app and open a photo** 🐾⁵

☞ **If necessary, tap the photo**

☞ **Tap** Edit

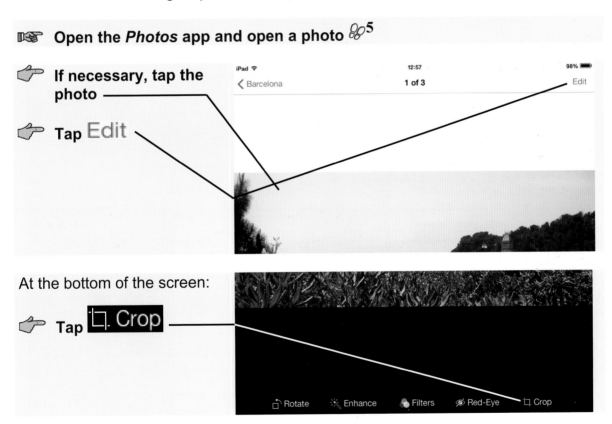

At the bottom of the screen:

☞ **Tap** 🔲 Crop

In this example we will be cropping a building:

You will see a transparent
frame with nine squares,
overlaying the photo:

You can move this frame:

 **Drag the top right-
hand corner to the
bottom left a bit**

You will see that the view of
the photo will be adapted to
the frame at once.

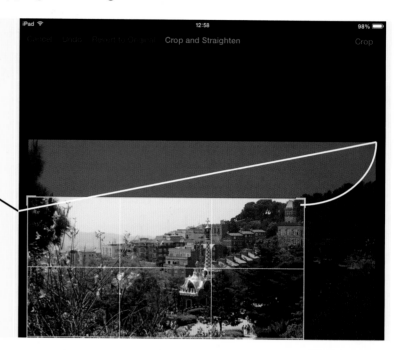

 **Drag the top left-hand
corner to the top right
a bit**

Now the height/width ratio of
the photo is no longer correct.
Select the desired ratio:

 **Tap** (Aspect Ratio)

The iPad's screen has a 4 x 3
ratio:

 **Tap** 4 × 3

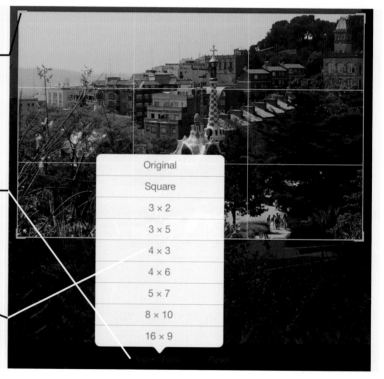

The selected ratio has been applied to the cropped section.

If necessary, you can move the photo in order to position the object on the correct spot in the frame.

With the Revert to Original button you can restore the original photo:

You may need to practice the cropping operation for a while before getting a good result.

To actually crop the photo:

 Tap Crop

You will see the cropped photo:

To save the photo:

 Tap Save

 Please note:

If you have transferred photos to the iPad from your computer, you still need to tap Save to Camera Roll. Then a copy of the photo will be saved in the camera roll.

To view the photo you have saved, you need to do the following:

 Tap the name of the album, for example ❮ Barcelona

 Tap the last photo

You will see the edited photo.

5.11 Other Photo Editing Apps

You may find the photo editing options offered by the standard *Photos* app to be somewhat limited. There are many more apps that can be used for editing photos which have more extensive options.

In the *App Store* you can find all the photo (and video) apps by tapping Featured, More, and Photo & Video.

One good example of a free app is the *Photo Editor* app by *Aviary*. With this app you can crop and enhance photos, edit the colors and exposure, frame the photos, add text and do many other things as well.

At the bottom of the screen you see the components of this app:

At the top you see a settings button for the app:

You can also use the Share button at the bottom to share photos with others:

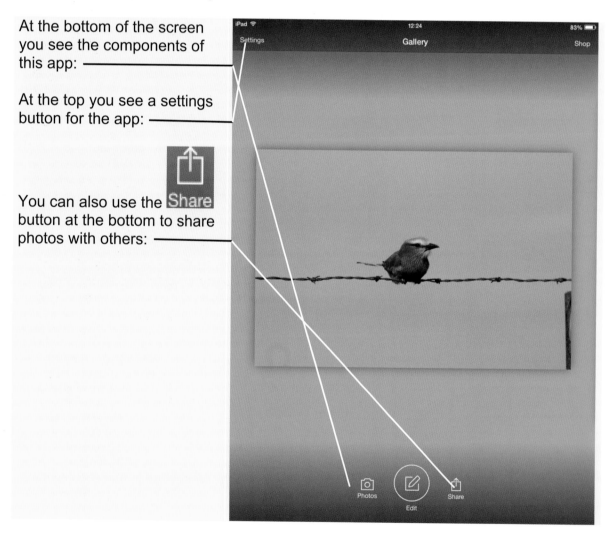

Here is the screen with the editing options: —————

At the bottom you will see various options. By dragging across the bar at the bottom you can display even more options.

Tap an option to apply it, or to change the settings for this option. Some options also give an explanation.

5.12 Photo Stream on Your iPad

With the *Photo Stream* function you can synchronize your photos using *iCloud*. *Photo Stream* will automatically send the photos on your camera roll to *iCloud* when you are connected to the Internet. These photos will then be downloaded automatically to all other devices or locations you have set up in *iCloud* and *Photo Stream*. In this way, you can view your photos on all of your devices, or save the photos you have taken with your iPad on your computer by copying them to a different folder.

Please note:
You will need to have *iCloud* already set up (if you wish, read *section 1.22 Find My iPad* to review how to set up *iCloud*) and have your *Apple ID* at hand.

☞ **Open the *Settings* app** [1]

👉 Tap ☁ iCloud

👉 Tap ✳ Photos

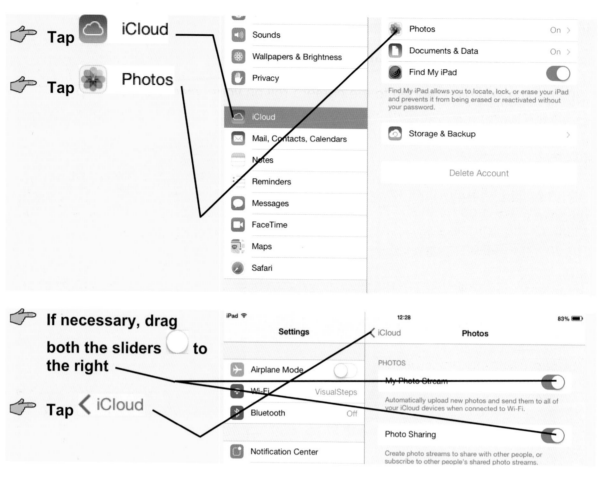

👉 **If necessary, drag both the sliders ◯ to the right**

👉 **Tap ‹ iCloud**

From now on, the pictures you take with the *Camera* app will be synchronized with *iCloud* and with all the other devices on which you have set up *iCloud*.

👉 **Open the *Camera* app** 👣¹

👉 **Take a few pictures** 👣⁹

👉 **Open the *Photos* app** 👣¹

👉 Tap My Photo Stream

👉 **Tap the album**

When you open the *Photos* app on the other devices where you have enabled *Photo Stream* and Wi-Fi, you will see the *My Photo Stream* album there too.

Tip

Content of the My Photo Stream album
The content of the album called *My Photo Stream* will automatically change: the last 1.000 photos you have added to the camera roll on your devices will be displayed. New photos will be saved in *iCloud* for 30 days.

 Tip

Edit and delete
You can edit and delete the photos in the *My Photo Stream* album in the same way as you edit the photos on your camera roll. If you save an edited photo this will also be added to your camera roll. And the edited photo on your camera roll will be copied automatically to the *My Photo Stream* album.

If you want to permanently save a photo that has been added to your *Photo Stream* on another device, you need to save this photo to the camera roll in the *My Photo Stream* album. Here is how you do that:

☞ **Tap the desired photo**

☞ **Tap** ⬆️

☞ **Tap** Save to Camera Roll

The photo will be saved in the camera roll on your iPad.

If you have saved an unedited photo from *My Photo Stream* in your camera roll, this photo will not be added to the album for a second time. This prevents the *My Photo Stream* album from containing duplicate photos.

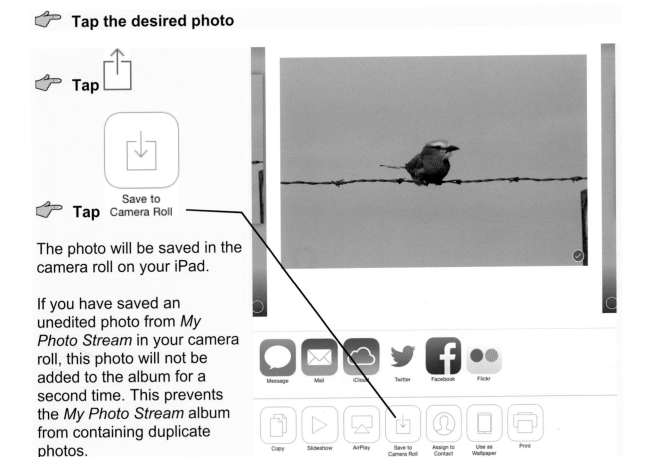

5.13 Photo Stream on Your Computer

At the time we were writing this book, it was not possible to view the photos in *Photo Stream* on the www.icloud.com website. If you own a *Windows* computer you will be able to synchronize the photos by using the *iCloud control panel*. This is a small program from the *Apple* website that you can download and install onto your computer. This is how you do that:

☞ **Open the www.apple.com/icloud/setup/pc.html website** ✂️4

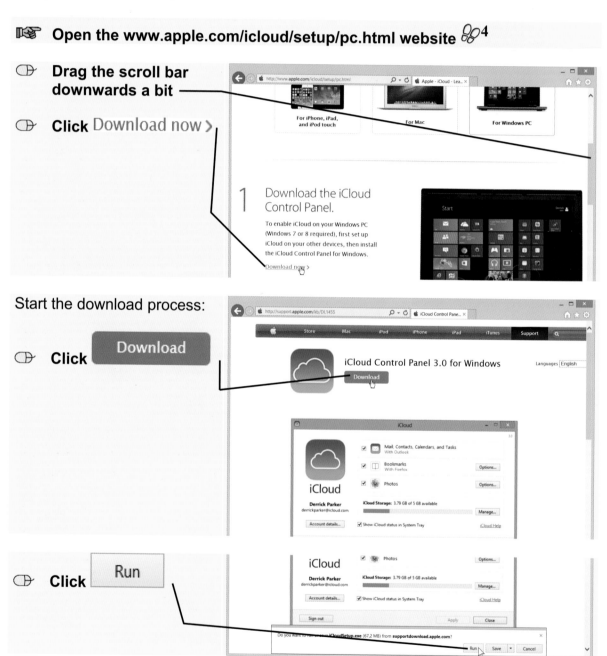

Drag the scroll bar downwards a bit —

Click Download now ➤

Start the download process:

Click **Download**

Click Run

The program is downloaded. When that has finished, you will see the window of the installation program:

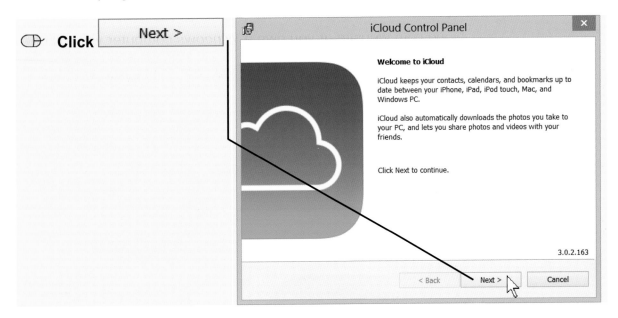

Agree to the license terms:

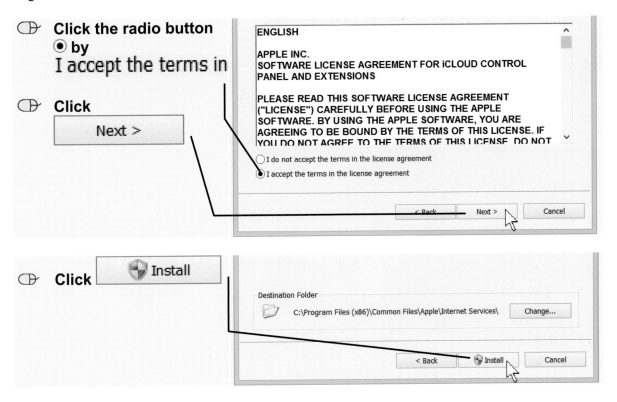

Your screen may turn dark and you will be asked to give permission to continue:

☞ Give permission to continue

You will see the progress of the installation:

After the installation has finished you will see this window:

☞ **Click** Finish

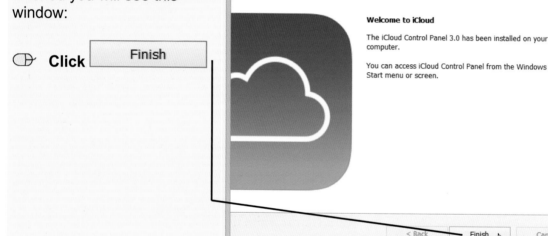

You have to restart your computer:

☞ **Click** Yes

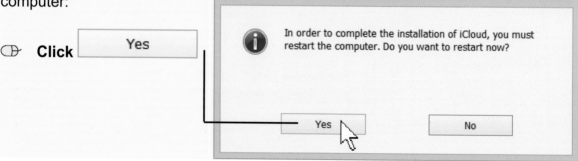

Your computer will restart. Next, you will be able to sign in with your *Apple ID*:

Type your *Apple ID*

Type your password

Click Sign in

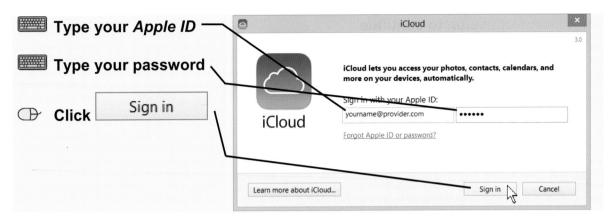

You may see this window:

If necessary, click the desired option

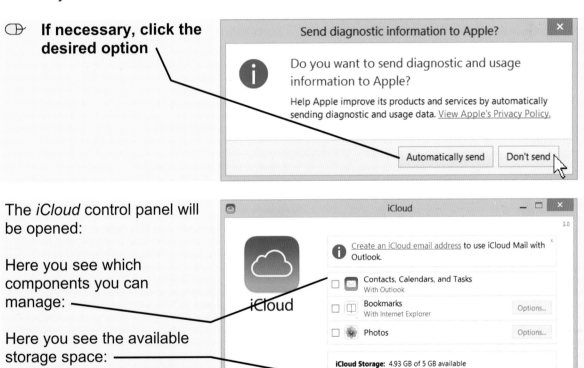

The *iCloud* control panel will be opened:

Here you see which components you can manage:

Here you see the available storage space:

By default, the *iCloud* status is displayed in the bottom right-hand corner of your computer screen:

Now you can set up *Photo Stream*:

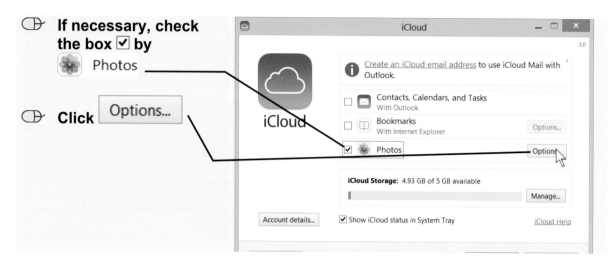

If necessary, check the box ☑ by
   ❋ Photos

Click Options...

Two new folders will be created for *Photo Stream*, an upload and a download folder. They are placed by default in the (*My*) *Pictures* folder of your computer. The pictures you take with your iPad or save in the camera roll will automatically be put in the download folder. In the upload folder you can place the photos you want to send to *Photo Stream*. These photos will then appear in the *Photo Stream* album on your iPad.

Here you see the location of the download and upload folders:

If you wish, you can change the location of these folders. For now, this will not be necessary:

Click OK

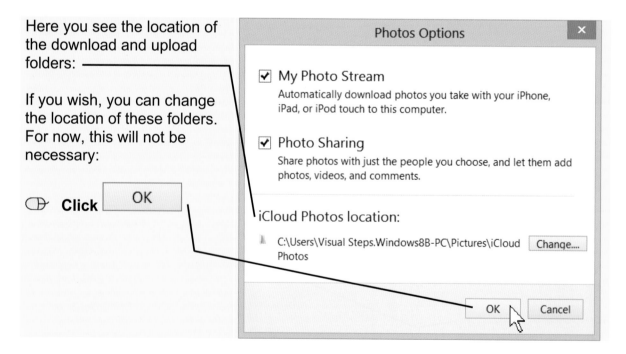

Apply the changes:

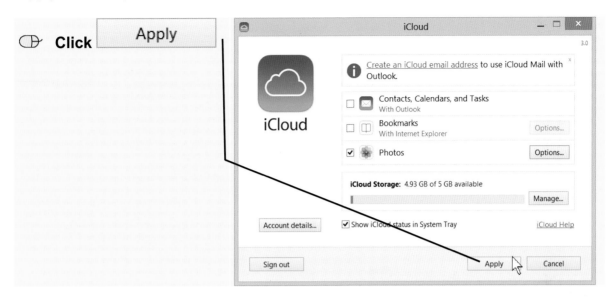

Close the *iCloud* control panel:

☞ **Close the Internet browser window** 👣**3**

The photos will automatically be copied from *Photo Stream* to the download folder on your computer. You can verify this.

In *Windows 7* and *Vista*:

In *Windows 8* on the taskbar:

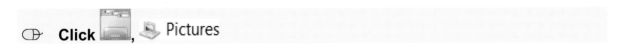

The *Pictures* folder will be opened. The content of this folder on your own computer may look different from this example.

Double-click

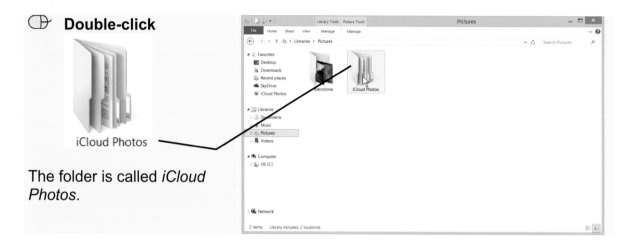

The folder is called *iCloud Photos*.

The *Photo Stream* folder contains two subfolders, *My Photo Stream* and *Uploads*:

Double-click

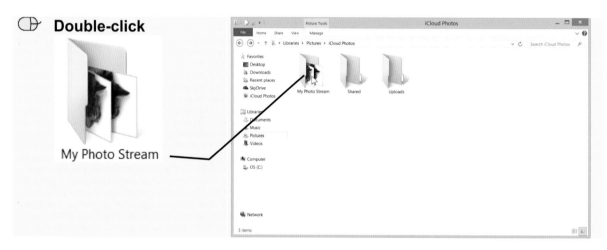

You will see the photos that have been added to *Photo Stream* on your iPad:

Please note:

The content of the *My Photo Stream* folder is continuously updated. It can contain up to 1000 photos. A new photo will be saved for no longer than 30 days. If you want to save a photo for longer periods of time you will need to copy it to a different folder on your computer.

The photos in the *Uploads* folder will automatically be added to the *Photo Stream*. You can give it a try. You can use one of your own photos:

⬚ **Click** ⬅ **twice**

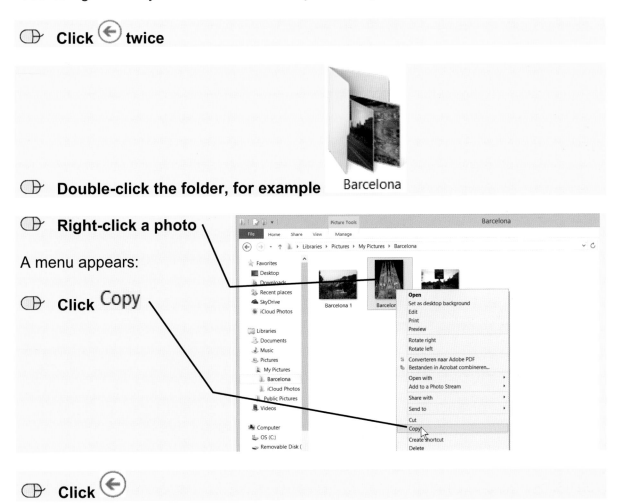

⬚ **Double-click the folder, for example** Barcelona

⬚ **Right-click a photo**

A menu appears:

⬚ **Click** Copy

⬚ **Click** ⬅

Open the *Uploads* folder:

⬚ **Double-click** iCloud Photos , Uploads

Paste the photo into the *Uploads* folder:

☞ **Right-click an empty part of the window**

☞ **Click** Paste

Now the photo has been added to the *Uploads* folder:

☞ **Close the *Uploads* window** 𝒢³

The photo will be uploaded to *iCloud* automatically and from there it will be added to the *My Photo Stream* album on your iPad. You can check this on your iPad:

☞ **Open the *Photos* app** 𝒢¹

☞ **If necessary, tap my** My Photo Stream

You will see that the photo has been added to the *My Photo Stream* album.

☜ **Please note:**

If you delete a photo in the *My Photo Stream* folder on your computer, this photo will not be deleted from the *My Photo Stream* album on your iPad or on any other device. But if you delete a photo in the *My Photo Stream* album on your iPad, this photo will be deleted from the *My Photo Stream* folder and from the *My Photo Stream* album on any other device.

You can delete all the photos in the *Photo Stream* on your computer at once, by resetting the *Photo Stream*.

If you do not intend to use *Photo Stream* in future, you can drag the slider in the iPad's *Settings* app back to the left. From then on, the pictures you take will no longer be synchronized with *iCloud*. The *My Photo Stream* album will no longer appear on your iPad, but the *Photo Stream* on *iCloud* will still be there.

5.14 YouTube

YouTube is the name of the extremely popular website where literally millions of videos can be found in all sorts of categories. You can watch these videos on your iPad using the *Safari* app or with *YouTube's* own dedicated app. It can be downloaded for free in the *App Store*. This app also lets you upload your own videos to the *YouTube* website. In this section, we will explore some of the features of the *YouTube* app.

☞ **Open the *YouTube* app** 🐾¹

You can use the search box to search for videos:

You will see the search results on the screen:

☞ **Tap a video**

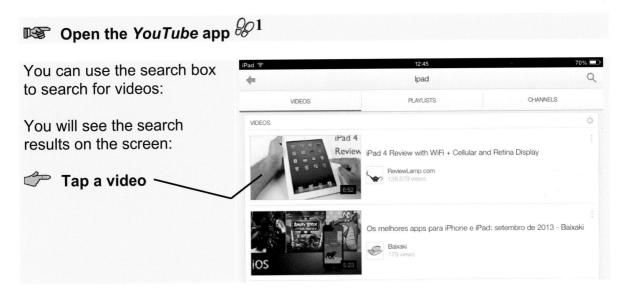

The video will be played automatically.

Below the video you will see the playback buttons:

You can display the video in full-screen mode, if you wish:

You will see various buttons for reviewing and sharing the video:

You can also view the comments the video has received and watch other recommended videos:

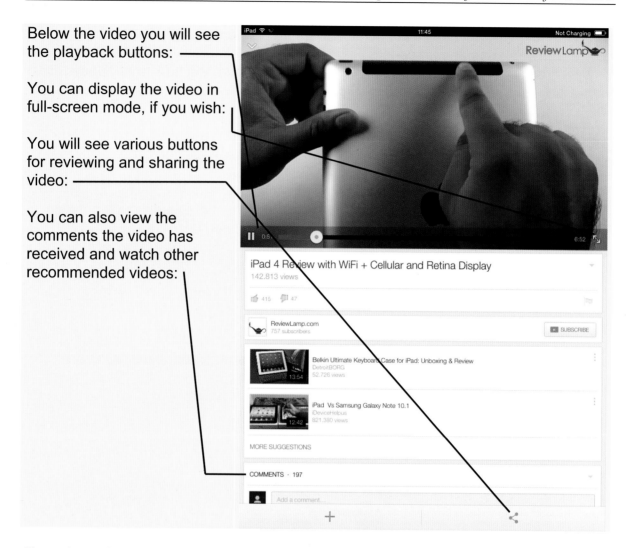

If you have found an interesting video on *YouTube* you can add it to the 'Watch Later' list or add it as a favorite to your favorite list.

 **Please note:**

To use this option, as well as several others on *YouTube*, you need to have a *Google* account. You can create such an account on www.youtube.com, **Sign in** and **CREATE AN ACCOUNT**.

This is how you sign in:

 **Tap** SIGN IN

⌨ **Type your email address and password**

☞ **Tap** Sign in

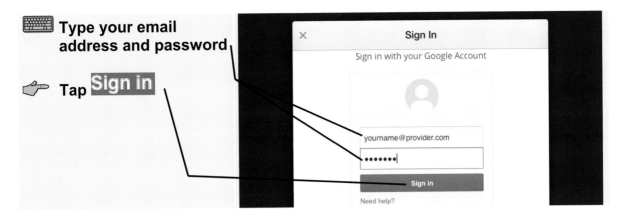

You will see this window:

☞ **Tap the desired option**

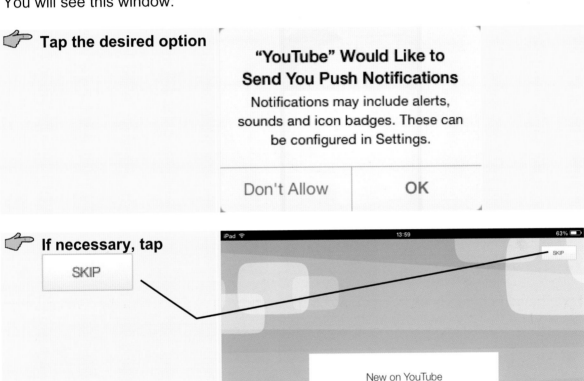

☞ **If necessary, tap** SKIP

You will see options by the
+ and < buttons:

There are millions of videos on *YouTube*. A large part of these have been added by individual people. This can be done not only with a computer, but also with an iPad as well. This is how you upload a video:

☞ **Open the video in the *Photos* app** 👣⁵

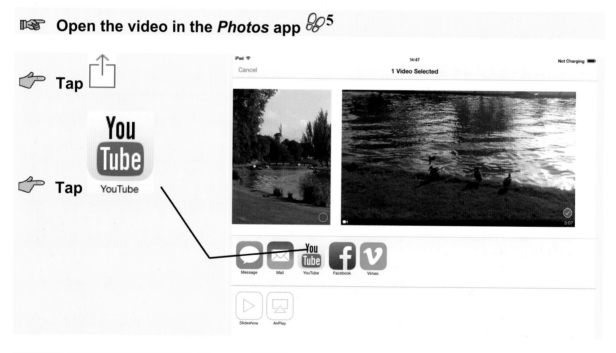

☞ **Sign in with your *YouTube* account and follow the instructions in the next few screens**

5.15 Watching Online TV on Your iPad

Since television broadcasts have been digitized, the options for watching TV on your computer or tablet have increased enormously. You can also watch TV shows on the iPad, provided you use the right apps. These apps will let you watch clips, full episodes of old TV shows, or even live broadcasts, depending on the network or broadcasting corporation. Getting these live images from the Internet is called streaming.

Unfortunately, there is no app available that presents you with an overview of all the television shows in English-speaking countries; each country or network has its own apps. For example, the *BBC iPlayer* and the *ITV Player* app are available for the iPad in the UK and the Australian Broadcasting Corporation has its own app for Australia. Many of the American networks have their own apps as well, such as the *Watch ABC* app and the *TV.com* app by CBS.

Almost all of these apps are free of charge and can be downloaded from the *App Store* using *iTunes*.

With the *BBC iPlayer* app you can find all the BBC programs:

You can search for a specific program by using the search function:

At the bottom of the screen you will see other options that will help you find your favorite programs. For example, the Genre option:

After you have selected a video, tap [▷] and playback will start.

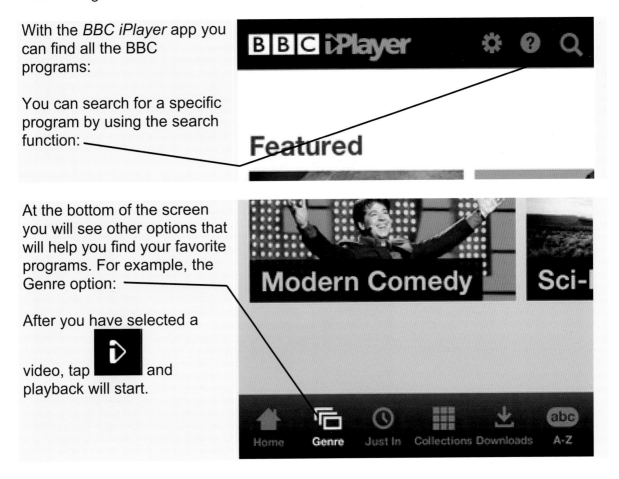

At the bottom you can see the playback buttons and the progress of the video clip: ——

While you are playing a TV show it is recommended that you hold the iPad horizontally (landscape orientation). If you want to watch the video full screen, tap ⊞:

After you have finished, you tap the screen and tap the icon in the bottom right of the screen to go back to the previous screen.

The American *DIRECTV* app has options for watching various TV channels, although the programs are limited. You can watch favorite TV shows and movies, and create playlists.

These are some of the control buttons:

Another possibility for watching TV on your iPad is with an app provided by your cable provider. The app is usually free, but you need to subscribe to a cable provider before you can watch TV on your tablet or computer. You can download the app from the provider's website or from the *App Store*.
Examples of these types of apps are *HBO GO*, *TWC TV*, and *Sky* in the UK. On the cable provider's website you can check various options and find out whether they offer online TV options. Furthermore, there are specialized services such as *Hulu* and *Netflix* that provide all sorts of online TV and movie streams, at a fee. You need to subscribe to these services to watch their content on the iPad.

Watching TV on your iPad is a lot like watching TV on your television set. Not only can you can zap through the channels, you can also watch previously recorded programs as well, and you may even be able to purchase premium content such as movies that have just been released. There are some restrictions though compared to your TV. Not all of the TV channels will be available on your iPad. And some digital services such as renting and watching videos require a regular TV or a setup box.
If you want to use online TV you need to have a wireless Internet connection and you need to be at home. You will not be able to watch TV while you are travelling by train or by car. But watching your favorite show at home is no problem at all.
If you subscribe to a cable provider, you will usually need to sign in with a user name and a password, in order to use their online TV service. Otherwise anyone would be able to use the app or website to watch the channels offered by the provider.

5.16 Apple TV

An iPad is very suitable for playing videos. The quality of the onscreen image is very high. But unfortunately the size of the screen is limited. If you want to use your iPad to watch Internet videos on your television, you can use Apple TV. You can buy Apple TV at your local Apple supplier.

Apple TV is a small square box of about 4 x 4 inches. It is connected to a TV and can wirelessly receive the video images and sounds of an iPad. You can also use this device to watch *iTunes* or *YouTube* videos on your TV.

Notes

Write your notes down here.

6. Entertainment

Do you often listen to music on your iPad? You may be able to enjoy your music even more by applying some additional settings. For instance, you can set a volume limit so that your music is never played too loudly or use the sound check option to play your songs at approximately the same volume level. If you have songs saved on your computer in *iTunes*, you can apply the home sharing option and play them on your iPad.

Your iPad contains an extensive music player in the form of the *Music* app. If you have saved music on your computer, you can transfer tracks using *iTunes* to your iPad. You can even create playlists with your favorite songs, if you wish.

We also have some good suggestions for a number of other music apps. A nice alternative to using *iTunes* is the *Spotify* app. You can get a free or paid subscription to this app and then listen to music on your iPad. If you like to listen to local, talk and sports radio stations, you will have a lot of choice by downloading the free *TuneIn Radio* app. It offers thousands of stations from around the globe.

Besides this there is the possibility of reading digital books (ebooks) on your iPad. We will show you how to transfer ebooks to the iPad. You can also use the *Newsstand* app to read magazines and newspapers that are free or subscription based.

In this chapter we will give you tips on the following subjects:

- setting the volume for playing music;
- setting up home sharing;
- creating a playlist in the *Music* app;
- transferring purchases to *iTunes*;
- importing CDs into *iTunes*;
- transferring songs from the computer to the iPad;
- listening to the radio on the iPad with *TuneIn*;
- purchasing music and listening to music with *Spotify*;
- making music with *Garageband*;
- transferring ebooks to the iPad;
- reading magazines and papers with *Newsstand*.

6.1 Sound Settings for Playing Music

You are used to controlling the volume on your iPad by using the volume control slider within an app or the volume buttons along the edge. There are also other options available for controlling the volume. When you play multiple music tracks one after the other using a playlist, (see *section 6.3 Creating a Playlist*), you will often notice that the songs are played with different volume levels. By turning the Sound Check option on, all the songs will be played at approximately the same volume level:

☞ **Open the *Settings* app** 🦶[1]

👉 **Drag upwards across the left side of the screen**

👉 **Tap** 🎵 Music

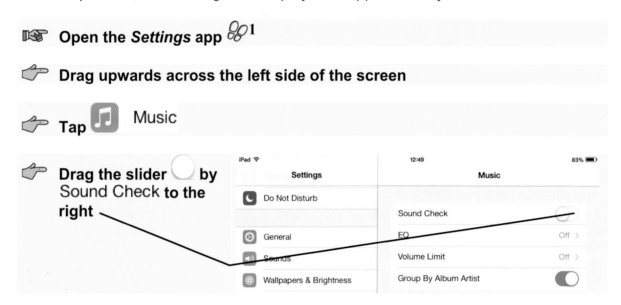

👉 **Drag the slider ◯ by Sound Check to the right**

The EQ function (equalization) allows you to set the volume for different tones (frequencies) in a song. There are several different options to choose from:

👉 **Tap EQ**

☞ **Tap one of the equalizer options**

For example, choose an equalizer effect that matches the type of music you want to play.

Now the equalizer will be set for that type of music.

Try out different EQ effects as you listen to other types of music.

☞ **Tap** ❮ Music

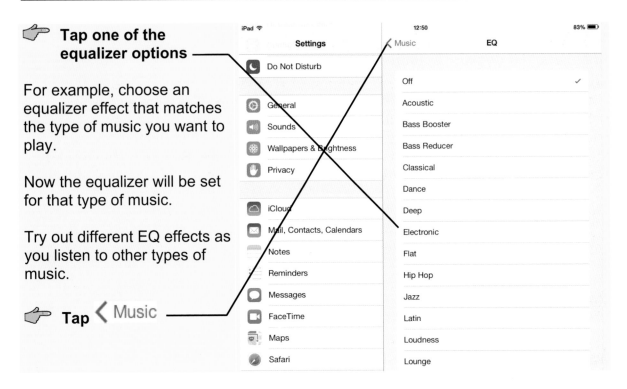

You can set a limit to the volume level and make sure the music is not played any louder than you want it to be:

☞ **Tap** Volume Limit

☞ **Drag the slider ◯ by to the desired volume**

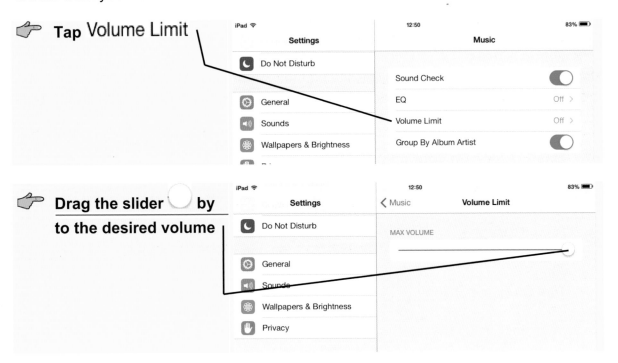

Tip

Speakers and docking station
The iPad is often used for playing music. Unfortunately the sound quality of the built-in speakers is rather limited. You can achieve better listening pleasure by using stand-alone speakers.

Wired speakers can be connected with a cable to the iPad's headphone jack. The downside of this method is that the cable often gets in the way. A wireless speaker or speaker set is much easier to use. Bluetooth speakers have a range of about 10 meters (30-35 feet) and can be used anywhere. Wireless speakers that use the Apple AirPlay system use an existing wireless network. Without such a network you will not be able to use this type of speaker.

Another type of speaker is the built-in kind that can be found in docking stations. A docking station is primarily intended for charging the iPad. But many times you can play music through the built-in speakers once the iPad is 'docked'. Many docking stations also come with a remote control.

6.2 Setting Up Home Sharing

If you use the home sharing option you can play music that is stored on your computer on your iPad, or on any other device made by Apple. You will need to use *iTunes* for this. This is how you set up home sharing:

Please note:
Home sharing uses the wireless AirPlay connection provided by Apple. To use such a connection you will need to have an active wireless home network. You will also need to turn the computer on and have the *iTunes* program open.

Open *iTunes* on your computer

Click **Click Library**

Click Turn On Home Sharing

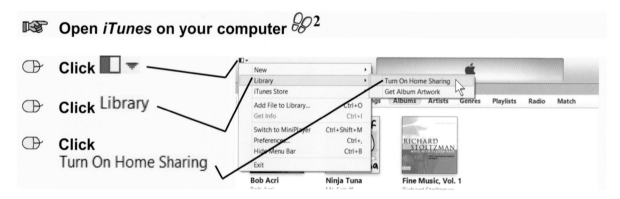

Type your *Apple ID* and password

Click

Turn On Home Sharing

You can activate home sharing on a maximum of 5 computers:

If your computer has not yet been authorized:

Click Authorize

Your computer will be authorized:

If necessary, click OK

Click Done

You will also need to change some settings on your iPad:

Open the *Settings* app 🦶1

Tap 🎵 Music

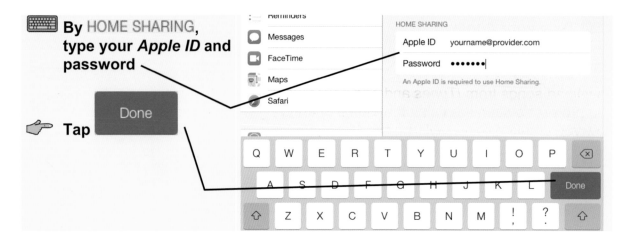

By HOME SHARING,
type your *Apple ID* and
password

☞ **Tap** Done

Now you can use the *Music* app to view and play any of the shared tracks:

☞ **Open the *Music* app** 🐾1

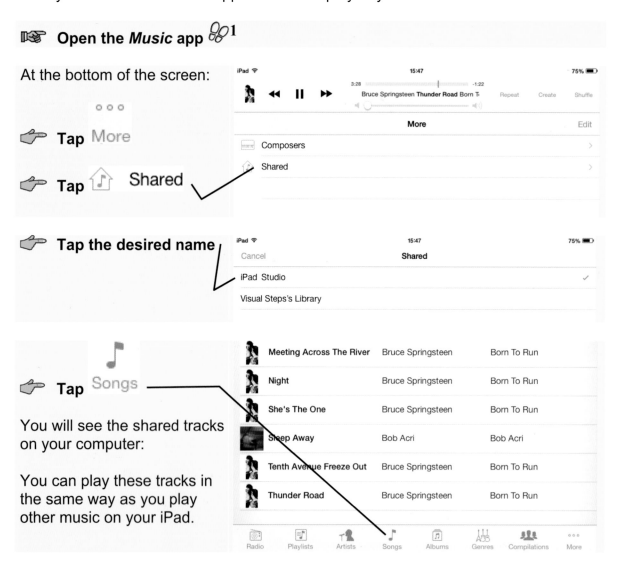

At the bottom of the screen:

☞ **Tap** More

☞ **Tap** 🏠 Shared

☞ **Tap the desired name**

☞ **Tap** Songs

You will see the shared tracks
on your computer:

You can play these tracks in
the same way as you play
other music on your iPad.

6.3 Creating a Playlist

One of the nice features of the *Music* app is the ability to create a playlist. You can download songs from *iTunes* and add your favorite songs to a playlist, in the order you prefer. You can then play the tracks in the playlist as often as you like. This is how you create a new playlist in the *Music* app:

☞ **Open the *Music* app** 👣1

In the bottom of the screen:

👉 **Tap** Playlists

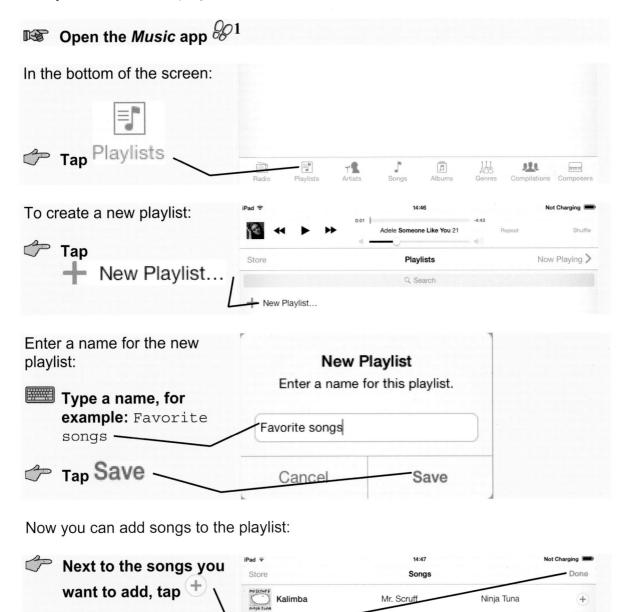

To create a new playlist:

👉 **Tap** + New Playlist...

Enter a name for the new playlist:

⌨ **Type a name, for example:** Favorite songs

👉 **Tap** Save

New Playlist

Enter a name for this playlist.

Favorite songs|

Cancel   Save

Now you can add songs to the playlist:

👉 **Next to the songs you want to add, tap** ⊕

👉 **Tap** Done

Songs

Kalimba   Mr. Scruff   Ninja Tuna   ⊕

Maid with the Flaxen Hair   Richard Stoltzman/Slov...   Fine Music, Vol. 1   ⊕

Sleep Away   Bob Acri   Bob Acri   ⊕

You will see the playlist. If you want to remove a song from the playlist:

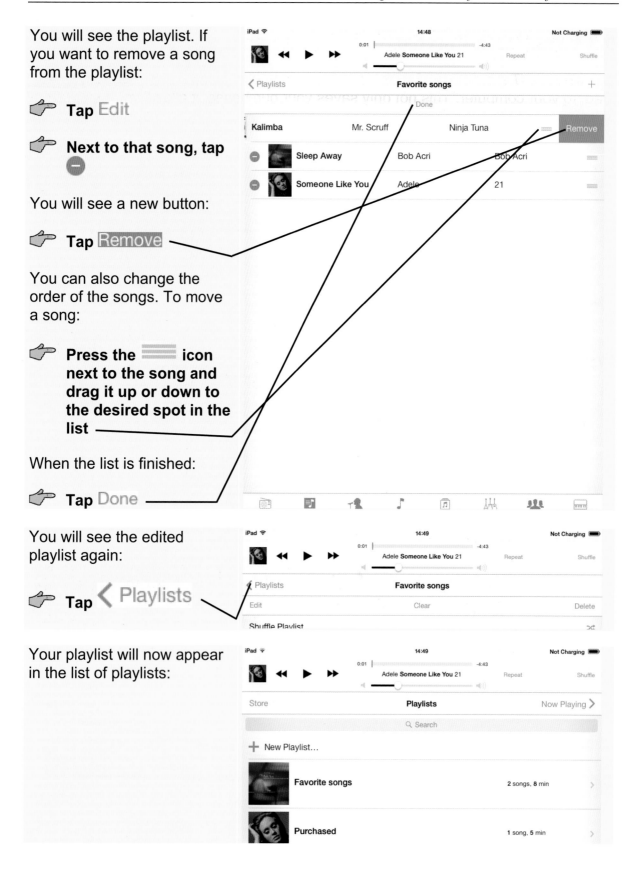

☞ **Tap** Edit

☞ **Next to that song, tap** ⊖

You will see a new button:

☞ **Tap** Remove

You can also change the order of the songs. To move a song:

☞ **Press the** ☰ **icon next to the song and drag it up or down to the desired spot in the list**

When the list is finished:

☞ **Tap** Done

You will see the edited playlist again:

☞ **Tap** ‹ Playlists

Your playlist will now appear in the list of playlists:

6.4 Transferring Purchases to iTunes

You can use *iTunes* to transfer music, apps, and books you have purchased on your iPad, to your computer. This not only saves your purchases, it allows you to use them on your computer as well.

☞ **Connect your iPad to the computer**

☞ **Open *iTunes* on your computer**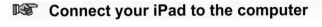

If necessary, display the menu bar. You can do that with a keyboard shortcut:

⌨ **Simultaneously press**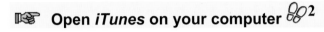

The menu bar will be displayed:

⊕ **Click File**

⊕ **Click Devices**

⊕ **Click**
Transfer Purchases from "iPad \

⊕ **If necessary, click** 📱 **iPad** ⏏

At the top of the window:

⊕ **Click On This iPad**

The songs you have purchased will appear in the library:

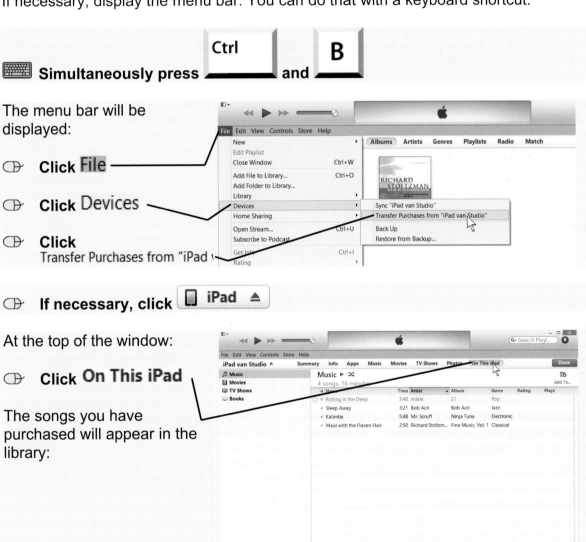

6.5 Importing CDs into iTunes

You can also transfer music tracks from CDs to your computer. But first you will need to import these tracks into *iTunes*. This operation is also called ripping. Once the tracks are imported you can copy them to the iPad.

 Please note:

Some CDs have copy protection, to prevent people from making illegal copies. These types of CDs cannot be transferred to the iPad.

Open *iTunes* on your computer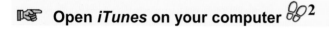

Insert a music CD from your own collection into the CD/DVD drive of your computer

You will see a list of the tracks on the CD:

iTunes will ask if you want to import the CD:

 Click | Yes

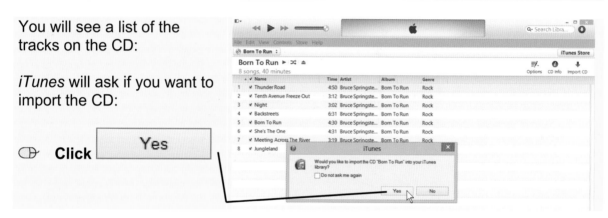

You can tell that a track is being imported by the symbol that appears next to the name of the song:

In the top of the window you can also see which track is being imported and how long the operation will take:

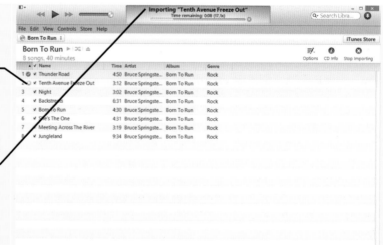

By default, all tracks will be selected, so they will all be imported. If you want, you can uncheck the boxes ✔ next to the tracks you do not want to import.

After the CD has been imported, you will hear a sound signal. All tracks are now marked with a ✅. This means the import operation has been successfully concluded. Now the songs have been added to the *iTunes* Library.

Once the tracks have been imported into *iTunes* you can add them to your iPad.

6.6 Transferring Songs from the Computer to the iPad

It is a good idea to have the *iTunes* sidebar and menu bar in view. You can display the menu bar easily using a keyboard shortcut:

Simultaneously press **Ctrl** and **B**

☞ Click **View**

☞ Click **Show Sidebar**

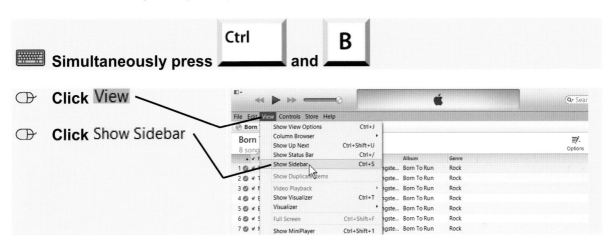

☞ **Connect your iPad to the computer**

The iPad is listed in the *iTunes* sidebar under Devices:

Now you can select the tracks to be transferred. Click ♫ **Music** to display the music stored in *iTunes*:

In this example we will transfer the tracks from the CD we ripped in the previous section:

☞ **Click** 🎵 **Music**

☞ **Click Albums**

☞ **Click the imported CD**

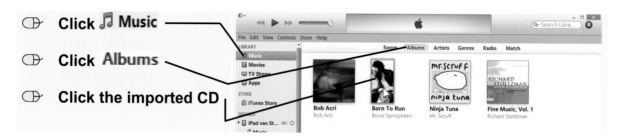

The method is the same for all types of tracks.

Select the tracks you want to transfer:

☞ **Click the first track**

⌨ **Press** `Ctrl` **and hold it down**

☞ **Click the other tracks**

⌨ **Release** `Ctrl`

💡 **Tip**
Select tracks in a list

You can select multiple consecutive tracks in the list by pressing the `Shift` key and holding it down.

The tracks have been selected. Now you can copy them to your iPad:

☞ **Drag the selected tracks to your iPad**

☞ **Release the mouse button**

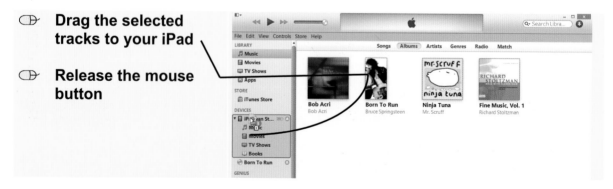

After a few seconds the songs from the CD will have been copied to your iPad and can be played with the *Music* app. You can now safely disconnect the iPad from the computer.

6.7 Listen to the Radio on the iPad with TuneIn

If you are familiar with the use of *iTunes* on the computer you will also know that you can play streamed Internet radio with this program. Unfortunately, this feature is not available in either the *iTunes* app or the *Music* app on the iPad.
If you still want to listen to radio on your iPad you will need to download a separate app from the *App Store*. Many radio stations have developed their own special apps. If you use the search box at the top to look for your favorite radio station, you may find that there are one or more apps available.
A great alternative is to use the free *TuneIn Radio* app. This app has literally thousands of stations available from all around the world:

☞ **Open the *TuneIn Radio* app** 🐾¹

You may see a message asking you to let the app use your current location and send you messages:

☞ **Select the option you prefer**

Next, you will see the app's window:

You can start searching for a station on the Browse page:

👉 **Tap a category**

Another option is to enter a keyword with 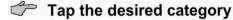:

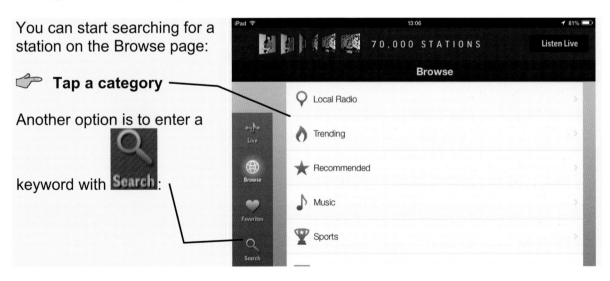

You may see even more categories:

👉 **Tap the desired category**

You will see a list of radio stations:

☞ **Tap the desired station** ———

The radio station will be played on the player at the bottom of the screen. Use the buttons to control the player:

If you want to find another

station, tap ⬅ :

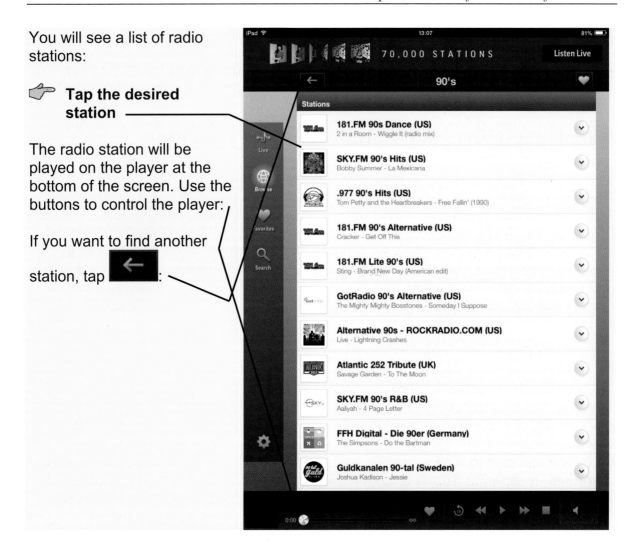

6.8 Buying Music and Listening to Music with Spotify

With the *iTunes* app you can purchase a lot of music. Rather than purchasing tracks or albums one at a time you may want to consider a music service. The *Spotify* app for the iPad allows you to listen to full albums at once.

One of the advantages of *Spotify* is that you can get a subscription and you will no longer need to pay for individual tracks. You will not own the tracks, but you can play them where and whenever you want through the streaming technique. This means that the music will be sent to your iPad while it is playing.

There are three options for listening to music with *Spotify*:

- A free subscription: you can listen to music on your desktop or laptop, but every once in a while you will see banners or advertisements. You cannot download tracks or play them without using the Internet.
- A regular subscription: you can listen to music on your desktop or laptop without any advertising. You cannot download tracks and play them without using the Internet.
- A premium subscription: you can listen to music without advertising. You can download tracks and play them offline as well.

Unfortunately the use of this service on mobile devices, such as an iPad, is restricted. You can stream music to a regular computer for free, but for an iPad you need to have the premium subscription. But this will still be a lot cheaper than purchasing each individual track.
You can try *Spotify* on your iPad for free, for 48-hours:

☞ Open the *Spotify* app 1

You can select an option to allow messages:

☞ Select the option you prefer

Next, you can sign in. There are two ways of doing this: through a *Facebook* account or through a separate *Spotify* account. The advantage of signing in with your *Facebook* account is the option of easily sharing your music preferences with your friends on *Facebook*. You will not need to create a new, separate account.
If you do not have a *Facebook* account, or prefer not to use this account for *Spotify*, you can create a separate *Spotify* account.

In this example we have signed in with a *Facebook* account:

☞ Tap the desired option

If you want to sign in with a *Spotify* account you will need to create an account first, on the www.spotify.com/ signup web page

☞ Sign in with your *Facebook* data

You can search for a song or an artist:

👉 Tap Search

⌨ **Type the keyword in the search box**

👉 Tap **Search**

You will see an overview of all the tracks and artists that have been found:

👉 **Tap the desired item**

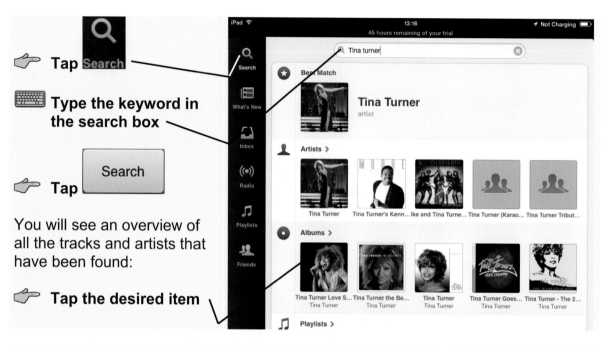

If you tap an album, you will see this album:

👉 **Tap a track**

The track will be played, and you can control playback with the player buttons:

You can also listen to the radio with this app (US only):

And you can create playlists of your favorite songs:

Take your time to use this option and try out some of the other options as well. If you are a music lover, this may be just the right app for you.

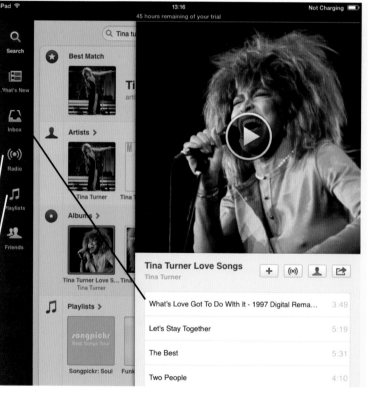

6.9 Making Music with Garageband

Do you like to make music yourself? With the *Garageband* app you can turn your iPad into a studio and use different instruments. You can play various instruments such as a piano, a guitar, or drums by using the touchscreen. Through a Wi-Fi connection, you can even play together in a band with other iPads.

You can record and edit the music with the recorder, and mix it up with professional music samples, if you like. After you have finished creating your song you can turn it into a ringtone for your phone, for example, or share the music with others through *Facebook* or *YouTube*.

You can select various musical instruments:

After you have recorded the music, you can edit it:

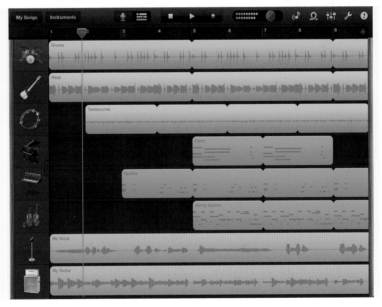

6.10 Transferring Ebooks to the iPad

One of the apps that can be used to read ebooks on the iPad is *iBooks*. You can download this app in the *App Store* for free. Ebooks may be purchased directly through this app, through other ebooks apps, or through an online bookstore. Maybe you already have some ebooks saved on your computer. You can use *iTunes* to copy these ebooks to your iPad.

☞ **Open the *iTunes* program on the computer** ✇²

⊕ **Click**

⊕ **Click**
    Add File to Library...

☞ **Open the folder with the ebooks**

⊕ **Click the desired file**

⊕ **Click** | Open |

☞ **Connect your iPad to the computer**

In the *iTunes* window:

⊕ **If necessary, click View, Hide Sidebar**

⊕ **Click** | ☐ iPad ⏏ |

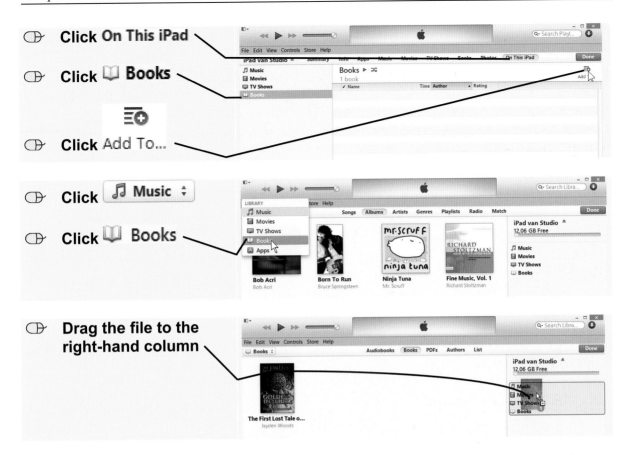

Click On This iPad

Click 📖 Books

Click Add To...

Click 🎵 Music ⇕

Click 📖 Books

Drag the file to the right-hand column

The file will be copied to the iPad at once. You can view it on the iPad:

👉 **Open the *iBooks* app**

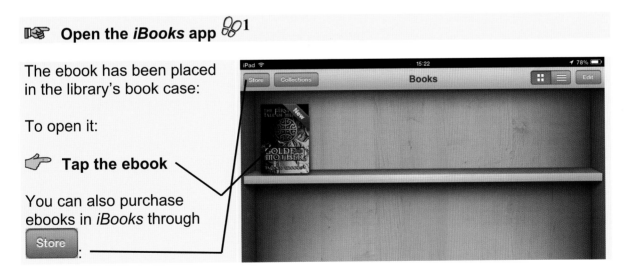

The ebook has been placed in the library's book case:

To open it:

👉 **Tap the ebook**

You can also purchase ebooks in *iBooks* through **Store** :

At the bottom of the screen you see the page you are reading:

Swipe your finger across the screen from right to left to turn a page or use the bar at the bottom:

Go back to the library:

View table of contents:

Edit the view settings:

Search for words or pages:

Insert a bookmark:

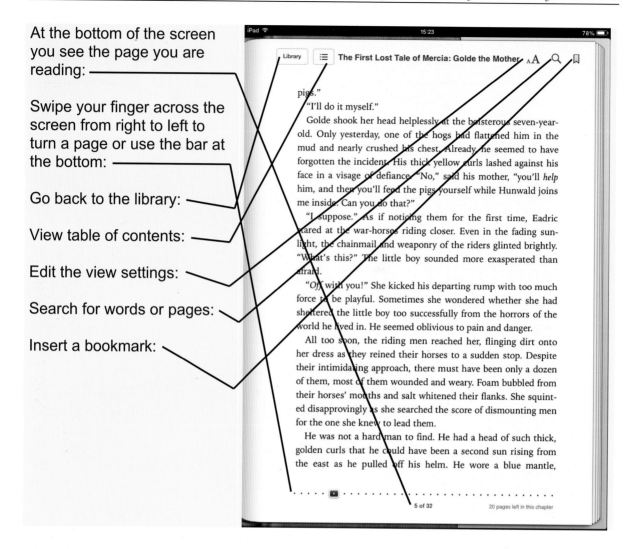

6.11 Reading Magazines and Papers with Newsstand

In the standard *Newsstand* app you can read and manage your newspapers and magazines. You will often need to have a subscription or purchase single copies in order to do this, but there are a few free papers and magazines available as well.

☞ **Open the *Newsstand* app** 🐾¹

If you have not yet purchased any magazines or papers, the *Newsstand* app will be empty:

You can purchase these items in the store:

☞ **Tap** Store

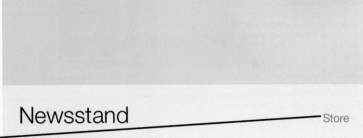

You will see the *Newsstand* apps of the newspapers and magazines that offer digital subscriptions or single copies:

☞ **Swipe from the right to the left across the magazines until you see *Huffington***

☞ **Tap**

Huffington
News
FREE

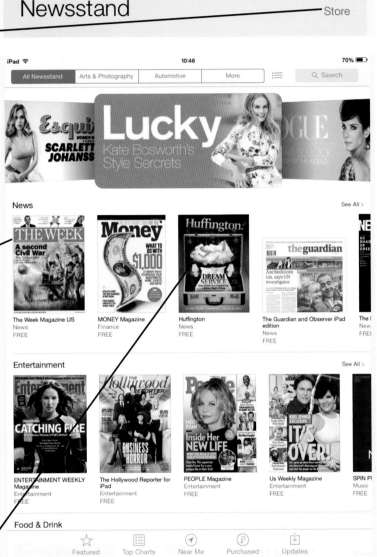

You will see additional
information about *The New
Yorker Magazine* app:

☞ **Tap** ⁺FREE

☞ **Tap** INSTALL

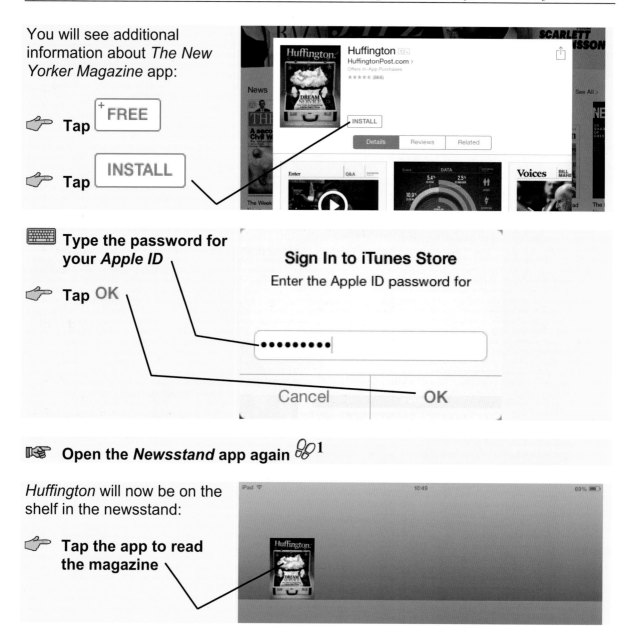

Type the password for
your *Apple ID*

☞ **Tap** OK

Sign In to iTunes Store

Enter the Apple ID password for

•••••••••

Cancel   OK

☞ **Open the *Newsstand* app again** 👣1

Huffington will now be on the
shelf in the newsstand:

☞ **Tap the app to read
the magazine**

Each *Newsstand* app offered by a newspaper or magazine will look different. You
can also purchase single copies with your *iTunes* credit and download them. Many
papers offer digital subscriptions, or free access to the digital edition if you subscribe
to the regular newspaper. You can enter your account information for the digital
edition in the *Newsstand* app. Then new issues will be downloaded automatically.
You will also be able to read these issues through the app of the newspaper or
magazine you have downloaded.

The *Newsstand* app gives a quick overview of all the issues you have downloaded.

7. Communication and Sharing

The iPad is used frequently to share, collaborate and exchange information. The ability to share news and photos using social media apps such as *Facebook* and *Twitter* is especially popular. You can turn various settings on or off on your iPad for these social media apps to safeguard privacy and to update profile and status information. Other standard apps like *Contacts* and *Calendar* offer optional integration with social media apps. This can make it even easier and faster to share information with others.

The iPad comes with various communication apps. *Messages* lets you send short text messages to other people who use the same app. *FaceTime* is a video chatting app that lets you have face-to-face conversations with other *FaceTime* users.

The *Notification Center* is the place where you can quickly see if you have any new messages, calendar events or other types of alerts. You can decide for yourself which apps will be allowed to show you messages in the *Notification Center*. And if you ever want to temporarily turn off the alerts, you can do that with the Do Not Disturb option.

In this chapter we will provide you with tips on the following subjects:

- using the *Notification Center*;
- setting up messages in the *Notification Center*;
- the Do Not Disturb option;
- using *Facebook* and *Twitter* in other apps;
- settings for *Facebook* and *Twitter*;
- video chatting with *FaceTime*;
- sending messages with the *Messages* app;
- *Facebook* in the *Calendar* and *Contacts* apps;
- create your own magazine with *Flipboard*.

 Please note:

In order to follow the operations in some of the sections in this chapter you need to have downloaded the *Facebook* and *Twitter* apps, and have them set up on your iPad. If necessary, you can download these apps through the *Settings* app, and

 Facebook or Twitter .

7.1 Using the Notification Center

You can display and arrange the messages you receive on your iPad such as new email messages, appointments and reminders in the *Notifications Center*. This is how you open the *Notifications Center*:

☞ **Swipe your finger from the top of the screen to the bottom**

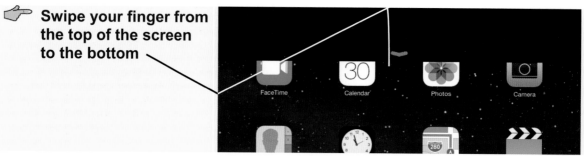

The *Notification Center* will be opened:

Here you can see a notification about Tennis lessons in the

Today view:

There are two other views: "All" notifications or "Missed" notifications:

To open a message:

☞ **Tap a message, for example, the event**

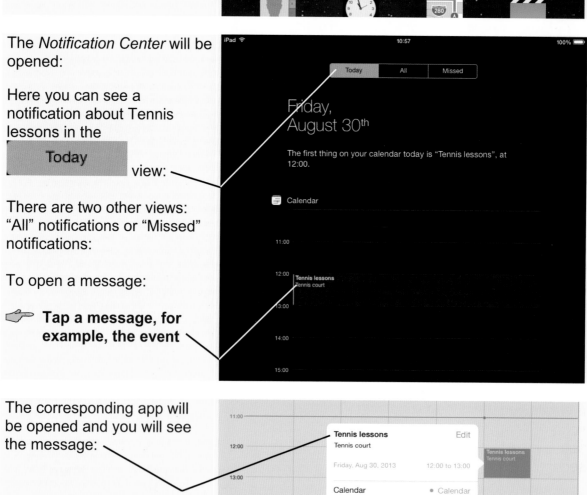

The corresponding app will be opened and you will see the message:

To close the *Notification Center*:

☞ **Swipe your finger from the bottom of the screen to the top**

7.2 Message Settings in the Notification Center

In the *Settings* app you can choose which messages you want to display in the *Notification Center*, like email messages, for example:

☞ **Open the *Settings* app** ℘¹

☞ **Tap**

Notification Cen

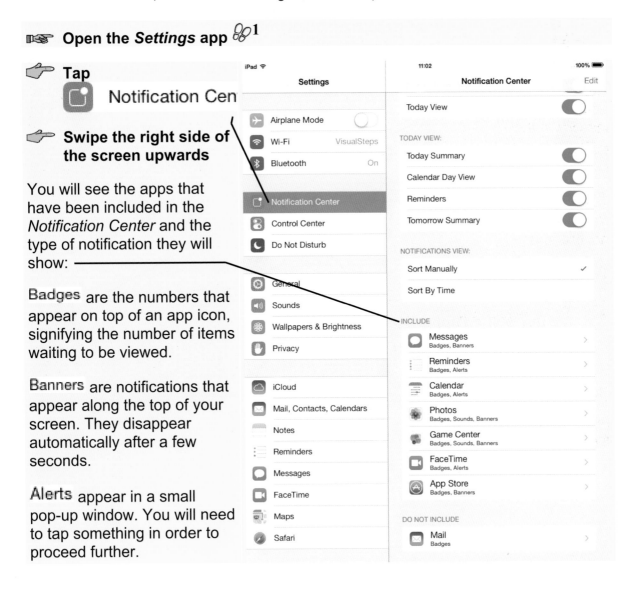

☞ **Swipe the right side of the screen upwards**

You will see the apps that have been included in the *Notification Center* and the type of notification they will show:

Badges are the numbers that appear on top of an app icon, signifying the number of items waiting to be viewed.

Banners are notifications that appear along the top of your screen. They disappear automatically after a few seconds.

Alerts appear in a small pop-up window. You will need to tap something in order to proceed further.

This is how to include an app in the *Notification Center*:

☞ **By** DO NOT INCLUDE, **tap the app, for example**

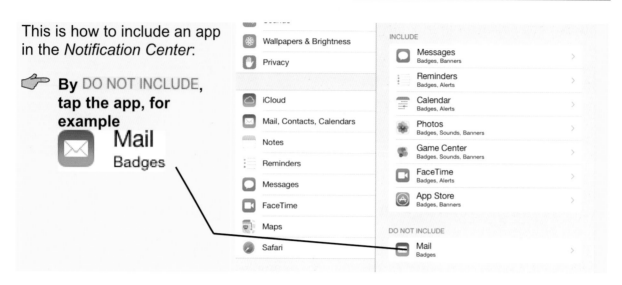

☞ **If necessary, tap the desired email account**

☞ **Drag the slider ⬭ by Show in Notification Center to the right**

Your new email messages will now be displayed in the *Notification Center*.

Here you can select the type of notification you want to see when a new message is received:

☞ **Tap the desired option**

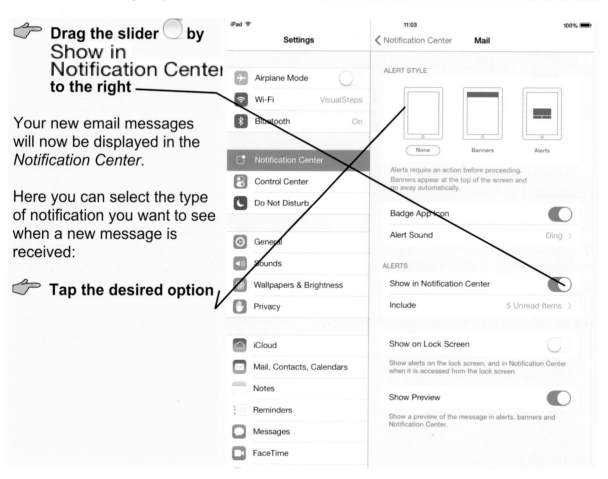

You can edit various other settings:

By default, a preview of the message will be displayed:

You can also set the message to be displayed on the lock screen:

Here you can set the message sound:

If you do not want to hear any sounds, tap Off.

☞ **Edit the settings as desired**

You can change these settings for each individual app.

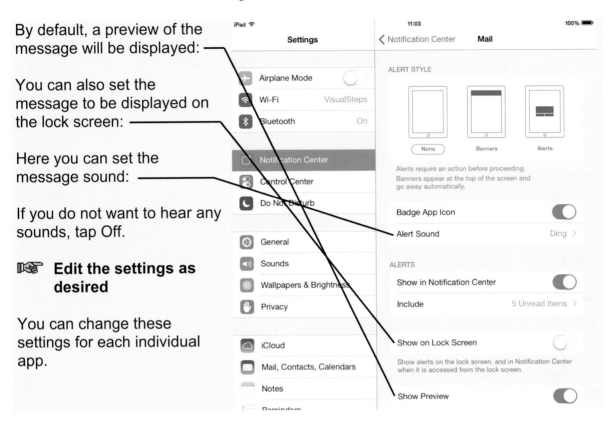

7.3 Using the Do Not Disturb Option

If you regularly use the iPad to keep in touch with others you will probably be notified of new messages. For example, one of your contacts has just sent you a message. A notification about this message will be displayed on your iPad and if the sound is turned on, you will hear a beep or other sound signal.

There may be times when you do not want to be disturbed by any messages, beeps or other sound signals. If you want to continue to receive these messages on your iPad but without being disturbed, you can turn on the Do Not Disturb option:

☞ **Open the *Settings* app** 👣¹

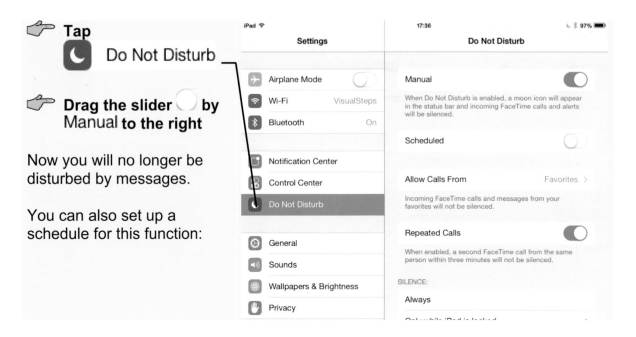

👉 **Tap** 🌙 Do Not Disturb

👉 **Drag the slider** ⚪ **by Manual to the right**

Now you will no longer be disturbed by messages.

You can also set up a schedule for this function:

7.4 Using Facebook and Twitter from Other Apps

Facebook and *Twitter* are integrated into several of the iPad's standard apps such as *Photos*, *Safari* and *Maps*. In this section we will explore a number of options and settings for these apps.

You can easily share a photo from the *Photos* app with *Facebook* or *Twitter*:

👉 **Open the *Photos* app and open a photo** 👣[5]

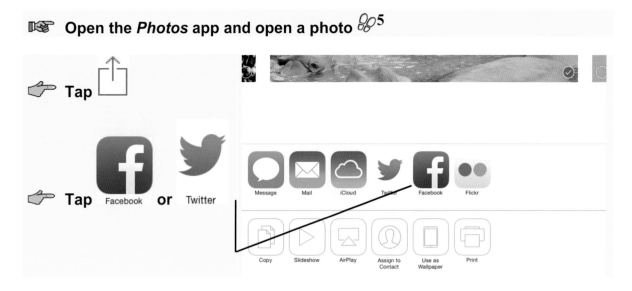

👉 **Tap** ⬆️

👉 **Tap** Facebook **or** Twitter

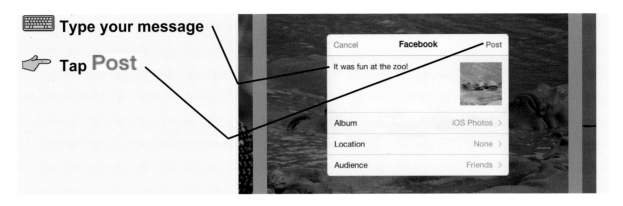

Type your message

☞ **Tap** Post

In the same way, you can share a link to an interesting web page while you are using *Safari*:

👉 **Open the *Safari* app and open a random web page** 🦶⁶

☞ **Tap** ⬆️

☞ **Tap** Facebook **or** Twitter

Type your message

☞ **Tap** Post

👉 **Go back to the home screen** 🦶¹⁰

In *Maps* you can share an interesting location with *Facebook* or *Twitter*.

👉 **Open the *Maps* app** 🦶¹

Type a location

By location, tap ⓘ

Tap Share

Tap Facebook **or**

Twitter

Type your message

Tap Post

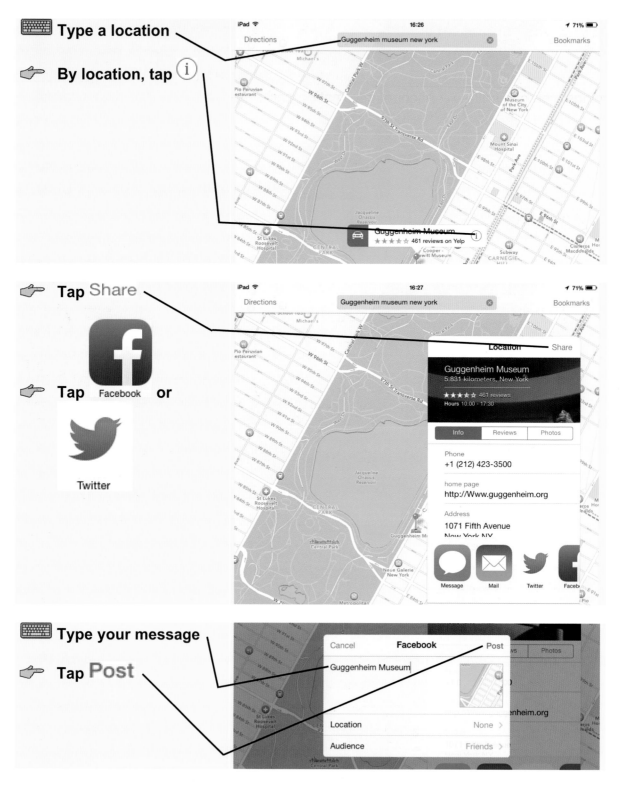

There are several other apps that will let you post messages to *Facebook* or *Twitter* in a similar way.

7.5 Settings for Facebook and Twitter

You can set a number of options for the *Facebook* and *Twitter* apps. Among other things, you can edit your account information and set privacy options.

This is how you view the *Facebook* settings:

☞ **Open the *Facebook* app** 🎴**¹**

⌨ **If necessary, type your user name and password**

👉 **Tap** ▤

On the left-hand side of the screen you will see a menu :

👉 **Drag the left side of the screen upwards**

👉 **Tap**
⚙ **Account Settings**

A list of categories appears:

👉 **Tap the desired category**

☞ **Edit the settings as desired**

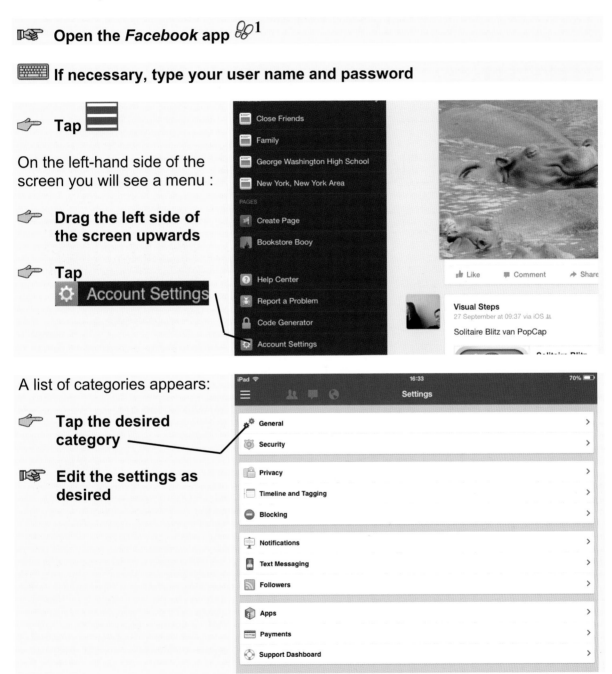

After you have finished you can quit the *Settings* screen by tapping and ███.

You can also set a number of options for the *Facebook* app in the *Settings* app:

☞ **Open the *Settings* app** 🦶¹

☞ **Drag the left side of the screen upwards**

☞ **Tap** 📘 Facebook

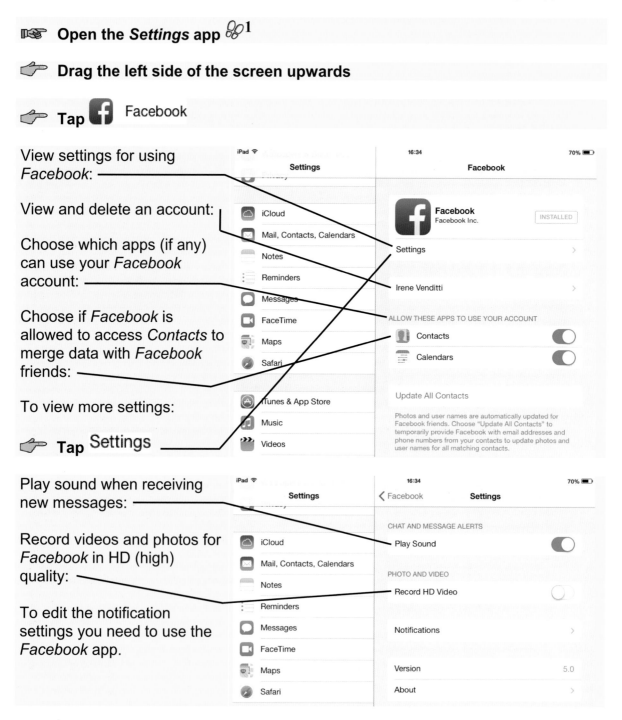

View settings for using *Facebook*:

View and delete an account:

Choose which apps (if any) can use your *Facebook* account:

Choose if *Facebook* is allowed to access *Contacts* to merge data with *Facebook* friends:

To view more settings:

☞ **Tap** Settings

Play sound when receiving new messages:

Record videos and photos for *Facebook* in HD (high) quality:

To edit the notification settings you need to use the *Facebook* app.

☞ **Edit the settings as desired**

This is how you view the *Twitter* settings in *Twitter* app:

☞ **Open the *Twitter* app** 👣**1**

⌨ **If necessary, type your user name and password**

☞ **Tap**

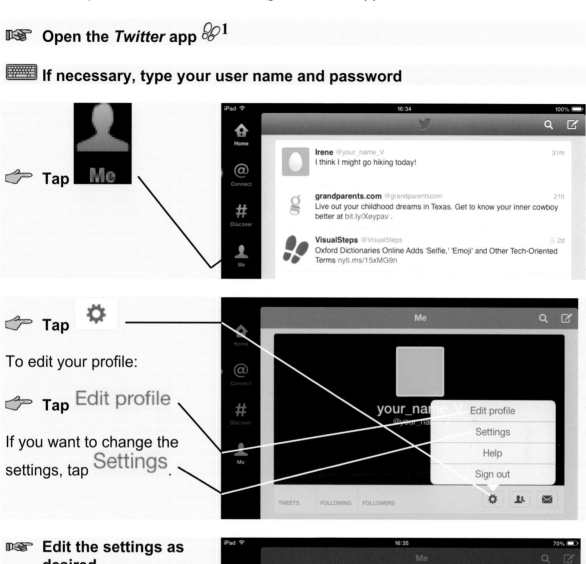

To edit your profile:

☞ **Tap** Edit profile

If you want to change the settings, tap Settings.

☞ **Edit the settings as desired**

☞ **Tap** Save

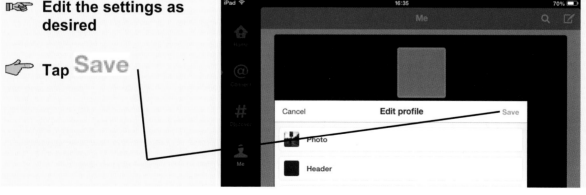

You can use the *Settings* app to edit other settings for *Twitter*:

☞ **Open the *Settings* app** 🦶¹

☞ **Drag the left side of the screen upwards**

☞ **Tap** 🐦 Twitter

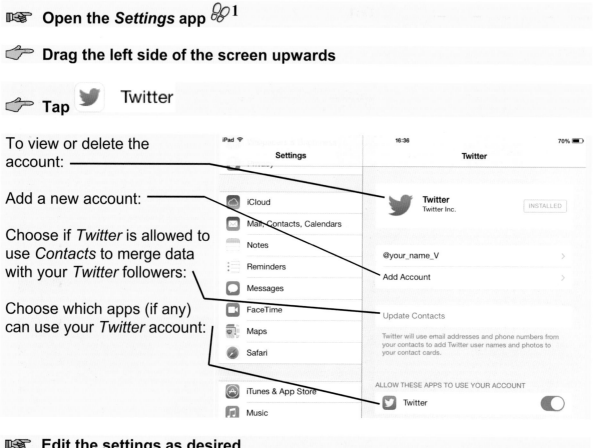

To view or delete the account:

Add a new account:

Choose if *Twitter* is allowed to use *Contacts* to merge data with your *Twitter* followers:

Choose which apps (if any) can use your *Twitter* account:

☞ **Edit the settings as desired**

7.6 Video Chatting with FaceTime

Your iPad has its own app for video chatting called *FaceTime*. You can use this app to make (video) calls to another iPad, iPhone, iPod touch or Mac computer. You need to have an *Apple ID* to use *FaceTime*.

 Tip

The Skype app
Video chatting is also possible with the *Skype* app. The *Skype* app does not require an *Apple ID* but instead a *Skype* user account. *Skype* can also be used on a *Windows* computer and other types of tablets and smartphones.

This is how you use *FaceTime*:

☞ **Open the *FaceTime* app** 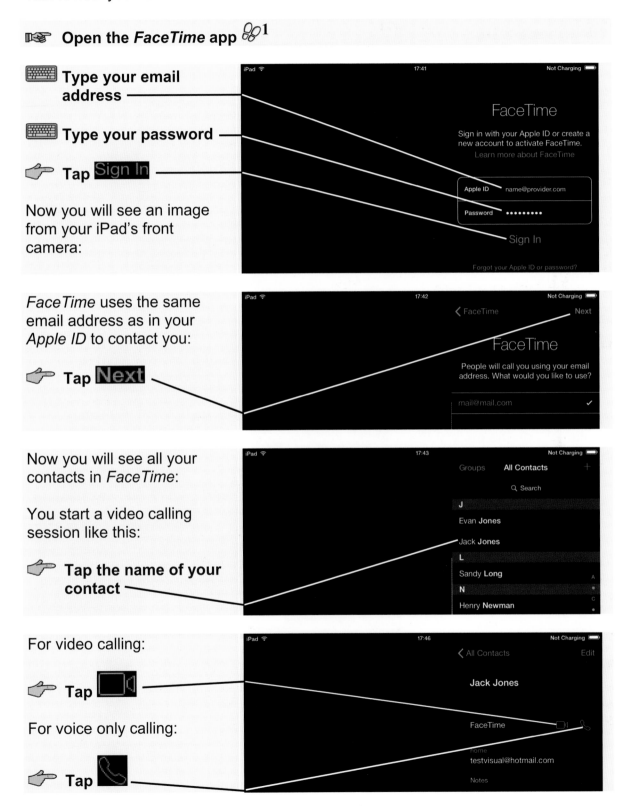**1**

⌨ **Type your email address** ──────

⌨ **Type your password** ──────

☞ **Tap** `Sign In` ──────

Now you will see an image from your iPad's front camera:

FaceTime uses the same email address as in your *Apple ID* to contact you:

☞ **Tap** `Next`

Now you will see all your contacts in *FaceTime*:

You start a video calling session like this:

☞ **Tap the name of your contact** ──────

For video calling:

☞ **Tap** ──────

For voice only calling:

☞ **Tap** ──────

The iPad will try to make a connection. You will hear the phone ring.

 Please note:
The contact needs to be online and needs to have added your name and email address to his contacts.

Once the connection has been made, you will be able to see and hear your contact:

Tap the [icon] icon to mute the sound of your microphone:

If you want to end the conversation:

👉 **Tap** [End]

Tap the [icon] icon to use the camera on the back of the iPad:

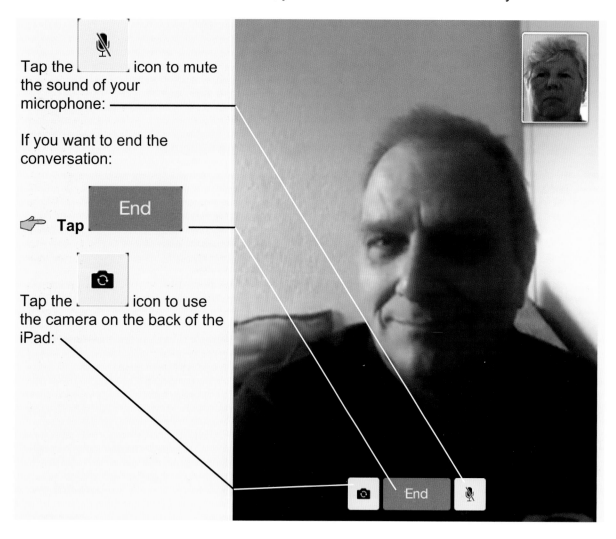

In this way you can have a face-to-face conversation with contacts from all over the world.

7.7 Sending Messages with the Messages app

The *Messages* app allows you to send *iMessages* (text messages) to other people who own an iPad, iPhone, iPod Touch or Mac computer using Wi-Fi or a mobile data network. To be able to use the *Messages* app you will need to have an *Apple ID*.

This is how you send an *iMessage* with the *Messages* app:

☞ **Open the *Messages* app** 𝒪𝒪¹

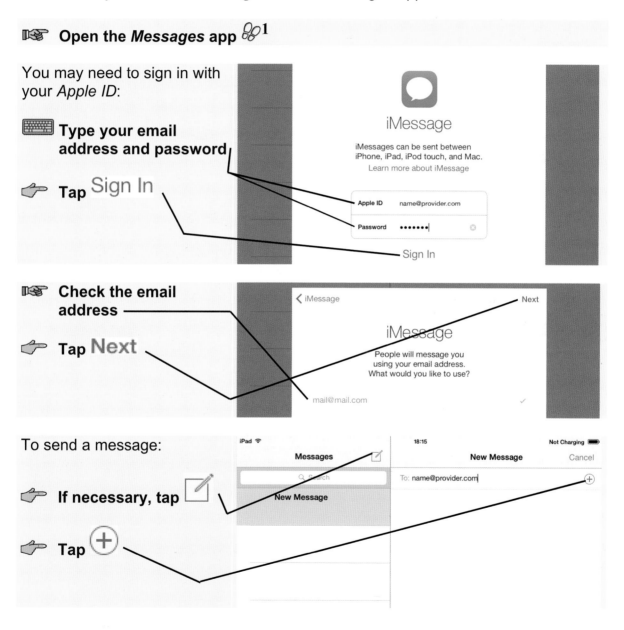

You may need to sign in with your *Apple ID*:

⌨ **Type your email address and password**

☞ **Tap** Sign In

☞ **Check the email address** ————

☞ **Tap Next**

To send a message:

☞ **If necessary, tap** ▱

☞ **Tap** ⊕

☞ **If necessary, tap**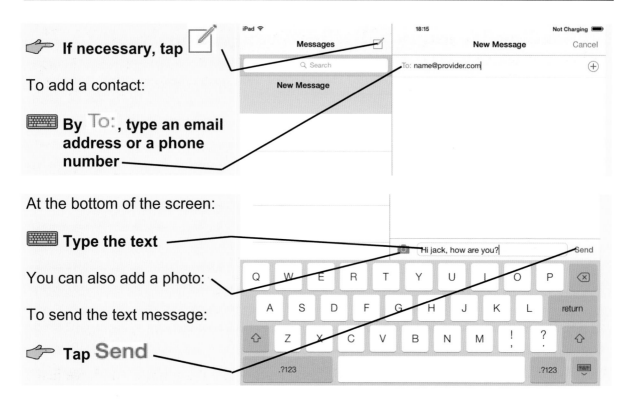

To add a contact:

⌨ **By To:, type an email address or a phone number**

At the bottom of the screen:

⌨ **Type the text**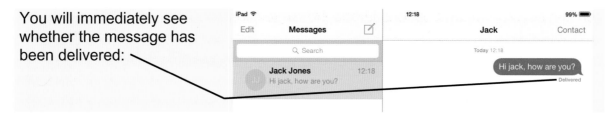

You can also add a photo:

To send the text message:

☞ **Tap Send**

As soon as the message is sent you will hear a sound signal.

You will immediately see whether the message has been delivered:

☞ **Go back to the home screen** 🐾10

When a reply is received you will hear a sound signal and see a message on the login screen:

If the iPad is unlocked you will see a badge appear on the app icon: ———

When you open the app you will see the answer displayed below your message:

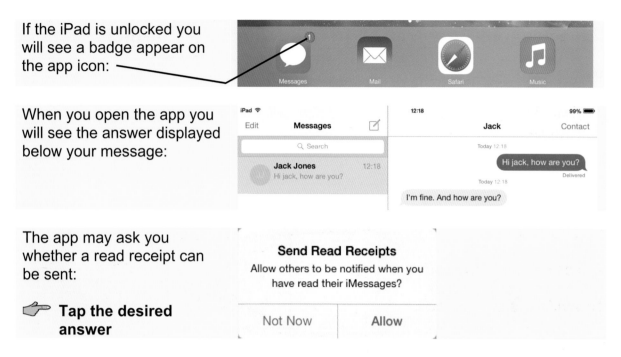

The app may ask you whether a read receipt can be sent:

☞ **Tap the desired answer**

Send Read Receipts

Allow others to be notified when you have read their iMessages?

| Not Now | Allow |

When you reply to such a message, it will be placed below the answer you have just received. This way, you can view the ongoing conversation with this contact with the messages neatly placed one below the other.

You can set a number of options for the *Messages* app:

🖙 **Open the *Settings* app** 👣¹

☞ **Tap** 💬 Messages

Temporarily disable sending messages: ———

Send a read receipt to the sender: ———

Set up your email addresses:

Add a subject to a message:

7.8 Facebook Integration in Calendar and Contacts

If you have installed and set up the *Facebook* app on your iPad, it will be linked automatically to the *Calendar* and *Contacts* apps. Among other things, this means that birthdays or invites for events from *Facebook* will be displayed in the *Calendar* app:

☞ **Open the *Calendar* app** 𝒫¹

👉 **Tap** Calendars

👉 **Drag the *Show Calendars* window upwards**

You will see that separate calendars have been added for *Facebook* events and birthdays:

In this example you will also see a birthday:

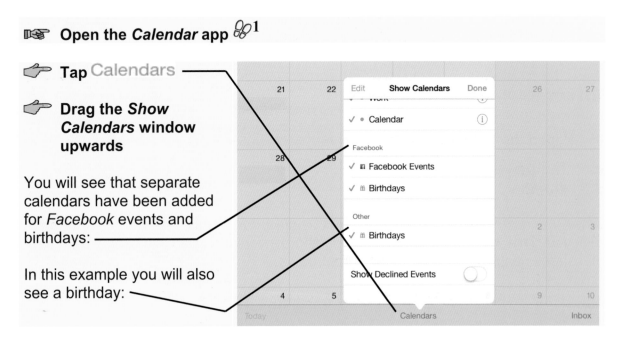

By default, your *Facebook* friends will be added to the *Contacts* app:

☞ **Open the *Contacts* app** 𝒫¹

You will see that your *Facebook* friends have been added to your contacts list:

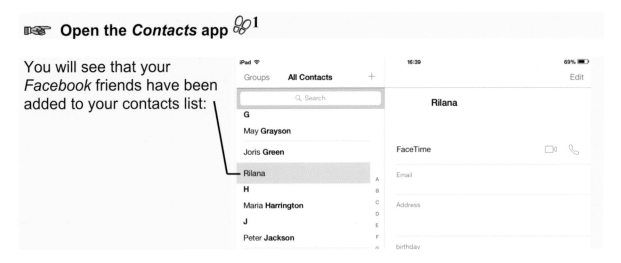

Tip

Update contacts

If you grant *Facebook* access to your contact data just a single time, the photos of existing contacts will be updated on the basis of their profile photo in *Facebook*:

If you do not want the *Calendar* and/or *Contacts* apps to use your *Facebook* account, you can turn off this option:

☞ **Open the *Settings* app** 🐾¹

☞ **Tap** 📘 **Facebook**

☞ **Drag the slider ◯ by**

🗓 **Calendars**

and/or 👤 **Contacts**

to the left ——

The *Facebook* calendar and/or the contact data will be deleted.

Your iPad may contain other apps that use *Facebook*. You can turn off this setting for these other apps in the same way.

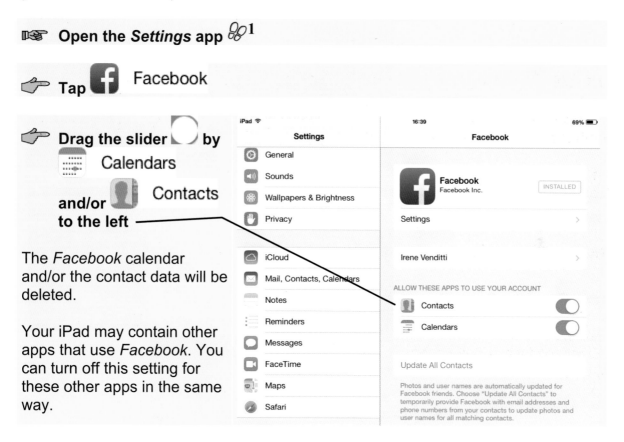

7.9 Creating Your Own Magazine with Flipboard

For most computer users, their news and information is gathered from different sources, ranging from news websites to *Facebook*. Instead of visiting all these different websites, you can use the free *Flipboard* app to collect the information in your own online magazine. You can download this app from the *App Store*.

Every day you will get an automatic update of your favorite news sites in images and text. Everything is arranged on multiple pages, so you can quietly browse through the pages, just like you do with an actual paper magazine.

☞ **Open the *Flipboard* app**

You will see the app's home screen:

☞ **Tap** **< FLIP**

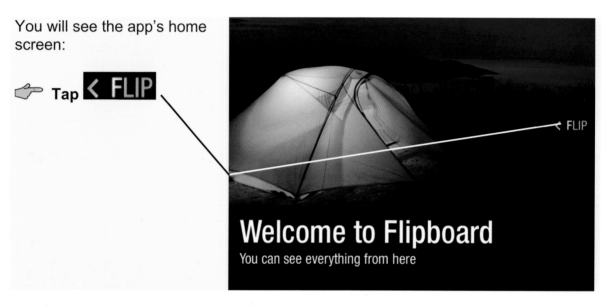

Here you see the items that have been set up in this example. To add new items yourself:

☞ **Tap** More >

Or:

☞ **Tap**

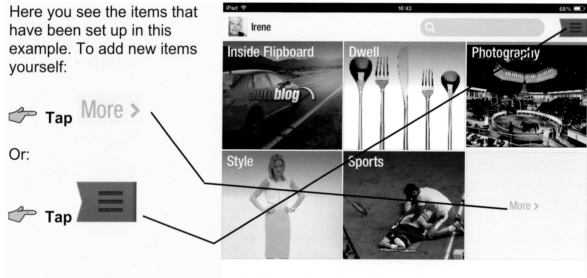

👉 **Tap the desired category**

To subscribe for free:

👉 **Tap 🔖 by the desired item**

Tap an item in order to view it.

This is what an item in your *Flipboard* magazine may look like:

7.10 Visual Steps Website and More Books

By now we hope you have noticed that the Visual Steps method is an excellent method for quickly and efficiently learning more about tablets, computers and other devices and their applications. All books published by Visual Steps use this same method.

In various series, we have published a large number of books on a wide variety of topics, including *Windows*, *Mac OS X*, the iPad, the iPhone, Samsung Galaxy Tab, photo editing and many other topics.

On the **www.visualsteps.com** website you can click the Catalog page to find an overview of all the Visual Steps titles, including an extensive description. Each title allows you to preview the full table of contents and a sample chapter in a PDF format. In this way, you can quickly determine if a specific title will meet your expectations. All titles can be ordered online and are also available in bookstores across the USA, Canada, United Kingdom, Australia and New Zealand.

Furthermore, the website offers many extras, among other things:
- free computer guides and booklets (PDF files) covering all sorts of subjects;
- frequently asked questions and their answers;
- information on the free Computer Certificate that you can acquire at the certificate's website **www.ccforseniors.com**;
- a free email notification service: to let you know when new books are published.

There is always more to learn if you want. Visual Steps offers lots of other books on computer-related subjects. And remember, each Visual Steps book is written using the same step-by-step method with short, concise instructions and screen shots illustrating every step.

Appendix A. How Do I Do That Again?

The actions and exercises in this book are marked with footsteps: 1
Read how to do something once more by finding the corresponding number in the appendix below.

$\mathscr{C}\!\mathscr{C}$ 1 **Open an app**
- Tap the app

$\mathscr{C}\!\mathscr{C}$ 2 **Open *iTunes* on a computer**
In Windows 7, Vista, and XP:

- Click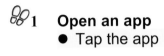

- Click ▶ All Programs

- Click 📁 iTunes

- Click 🎵 iTunes

In Windows 8, on the Start screen:

- Click **iTunes**

$\mathscr{C}\!\mathscr{C}$ 3 **Close a window**
- Click **X**

$\mathscr{C}\!\mathscr{C}$ 4 **Open a website on a computer**
On the taskbar:

- Click 🌐

- Type the web address in the address bar

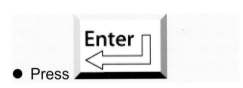

- Press

$\mathscr{C}\!\mathscr{C}$ 5 **Open the *Photos* app and a photo or a video**

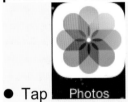

- Tap **Photos**

- Tap a photo or a video

$\mathscr{C}\!\mathscr{C}$ 6 **Open the *Safari* app and a web page**

- Tap **Safari**

- Type the web address in the address bar

- Tap **Go**

 7 **Open the *Mail* app and an email message**

- Tap

- Tap an email message

8 **Safely disconnect the iPad in *iTunes***
- By the name of the iPad, click
  ⏏

9 **Take a picture**
- Point at the subject you want to photograph

- Tap

10 **Go back to the home screen**
- Press the Home button

Appendix B. Dictionary

Below you will find a list of terms that have been used in this book.

Dictionary

Access point	A device that acts as an intermediate station (router) for your Internet connections, so you can connect other devices to it with a network cable or to wireless devices.
Accessibility settings	Settings you can use to make it easier to work with the iPad, in the case of certain impairments or disabilities, for example, a visual impairment.
AirPlay	A wireless data exchange system by Apple. It uses an existing wireless Wi-Fi network.
AirPrint	A function on the iPad with which you can print wirelessly to a printer that is suitable for *AirPrint*.
Album	A folder in the *Photos* app where you store photos and videos in different locations, for instance, an album with children's photos and an album with vacation photos.
App	Short for application, a small program.
Apple ID	A combination of an email address and a password, also called *iTunes App Store Account* that is needed to download apps from the *App Store* and for other Apple services.
App Store	Apple's online store, where you can download for free or purchase apps.
Apple TV	A small square device from Apple that measures approximately 4x4 inches. The box is connected to a TV and can stream video and audio files to and from the iPad. This device can be used to watch movies you have purchased in *iTunes*.
Attachment	A file, such as an image, that is sent with an email message. An attachment will be added to the email message from within the app in which the file is open.

Authorize	Ensure that a computer is able to save apps or play music that have been purchased in the *App Store* or through *iTunes*. You can authorize up to a maximum of five computers.
Auto-correct	A function that automatically displays corrections and word suggestions as you type.
Automatic lock	A function that will lock the iPad by default, if the device has not been used for a certain preset period of time. Also called sleep mode.
Backup copy	A copy of the settings, apps and various other data on your iPad. The backup copy is saved on the computer or in *iCloud*.
Badges	The numbers that appear on top of an app icon, signifying the number of items waiting to be viewed.
Banners	The notifications that appear along the top of your screen and which disappear automatically after a few seconds.
BBC iPlayer	An app with which you can watch the TV shows broadcasted by the BBC.
BCC	Blind Carbon Copy, that is to say, a copy of an email that is sent to multiple recipients. The addresses of the other recipients are not visible to one another.
Bookmark	A link to a website, saved in list. A bookmark allows you to jump quickly to the website whenever you want without any typing.
Bluetooth	An open standard for wireless connections over short distances between various devices. For example, you can connect a wireless keyboard or a headset to the iPad using Bluetooth.
Browser history	See History.
Calendar	One of the iPad's standard apps. It lets you keep a calendar of your activities and appointments.

Camera	One of the iPad's standard apps. You can take pictures and record video images with this app. You can use the camera on the front or on the back for this purpose.
Camera roll	The name of the folder that contains the pictures taken with your iPad, or saved onto your iPad, for instance from a website or an email attachment.
CC	Carbon Copy, a copy of an email that is sent to multiple recipients. The addresses of the other recipients are visible to one another.
Clock	One of the iPad's standard apps. It displays a clock for different time zones. The app can also be used as an alarm clock, a stopwatch or a timer.
Code lock	A safety measure to protect and lock the iPad with a code made up of numbers and letters.
Contacts	1. One of the iPad's standard apps. The app allows you to add, edit, delete and otherwise manage your contacts. 2. The people you communicate with and have saved in a list.
Cookies	Small files that are stored on your computer by the websites you have visited in order to make it easier to surf these websites later on. These cookies may contain personal information regarding your surfing behavior.
DIRECTV	An app that will let you watch various (American) TV channels on your iPad.
Docking station	A device into which you can insert your iPad in order to charge it. Some docking stations allow you to play music files stored on the iPad.
Draft	A saved version of an email message that has not been sent.
Dropbox	A program and an app that saves files on a server that can be accessed from various computers and other devices that are connected to the Internet.
Ebook	A digital copy of a book that can be read with a special app, such as *iBooks*.
Email account	Such an account contains the email address and password, the server name and user name necessary to connect to a mail server. This enables you to receive email messages.

Email server	See Mail server.
Equalizer	A device or function with which you can set the volume of different tones (frequencies) in a music file.
Event	This is the name for an appointment in the *Calendar* app.
Facebook	A popular social network site that offers a free app for the iPad.
FaceTime	One of the iPad's standard apps. A video chatting app that lets you conduct face-to-face conversations with other contacts that also use *FaceTime.* It can be used on an iPad, iPhone, iPod touch or a Mac computer.
Favorites Bar	A bar in *Safari* where you can save bookmarks.
Fetch	The traditional way of retrieving new email messages: you open your email program and connect to the mail server. You can set the program to check for new messages at regular intervals while the email program is opened.
Find My iPad	An option on the iPad with which you can locate your iPad on a map. You can use this option if you misplace your iPad or if it has been stolen.
Flipboard	An app that can be downloaded from the *App Store.* It can collect news and information from different sources.
Flyover	A function in the *Maps* app that lets you view various cities and places of interest in 3D.
Fraudulent website	Also called a phishing website. A website that is disguised as an official website, for example, a banking website, that entices you to enter your personal data, such as your user name and password and use them for defrauding purposes.
Garageband	An app with which you can make music on your iPad. You can use various instruments. The music you have recorded can be edited later on.
Gmail	A free email service offered by the same company that developed the well-known *Google* search engine.
GoToMyPC	An app that lets you access your computer through your iPad.

Google Maps	An app with which you can find locations and addresses, view satellite photos and get directions.
History	In the (browser) history, links are saved to all the websites you have recently visited. You can use these links to quickly find a website you previously visited.
Home sharing	An *iTunes* setting that allows you to play music on your iPad from the files saved in *iTunes* on your computer.
Hybrid	A view in the *Maps* app where a satellite photo is displayed combined with a view of the street names.
iBooks	An app you can download for free from the *App Store* and which can be used to read ebooks (digital books) on the iPad.
iCloud	Storage space on one of the servers owned by Apple. This service provides access to your documents and data on various Apple devices. You can use *iCloud* to save backups, share photos and more.
iMessage	A function that lets you send messages to any Mac, iPhone, iPad and iPod touch user for free using a mobile data network (3G or 4G) or Wi-Fi. If you send a message through 3G/4G you will need to pay for the data traffic but a text message is usually not larger than 140 bytes.
Import	Files sent from a different program or from an external device. During this operation, the files will be copied to the iPad.
Inbox	A folder in *Mail* where you can view your incoming email messages.
Internet radio	A radio station that broadcasts through the Internet.
iOS	The operating system used on the iPad.
iTunes	A program that lets you manage the content of your iPad. You can also use *iTunes* to listen to music files, watch videos and import CDs. In *iTunes* you can find the *iTunes Store* and the *App Store* as well.
iTunes Store	An online store where you can download music, films and audio books for a fee. Some items are also available for free.
Library	An overview of all music tracks stored on your iPad.

Location Services	By using location services, apps such as *Maps* can collect and use information about your current location. The collected location data will not be linked to your personal data. If you are connected to the Internet and have turned on Location Services, the location information can be added to the pictures and videos you make with your iPad.
Lock	Puts the iPad into sleep mode. It is possible to secure this lock with a code.
Mail	One of the iPad's standard apps. It is used to send and receive email messages.
Mail server	A server owned by your provider on which the email messages are saved. When you retrieve or read messages on your iPad, this happens by means of the mail server.
Mailbox	A folder in *Mail* in which email messages are saved, such as the *Inbox* or *Drafts*.
Maps	One of the iPad's standard apps. It that lets you find locations and addresses, view satellite photos and get directions.
Mark	Mark an email in a mailbox with a marker, such as a flag or a symbol that indicates whether the message has been read or not.
Messages	An app that lets you send messages.
Money Journal HD	An app that you can purchase in the *App Store* and that will help you keep track of your income and expenses.
Multitasking gestures	A number of gestures you can make on the screen with your fingers in order to execute a certain operation.
Music	An app that lets you play music.
Music service	An online company that offers music for free or for a subscription fee. For example, *iTunes* and *Spotify*.
Near Me	An option to look for popular apps used by people in your current location.
Newsstand	An app with which you can manage subscriptions and singles copies of newspapers and magazines.

Notification Center	A central option that lets you display all the messages you have received on your iPad, such as email messages and notifications, in an orderly way. It gives you an overview of all your incoming messages. Open this option by dragging the screen from top to bottom.
Notifications	Messages sent by the iPad that appear on your screen in a pop-up window. Usually you will need to tap something in order to continue.
Outlook	A free email service from *Microsoft*.
Phishing	An illegal method with which computer users are deceived and coerced to reveal personal or financial information. A frequently used online phishing method starts by sending an email message that appears to be sent by a trusted source. In this message, the recipients are asked to enter personal information on a fake website.
Photos	An app with which you can view photos on the iPad.
Photo Stream	A function with which you can synchronize photos through *iCloud*. It enables you to view photos and videos on multiple devices.
Playlist	A collection of tracks, arranged in a certain order.
POP	POP stands for *Post Office Protocol*, which is the traditional way of managing email messages. After you have retrieved your email, the messages will be deleted from the server right away. However, the default setting of the POP accounts on your iPad is to save a copy on the server after you have retrieved your email messages. This means you can also retrieve these messages on your computer later on.
Pop-up	An extra window that opens automatically when you visit a certain website. These screens may contain unwanted advertisements.
Privacy mode	While surfing the Internet, the system will automatically save data concerning the websites you visit. User names, passwords and credit card information may also be stored. If you turn on the private mode, this data will not be saved.
Push	When push has been set, and is supported by your provider, the mail server will immediately send new email messages to your email program, right after they have been received. Even if your email program has not been opened and your iPad is locked.

Quickoffice Pro	An app with which you can create text documents, spreadsheets and presentations. The documents are compatible with *Microsoft Office*.
Reader	A component in the *Safari* browser with which you can hide advertisements and other elements while you are reading online articles. This feature is only available on web pages that contain articles.
Reading list	In the *Safari* app a list of saved web pages that can be read at a later time. Can be used without a data connection or when the iPad is in Airplane mode.
Regional settings	Settings for displaying the date, time, and phone numbers often vary per country. Some countries use a day-month-year notation, where other countries use a month-day-year notation. You can change these settings accordingly.
Rotation lock	This function locks the screen image when you rotate the iPad.
Safari	Web browser by Apple.
Screen shot	An image of the screen you see. You can make a screen shot by pressing the power button together with the Home button.
Side switch	If you hold the iPad in an upright position, you will find this switch on the top right-hand side of the iPad.
Signature	A standard salutation that is inserted at the end of all your outgoing email messages.
Siri	A function thats lets you give verbal instructions for the iPad to execute, and lets you ask the iPad for information too.
Sleep mode	You can lock the iPad by turning on the sleep mode, when you are not using it. When the iPad is locked, nothing will happen when you touch the screen. Music (or podcast) files will continue playing as usual, and you will still be able to use the volume control buttons. You can turn on the sleep mode with the sleep/wake button.
Slideshow	The automatic display of a collection of images.
Sound Check	A setting that makes your music tracks play at approximately the same sound level.
Spotify	An online music service that lets you play music using the streaming technique. You will need a premium subscription to use this service on your iPad.

Spotlight	The iPad's search function.
Status bar	The bar at the top of the screen of an iPad. It contains various icons that provide information about your iPad such as the time, battery level and wireless connection.
Streaming	A method of relaying data (audio and video) over the Internet and displayed to the viewer in real time.
Switch	A device that lets you connect computers and other devices to your wired network. A hub, switch or router may be integrated into a single device.
Synchronize	Uses *iTunes* to manage (sync) data between your *iTunes* library on your computer and your iPad, including music, contacts, photos, apps, ebooks and more.
Tuneln Radio	An app that lets you play Internet radio stations on your iPad.
Twitter	A popular social network site on which you can post short messages (tweets). A free app is available for the iPad.
Update	The most recent version of an app or the iPad's operating system. Updates may include bug fixes and are necessary in order to use the newest options and safety settings.
Video call	Face-to-face, live conversation over a network or the Internet.
Volume limit	A setting to limit the volume of the sounds made on your iPad.
Wall	A *Facebook* page where you can post messages and photos.
Weather Channel	An app with which you can view the weather forecast and other information regarding the weather in your area.
Wi-Fi	A network technology that allows computers and other devices to communicate over a wireless signal. May also be spelled WiFi, Wifi or wifi.
Wi-Fi enhancer/ booster	A device that receives a wireless network signal and enhances it before transmitting it further.
YouTube	The largest video website on the Internet. A *YouTube* app is also available. Apart from watching other people's videos, you can also upload your own videos to *YouTube*.

Source: iPad User Guide, Wikipedia

Appendix C. Index